Big Data Applications for Improving Library Services

Sangeeta Namdev Dhamdhere
Modern College of Arts, Science, and Commerce, Pune, India

A volume in the Advances in Library and Information Science (ALIS) Book Series

IGI Global
PUBLISHER of TIMELY KNOWLEDGE

Published in the United States of America by
IGI Global
Information Science Reference (an imprint of IGI Global)
701 E. Chocolate Avenue
Hershey PA, USA 17033
Tel: 717-533-8845
Fax: 717-533-8661
E-mail: cust@igi-global.com
Web site: http://www.igi-global.com

Library of Congress Cataloging-in-Publication Data

Names: Dhamdhere, Sangeeta N., 1975- editor.
Title: Big data applications for improving library services / Sangeeta Namdev Dhamdhere, editor.
Description: Hershey, PA : Information Science Reference, [2020] | Includes bibliographical references and index. | Summary: "This book explores the application of big data in library services"-- Provided by publisher.
Identifiers: LCCN 2019047066 (print) | LCCN 2019047067 (ebook) | ISBN 9781799830498 (hardcover) | ISBN 9781799830504 (paperback) | ISBN 9781799830511 (ebook)
Subjects: LCSH: Libraries--Information technology. | Big data. | Academic libraries--Information technology. | Public services (Libraries) | Librarians--Effect of technological innovations on.
Classification: LCC Z678.93.B54 B54 2020 (print) | LCC Z678.93.B54 (ebook) | DDC 025.50285--dc23
LC record available at https://lccn.loc.gov/2019047066
LC ebook record available at https://lccn.loc.gov/2019047067

This book is published in the IGI Global book series Advances in Library and Information Science (ALIS) (ISSN: 2326-4136; eISSN: 2326-4144)

British Cataloguing in Publication Data
A Cataloguing in Publication record for this book is available from the British Library.

Advances in Library and Information Science (ALIS) Book Series

ISSN:2326-4136
EISSN:2326-4144

MISSION

The **Advances in Library and Information Science (ALIS) Book Series** is comprised of high quality, research-oriented publications on the continuing developments and trends affecting the public, school, and academic fields, as well as specialized libraries and librarians globally. These discussions on professional and organizational considerations in library and information resource development and management assist in showcasing the latest methodologies and tools in the field.

The **ALIS Book Series** aims to expand the body of library science literature by covering a wide range of topics affecting the profession and field at large. The series also seeks to provide readers with an essential resource for uncovering the latest research in library and information science management, development, and technologies.

COVERAGE

- Library Buildings and Design
- Public Library Funding
- Ethical Practices in Libraries
- Corporate Libraries
- Outreach, Promotion, and Advocacy
- Diversity in Libraries
- Partnerships in Library Communities
- Community Outreach
- Evidence-Based Librarianship
- Recruitment of Library Professionals

IGI Global is currently accepting manuscripts for publication within this series. To submit a proposal for a volume in this series, please contact our Acquisition Editors at Acquisitions@igi-global.com or visit: http://www.igi-global.com/publish/.

The Advances in Library and Information Science (ALIS) Book Series (ISSN 2326-4136) is published by IGI Global, 701 E. Chocolate Avenue, Hershey, PA 17033-1240, USA, www.igi-global.com. This series is composed of titles available for purchase individually; each title is edited to be contextually exclusive from any other title within the series. For pricing and ordering information please visit http://www.igi-global.com/book-series/advances-library-information-science/73002. Postmaster: Send all address changes to above address.

Titles in this Series

For a list of additional titles in this series, please visit:
http://www.igi-global.com/book-series/advances-library-information-science/73002

Transforming Library Operations With ICT Tools
Okon Edet Ani (University of Calabar, Nigeria)
Information Science Reference • ©2021 • 300pp • H/C (ISBN: 9781799842798) • US $195.00

Open Access Implications for Sustainable Social, Political, and Economic Development
Priti Jain (University of Botswana, Botswana) Nathan Mnjama (University of Botswana, Botswana) and O. Oladokun (University of Botswana, Botswana)
Information Science Reference • ©2021 • 360pp • H/C (ISBN: 9781799850182) • US $195.00

Cases on Research Support Services in Academic Libraries
Viviana Fernández-Marcial (University of A Coruña, Spain) and Llarina González-Solar (University of A Coruña, Spain & General Secretariat of the Council of the European Union, Belgium)
Information Science Reference • ©2021 • 344pp • H/C (ISBN: 9781799845461) • US $185.00

Challenges and Opportunities of Open Educational Resources Management
S. Thanuskodi (Alagappa University, India)
Information Science Reference • ©2020 • 315pp • H/C (ISBN: 9781799835592) • US $195.00

Examining the Impact of Industry 4.0 on Libraries
Josiline Phiri Chigwada (Bindura University of Science Education, Zimbabwe) and Ngozi Maria Nwaohiri (Federal University of Technology, Owerri, Nigeria)
Information Science Reference • ©2020 • 300pp • H/C (ISBN: 9781799842255) • US $195.00

Emerging Trends and Impacts of the Internet of Things in Libraries
Barbara Holland (Brooklyn Public Library, USA)
Information Science Reference • ©2020 • 253pp • H/C (ISBN: 9781799847427) • US $195.00

For an entire list of titles in this series, please visit:
http://www.igi-global.com/book-series/advances-library-information-science/73002

IGI Global
PUBLISHER of TIMELY KNOWLEDGE

701 East Chocolate Avenue, Hershey, PA 17033, USA
Tel: 717-533-8845 x100 • Fax: 717-533-8661
E-Mail: cust@igi-global.com • www.igi-global.com

This book is dedicated to my beloved father, Late Shri. Namdev Maruti Dhamdhere

Editorial Advisory Board

Table of Contents

Detailed Table of Contents

The library plays a vital role for the students, researchers, and academician as a central data storage which is utilized for accessing any required data within less time and effort. Academic libraries are rich in primary and secondary data with lots of content, which may include data from other resources also such as internet and other media. This large amount of data must provide a valuable information to the user, but it may not be same format. Librarians need to transform and analyse all the available data to the same format so that it becomes easier for the user to facilitate the required knowledge. For example, they need to create a dataset in a manner that is easy to visualize and accessible. In this regard, big data analytics tools such as information visualisation tools help the user in mining the intended information. In any case, it is assumed that the confinements and conceivable outcomes of Big data innovation are being considered and that relationships are acknowledged as precise. This chapter focus on all the possibilities of various issues and challenges that may arise while using big data with library.

The chapter showcases the awareness of big data usage among librarians in Zimbabwe. The concept of big data is new, and librarians are building capacity to move with the current trends in librarianship. This chapter assists in pointing areas where big data can be applied in libraries. It also documents the challenges that are faced when

Information communication technology is growing at a faster speed and diversified way. Cloud computing, internet of things, 5G, and such technologies are gearing-up and resulting in proliferation of data. Data is a raw information and it has created a big data. To handle such data, big data techniques are emerging. Library and information science is a big-way service profession that mediates between the data/information and the users, letting them be students, researchers, technocrats. Big data, mostly digital data, is being generated through multiple on-line surveys and repositories. Digital and social media is the main source of generating such data. Analyzing such data according to user needs is a huge task. This is the challenge now a days to organize the data explosion, specially the volume and variety of data. Big data analytics proves to be a major help in organizing and fetching data sets pertaining to user query. The authors, in this chapter, deal with four major services of libraries, wherein time efficiency can be achieved through big data analytics. Authors have focused on thrust areas of library and information science and indicate the benefits of big data analytics for service efficiency.

The investigators have brought out the history of big data, its meaning, its different types such as web data, text data, location and time data, social network data, etc. The characteristics of big data such as volume, velocity, variety, and complexity are discussed. Application of big data in various fields in everyday life is discussed in different fields such detection of fraud, application in agriculture field, banking implication, healthcare implication. Entertainment and media industry is also using it effectively. Big data is also used in weather forecasting, transportation industry, education industry, and sports sector. Future of big data is bright. More data on everything is available today. One needs to analyse everything today in order to implement policies. Software is available to process such voluminous data. The chapter also discusses the influence of big data on Indian governance, digitalization in India, finance and banking sector. In conclusion, one can say there is bright future of big data in various private and public sectors. Today's problem is information overload. One has to be very dexterous in disseminating using information with the help of web tools and software one can use. The investigators also discuss the

Preface

In the recent past data has changed the world in an unbelievable way and made an impact on our lifestyles at an exceptional rate. Big data is now the latest science of exploring and forecasting human-machine behaviour dealing with a massive amount of associated data. It is now a day used in every field for quality improvement, problem solving and real time recommendation. Libraries are handling huge data and many new web-based services, online literature and databases. Use of Big Data for giving up to date and innovative real time services to library users is new change libraries are facing. It is possible for all modern libraries to apply Big Data in their libraries and improve their services. . While delivering new innovative services Big Data will play important role now a day. This book covers different areas of libraries Big Data can be applied. What many different services libraries can start using Big Data, Challenges and Issues, Case Studies, Big Data Analytics, Data Collection techniques, etc.

For this book we have received very good response from about 30 authors and 20 proposals. Out of them we have selected 12 chapters contributed by 20 authors in Library and Information and IT field from all over the globe.

First chapter in this book focuses on different issues related to big data like big data characteristics, data storage and transport issues, data management and processing time and technology issues. This chapter also discusses various challenges faced by big data like synchronization of disperse data, shortage of big data analysis professionals, big data storage and analysis, data security during storage and transmission, computational complexity, uncertainty of landscape for data management and technical challenges.

Second chapter showcases the awareness of big data usage among librarians in Zimbabwe. It assists in pointing areas where big data can be applied in libraries. It also documents the challenges that are faced when using big data applications and proffer solutions that can be applied to deal with those challenges. It answers the question of whether it is practical to utilise big data in any type of library on the basis of a qualitative study done using online questionnaire which was administered to twenty librarians in research institutions in Zimbabwe. The findings revealed and recommendations of requisite skills to equip librarians for capacity building are mentioned.

Third chapter discusses the results and recommendations of a study carried out with an intention to understand the intensity and the competencies of librarians in implementing Big Data initiative project in academic libraries by the Government of Karnataka State. This study also tries to understand the application of Big Data in these libraries, librarians completed the survey out of 78 respondents.

The objective of Chapter 4 is to familiarize Big Data and its application, and the opportunity and challenges in an academic library. Further, the article examines the application framework of big data in academic library based on large scale analysis.

Chapter 5 covers four major services of libraries where big data techniques are essential to be used for service efficiency and time efficiency are discussed.

In Chapter 6 authors have brought out the history of big data, its meaning its different types such as web data, text data, location and time data, Social network data etc.

In seventh chapter authors discussed about arrangement of big data to fulfil requirements of users effectively. The different segments of library including big data are explored. It also discusses the various problems, challenges and issues involved in big data of knowledge resource centre.

In Chapter 8, opportunities and challenges experienced while using big data applications in libraries are mentioned. The objective of the study was to examine the big data applications that are used in libraries. The big data concept is new and some librarians are not aware of it while others do not have the knowledge and skills of using big data applications. A structured literature review was done to examine how libraries use big data. The search term that was used was "big data AND libraries". The findings revealed and the challenges that are experienced by the authors are included along with author's recommendations to librarians for skill development.

Ninth chapter is a study attempted to map the Indian libraries' Twitter activity, taking academic libraries as case study. Selected Indian academic library tweets are collected form the Twitter using R programming language. The study further compares few develop countries' academic library tweets. Librarians all over the globe are increasingly using Social Twitter in their daily routine activities as well as the promotion of their system and services. In this chapter authors observations, sentimental analysis and recommendations to attract users are mentioned.

explores themes such as Data Visualization tools, data granularity and data visualization tools. It also explained the advantages of data visualization and the types of data African libraries should be collecting.

Tenth chapter explores themes such as Data Visualization tools, data granularity and data visualization tools. It also explained the advantages of data visualization and the types of data African libraries should be collecting.

Chapter 11 describes a case study about Real Time Recommendation Engine for users which includes data ingestion methods, challenges, metadata problem, analysis and consumption. In today's world, every reader or social media user has different choices/hobbies in terms of reading. For example, if any social media user is searching for a book to read without any specific idea of what s/he want, s/he waste a lot of time browsing around on the internet and crawling/trawling through various sites hoping that s/he might get good book. To avoid confusion, authors build a recommendation system for every reader user that helps to recommends book based on his choices, hobbies or what s/he had read previously that will be massive help for users instead wasting time on various sites. Data from social media is the powerful fuel that can be used to help in decision making and building a recommendation engine.

Chapter 12 is a scientometric evaluation which let us know how India is going forward in this research area with some specific statistics in scientific community. This chapter focuses the research landscape of big data research in India.

This will be a first attempt and book on application of big data in libraries. This will be useful to library professionals, Library and information Science students, Academic Professionals, Academicians, IT professionals, Big Data Professionals and all who are interested in Big Data concept and design.

I thank IGI Global for welcoming this concept and publishing this book. I also thank our college management for giving me infrastructure facility to complete this project. I thank all my family members, friends and colleagues for their constant support and motivation.

Chapter 1
Big Data Issues and Challenges

Shweta Kaushik
ABES Engineering College, India

ABSTRACT

The library plays a vital role for the students, researchers, and academician as a central data storage which is utilized for accessing any required data within less time and effort. Academic libraries are rich in primary and secondary data with lots of content, which may include data from other resources also such as internet and other media. This large amount of data must provide a valuable information to the user, but it may not be same format. Librarians need to transform and analyse all the available data to the same format so that it becomes easier for the user to facilitate the required knowledge. For example, they need to create a dataset in a manner that is easy to visualize and accessible. In this regard, big data analytics tools such as information visualisation tools help the user in mining the intended information. In any case, it is assumed that the confinements and conceivable outcomes of Big data innovation are being considered and that relationships are acknowledged as precise. This chapter focus on all the possibilities of various issues and challenges that may arise while using big data with library.

I. INTRODUCTION

Big Data

In today digital era, the data is generated enormously day by day from multiple resources such as social networking data, cloud computing data, online trading data etc. responsible for generating a large amount of data. The usage of the latest digital technologies and information system such as cloud computing, mobile computing,

DOI: 10.4018/978-1-7998-3049-8.ch001

IoT etc. is also responsible for the generation of large amount of data. This data generated by various technology is not always in the same format i.e, data may be structured, unstructured and semi-structured. This inconsistency of data raises many issues and challenges in front of the data management authority as they all need to deal with these numerous types of data. Previously, data warehouses are responsible for handling the large data storage and maintenance. User will acquire their required data by applying any of the data mining technique.

The primary requirement here was that all the data is stored in a predefined format which increase data warehouse efficiency and also reduce the time for searching any valuable data by data mining. Since, now data is not always stored in the same format and also due to its large volume it become infeasible to apply all these previously data mining technique. Usage of big data have their own technology and method to handle this issue, but still facing security issues and challenges regarding the data storage and finding the useful or required data for decision making purpose in less time. This chapter focus on these issues and challenges comes in front of big data technology.

Big Data in Library

There are few reasons for the adoption of big data technology in digital libraries for personalized services as:

- The consistent creation of huge measures of information makes acquiring successful data progressively troublesome. The data over-burden issue is ending up progressively visible comparative with restricted client data adequacy and time costs. In this manner, finding content that clients are really keen on from enormous scale information assets and separating unessential data to minimize the meaningless data screening expenses has turned out to be vital to improving client accomplishment in computerized libraries.
- The regularly expanding measure of information prompts consistently expanding information associations. Such associations cannot just improve our comprehension of information and encourage approaches to discover target information all the more successfully what's more, proficiently, yet additionally give the essential and fundamental conditions for further investigation and examination of concealed qualities which customary single-information assets can't give. In huge measures of information, there are an extraordinary number of relationships among the information, for example, the relationship among client social information, relationship among clients and clients, relationship among clients and assets, what's more, relationship among various assets. Such associations permit clients to get the necessary

help content all the more effectively and rapidly. Moreover, such associations can create new client data prerequisites and can be utilized to make new sorts of data benefits by joining existing client intrigue designs.

- Users get and break down information to acquire learning identified with a specific application. The comprehension and use of the learning substance are dictated by the information and furthermore relies upon the particular application condition and current data prerequisites. Connections, cooperation, and incorporation of semantic and application connections will significantly affect client understanding of the got information (Zhang, 2005).

II. CHALLENEGES IN BIG DATA

The data generation by the various organization is increasing at the very fast speed from 40-60% per year. Also, all this generated data is not useful for organization. This generation of enormous large volumetric data brought many challenges related to information security, computational complexity, data storage and scalability etc. There are many computational techniques as well as statistical methods which works well for small data but do not perform well in case of big data. Thus, it become a challenge in front of big data to handle all these issues. The various challenges faced by big data are, as shown in figure 1:

- **Synchronization of scatter information:** Tapping into enormous information can make segregation progressively predominant. While Big Data enables organizations to turn out to be better advertisers and specialist organizations, just as causing shoppers to acknowledge that they are being examined in detail consequently their better involvement, it makes them feel separated. The capacity to get to electronic data on clients' conduct on Internet exercises and inclinations could adversely influence an individual's chance, for example, on their bank credit application without giving an opportunity for that person to legitimize or guard oneself. It is out of line and not satisfactory to oppress individuals dependent on information that associations have gathered on people groups' lives. In this way, choices ought not be made exclusively out of electronic information, particularly those that adverse effect somebody.
- **Shortage of enormous information examination experts:** As new advancements become accessible in the market, new range of abilities are requested. Precise and noteworthy information mining and investigation, especially progressively, requires broad specialized abilities. It would be an extraordinary test for associations to discover gifted information investigators to utilize the associations' information. Despite the fact that information

experts were continually being required in the associations, the required examination aptitudes are diverse with enormous information. Associations need to shape a typical information examiner group either to outfit existing staff with the privilege range of abilities by consummation them to trainings and get fundamental accreditations, or source out for new workers who are spent significant time in enormous information as they can comprehend information from a logical point of view, the business and its clients, relate their information discoveries and apply legitimately to them. Other than the basic scientific abilities, they should be near items and procedures inside associations.

- **Big information stockpiling and investigation:** This is alluding to information being accessible and open a lot bigger and quicker progressively and crosswise over different ventures. This colossal measure of information should be prepared and dissected, and the assignments could be tedious as it requires some investment to examine. In this quick moving world, aftereffects of the investigation are requested very quickly. Associations need to have data from various assets. There might be situations when associations don't have adequate information to do the examination and would most likely look for or purchase information from outsiders that could possibly need to share the information. It is hard to think about that enormous information investigation consistently gives right outcomes as mistaken information could create erroneous outcomes bringing about misdirecting basic leadership.
- **Data security during capacity and transmission:** Security It is the most significant difficulties with Big information which is delicate and incorporates reasonable, specialized just as lawful noteworthiness. • The individual data (for example in database of a trader or long range informal communication site) of an individual when joined with outer huge informational indexes, prompts the deduction of new realities about that individual and it's conceivable that these sorts of realities about the individual are shrouded and the individual probably won't need the information proprietor to know or any individual to think about them.
    - Information with respect to the individuals is gathered and utilized so as to increase the value of the matter of the association. This is finished by making experiences in their lives which they are unconscious of.
    - Another significant result emerging would be Social stratification where an educated individual would take points of interest of the Big information prescient investigation and then again oppressed will be effectively recognized and treated more awful.

- Big Data utilized by law authorization will build the odds of certain labelled individuals to experience the ill effects of unfriendly outcomes without the capacity to battle back or in any event, having information that they are being segregated.

- **Computational Complexity:** Three of the key highlights of huge information, to be specific, multi-sources, gigantic volume, and quick changing, make it hard for customary figuring techniques, (for example, AI, data recovery, and information mining) to successfully bolster the handling, investigation and calculation of enormous information. Such calculations can't just depend on past measurements, investigation apparatuses, and iterative calculations utilized in customary methodologies for taking care of limited quantities of information. New methodologies should split away from presumptions made in customary calculations dependent on autonomous and indistinguishable circulation of information and sufficient testing for creating solid measurements. When taking care of issues including enormous information, we should reconsider and examine its processability, computational multifaceted nature, and calculations. New methodologies for huge information figuring should address huge information situated, novel and exceptionally effective registering standards, give creative techniques to handling and investigating enormous information, and bolster esteem driven applications in determined areas. New highlights in enormous information handling, for example, deficient examples, open and dubious information connections, and lopsided dissemination of significant worth thickness, give incredible chances, yet in addition present stupendous difficulties, to contemplating the processability of huge information and the advancement of new registering ideal models. To address the computational unpredictability of huge information applications, we should concentrate all in all life cycle of huge information applications so as to think about information driven figuring standards dependent on the attributes of huge information. We have to split away from conventional computing centric standards and build up information driven push-style processing ideal models and investigate feeble CAP system shared-information framework model and its arithmetical computational hypothesis. We should create calculations for disseminated and gushing processing and structure a major information arranged figuring system where correspondence, stockpiling, and registering are all around incorporated and streamlined. We should examine non-deterministic algorithmic hypothesis reasonable for enormous information and withdraw from the autonomous and-indistinguishably disseminated presumption made in customary measurable learning. We additionally need to investigate existing decrease based registering strategies where huge information is diminished on interest from being huge enough to being simply enough, and to being significant enough. At long last, we should create bootstrapping and examining based neighbourhood calculation and guess techniques and propose novel hypothetical reason for enormous information calculations that are adaptable to dealing with a lot of information.

Figure 1. Big data challenges

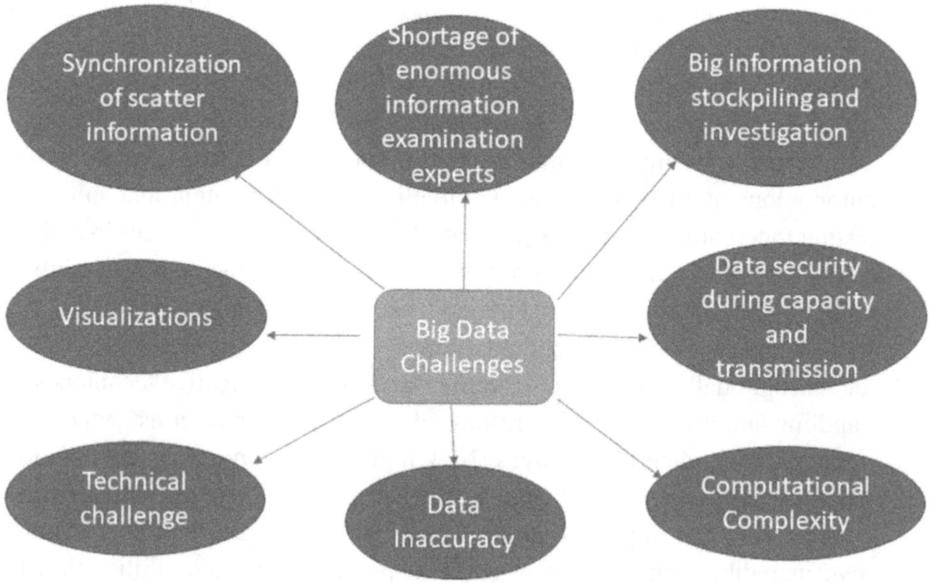

- **Data Inaccuracy:** Big information is good for nothing except if it is utilized for improved basic leadership. For that, associations must take essential activities to oversee information, for example, information securing, extraction and recording, information purging, information mix and total, just as information portrayal and examination including demonstrating, investigation and elucidations. Information that will be utilized to dissect originates from various sources and of various configurations. It might contain wrong data, duplication and logical inconsistencies. It is far-fetched that information of very second-rate quality can bring any valuable bits of knowledge or promising chances to association's exactness requesting business assignments. Deliberately organized information is fundamental for proficient and exact information investigation. Fragmented information can prompt wrong information examination bringing about poor outcome, judgment and choice. Information purging or information cleaning includes conflicting information, information got from heterogeneous sources, and information that are not exceptional or outdated. Information should be rinsed to be prepared for contemporary utilize and accessible for revelation and reuse.

- **Technical challenge:** Decision making about embracing new advancements can regularly take quite a while or to because of essential procedure to be pursued including levels of endorsements. It can likewise be befuddling to pick enormous information innovations available. Picking an innovation itself can be tedious and it develops to quick making associations difficult to stay informed concerning the most recent advances and patterns, bringing about poor basic leadership even from the earliest starting point of picking an item or answer for assistance them with real issues with enormous information the executives. Enormous information, being quick information, if its significance can be acquired, immediately examined, arranged and applied them once again into operational frameworks, at that point it can influence occasions as they are as yet unfurling. The capacity to settle on quick and right choices are significant as well. Information the executives for calculation might be a test and will require significant interest in data and correspondence innovation.
- **Visualizations:** A huge portion of huge information is created from individuals' observation, expectations, and wants. The motivation behind dissecting huge information is to assist associations with making choices. Be that as it may, depending on electronic information alone absent a lot of worry on its effect to individuals or nature, can prompt moral issues. Associations must be cautious when making end and judgment about what the information passes on. This is on the grounds that recognition, goals, and wants can change quickly. They should discover that choices ought to consistently be founded on how it will influence everybody included, and not just from the numbers and data appeared on papers. Other moral issues when taking care of enormous information could likewise incorporate issues of character, protection, proprietorship, and notoriety. Licensed innovation right issues additionally emerge during the accumulation, stockpiling, sharing, and preparing of huge information. Veracity is firmly identified with trust issues. All these moral contemplations are identified with each other. The circumstance is much progressively touchy when it has to do with individual and secret information, for example, restorative and budgetary records. From the procedure of huge information purifying up to investigation, the security might be compromised because of the introduction of this data to unapproved parties

The possible approach along with the limitation related to a particular challenge are described as described in Table 1.

Table 1. Big data challenges, approaches & limitations

S.No.	Challenge	Possible Approaches	Limitations
1	Shortage of big data analysis professionals	Establishment of special data force (SDF) with advanced analytical skills	Expensive but necessary to survive.
2	Synchronization of disperse data	Hadoop and MapReduce to load various formats of data in a distributed and synchronous mannerv	Heterogeneous nature of data is the reason which raised the challenge.
3	Visualization	Tableau, QlikView etc	Businesses use visualization tools to increase the throughput over big data.
4	Big data storage and analysis	Design of systems by taking user needs and technology under consideration	User interactive designs Satisfy customers. And a satisfied customer is itself an advertisement.

III. ISSUES IN BIG DATA

Analysis of big data application is becoming a research issue in front of academician and researchers. They all are trying to find a solution to implement the technology which is more efficient in terms of data handling, storage and integration with other technology. Various research issue related to big data are broadly categorized as, shown in figure 2:

- **Related to Big Data Characteristics:** Basic characteristics of big data are its volume, variety and velocity. Everyday a large amount of data is generated by the user ranging from terabytes to petabytes of different velocity which may include text, images, video etc. Also, the data is generated at very fast pace that our traditional approaches are not able to handle the data generated continuously. These issues need high consideration for effectively and efficient processing of data.
    - **Issues related to Data Volume** As information volume expands, the estimation of various information records will diminish in extent to age, type and amount among different components. The existing social networking websites are themselves delivering information in terms of

terabytes regular and this measure of information is certainly hard to be taken care by the current existing conventional frameworks.

- ◦ **Issues related to Data Velocity** The existing conventional frameworks are not able enough on playing out the investigation on the information which is continuously changing. Online business has quickly expanded the speed and lavishness of information utilized for various business exchanges (for instance, site clicks. Data velocity needs more consideration than a data transfer capacity issue.
- ◦ **Issues related to Data Variety** All this information is entirely unexpected comprising of raw, organized, semi organized and even unstructured data which is hard to be taken care of by the current customary systematic frameworks. From an expository point of view, it is likely the greatest limitation to adequately utilizing huge volumes of information.
- ◦ **Issues related to Data Value** As the information put away by various associations is being utilized by them for information investigation. It will create a sort of hole in the middle of the Business chiefs and the IT experts. The principle worry of business pioneers would be to simply enhancing their business and getting increasingly more benefit dissimilar to the IT heads who might need to worry with the details of the capacity and preparing.

- **Data storage and transport issues:** Large volumetric data is generated by all the user without any knowledge weather it is useful or not. For example, in social networking website a large volume of data is generated in terms of terabytes also. Out of this generated data most of the data is useless but still require storage space. Also, when this large data is transmitting from one place to another place for further processing also require lot of effort. This issue must be resolved so that only the data which is useful will store and reduce the data transmission time.

The distinction about the latest information blast, predominantly because of online life, is that there has been no new capacity medium. Besides, information is being made by everybody and everything, (from Mobile Devices to Super Computers) not only, as here to fore, by experts. Access to that information would overpower current correspondence systems. Expecting that a 1 gigabyte for each subsequent system has a compelling reasonable exchange pace of 80%, the economical transfer speed is around 100 megabytes. Accordingly, moving an Exabyte would take around 2800 hours, in the event that we accept that a supported exchange could be kept up. It would require some investment to transmit the information from a gathering or capacity point to a preparing point than the time required to really process it. To deal with this issue, the information ought to be prepared "set up" and transmit just the subsequent data. As it were, "carry the code to the data", unlike the customary technique for "carry the information to the code." (Kaisler, Armor, Espinosa, and Money, 2013)

- **Data management & Processing time:** Managing this large data is also becoming a challenging issue as it requires lot of effort in terms of data access, update etc. since data is available in multiple forms, it become a tedious task to arrange that data. Also processing this volumetric data require extra effort in terms of parallel processing of data. Otherwise, time to find the solution of any operation will be time consuming.

Settling issues of access, data usage, refreshing, administration, and reference (in productions) have demonstrated to be major hindrances. The sources of the information are differed - by size, by organization, and by technique for accumulation. People contribute advanced information in mediums agreeable to them like-archives, drawings, pictures, sound and video accounts, models, programming practices and so forth., with or without satisfactory metadata depicting what, when, where, who, why and how it was gathered and its provenance. In contrast to the gathering of information by manual strategies, where thorough conventions are regularly followed so as to guarantee exactness and legitimacy, Digital information accumulation is substantially slacker. Given the volume, it is illogical to approve each and every data item. New ways to deal with information capability and approval are required. The wealth of computerized information representation disallows a customized system for information accumulation. To summarize, there is no ideal huge information the board arrangement yet. This speaks to a significant hole in the exploration writing on enormous information that should be filled.

- **Technology issue:** In parallel to big data there are other technology in demand for data processing and benefit to user which may include IoT, Cloud Computing, Bio-Inspired computation etc. all these techniques generate numerous data which needs to be handle by the big data. Also, data store and manage by big data required by these techniques to process their task in efficient manner. But the issue arises here is extracting the data and transmit it from one format to another. For simplicity, assume that the complete information is divided into blocks of 8 words, so 1 Exabyte = 1K petabytes. Assume a processor consumes 100 instructions on one block at 5 gigahertz, the time required for start to finish preparing would be 20 nanoseconds. To process 1K petabytes would require an absolute start to finish preparing time of around 635 years. In this manner, viable preparing of Exabyte of information will require broad parallel handling and new examination calculations.

Figure 2. Big data issues

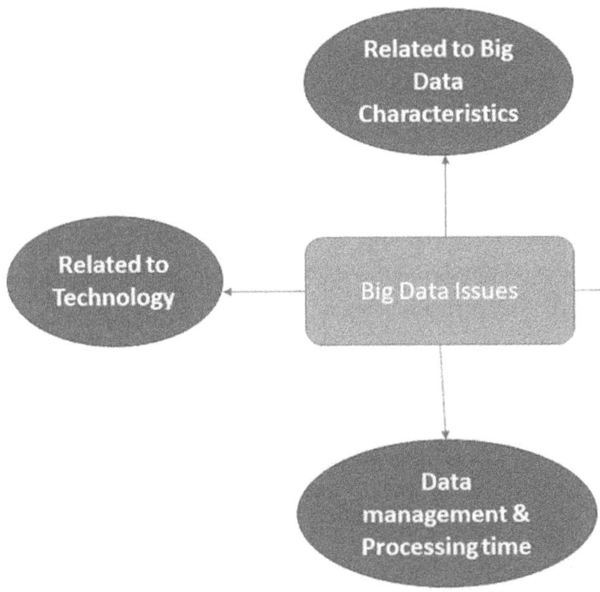

The glimpse of various issues occurs in Big data along with their possible solution and limitations (Wani, Jabin, 2018) are discussed in Table 2.

Table 2. Big data issues, solution and limitations

S.No.	Issue	Possible Solution	Limitations
1.	Characteristics	Hadoop MapReduce and Apache spark	Real time processing may be time consuming.
2.	Management	Quantum computing and in memory database management systems	Moving the whole business to the new platform can be very expensive and time consuming
3.	Storage	NoSQL, Distributed File Systems and Cloud Computing	Storing one exabyte needs 25000 no. of disk space which is complex and loading onto cloud is time consuming
4.	Processing	Advanced Indexing schemas, MapReduce and Simple scalable streaming systems (S4).	Processing of Zettabytes (1021) and even Exabytes (1018) of data is still seems a matter of concern
5.	Technical	Parallel Computing	Examination of broad parallel data processing and new result will be a matter of concern.

IV. LIBRARAY DATA AS BIG DATA

Three V's were first used to describe the Big Data. With further examination on Big Data, the "Three V's" have been extended to "Five V's": volume, velocity, variety, veracity (uprightness of information), value (handiness of information) and unpredictability (level of interconnection among information structures) by many researchers. In any case, the most significant are as yet the initial three. On the off chance that we just think about the static gathering in libraries, it may be difficult for us to relate it to big data. Also, the database the executive's frameworks ought to be sufficient to store what's more, to process library information, subsequently, in view of the definition of enormous information, there is no requirement for huge information innovation, for example, circulated frameworks to break down the information in library (Noor, 2013). In this segment, we attempt to break down the properties of information sets in library and to see how close they are connected to Big Data technology.

- **Volume:** As indicated by Wikipedia, 'Big Data' introduces to informational collections whose size is past the capacity of customary programming instruments for catching, overseeing, and preparing the information. In any case, the genuine size is a moving objective, which could extend from a just any dozen terabytes to numerous petabytes of information. The size of big data shifts relies upon the order. Some as of late grew enormous information applications incorporate medicinal services, transportation, and diversion, all of which include tremendous accumulations of information. It appears to us that every library has constrained accumulations. For instance, the National Geological Library of China has just 710,000 accumulations which are a lot littler than those in different fields. Then again, library gathers a ton of "little explore information", which are made by individual analysts. Those countless little information makers in total may well deliver as a lot of information (or more, estimated in bytes) as the enormous data. Additionally, library accumulations have a nearby bind to the connected information which structures bigger share of enormous information. English library examined the connected information of library accumulations and attempted to show the individuals, occasions, places which are identified with possessions in the library. The library could likewise gather the information that clients search or then again utilize the library information, and such information surely could have a volume like that of Twitter and others. As the size of accumulation volumes and the quantity of gathering traits increment, it could enable us to all the more quickly separate and in this way break down examples covered in the information. The so called "enormous information" in library could be utilized from numerous points of view, for example, improving ease of use, helping clients to discover the fascinating examples they need.

- **Velocity:** The speed attributes of big data could likewise be found in the information from library. Library keeps up various duplicates of documents on servers and on tape, in geologically circulated areas. Hence, there are developments of records between and inside associations. There are to an ever-increasing extent inquiry about going on and the examination information come in and join the dataset powerfully. Then again, the library information should be prepared quick so specialists could utilize it with worth and common clients could get the list items they need immediately.
- **Variety:** When all is said in done, libraries contain various sorts of information: books, diaries, reports, notes, maps, films, pictures, sounds and so on. Some are unstructured. Unstructured information comprises of language-based information (e.g., notes, twitter messages, books) also, non-language-based information (e.g., pictures, slides, sounds, recordings). In any event, for advanced research information, they have each possible shape and structure, from sweeps of chronicled negative photos to computerized magnifying lens pictures of unicellular creatures taken hundreds one after another at different profundities of field (Solo, 2010). On other hand, as usual libraries gather a host of utilization and value-based information made by clients as they associate with their frameworks and administrations. They are inundated with this kind of information – and are awakening the potential worth that can be extricated from what right now is to a great extent, unstructured information. Consequently, the qualities of assortment the huge information acquires could likewise be found in the library information. Other than those referenced qualities, the library information likewise has different properties.
- **Data Less Organized:** It appears to us that the information, for example, books, diaries in library are efficient since clients could utilize classifications to search for what they need. Notwithstanding, the circumstance is unique for that exploration information put away in libraries. The exploration information in libraries appear to be confused, less portrayed, and in arranges inadequately fit to long haul reuse (Solo,2010). Analysts are utilized to their own procedure to create this chaotic information. That information is frequently overseen by the task. Once undertakings complete with distribution of articles or reports, explore information are frequently secured in advanced storerooms being disorderly.
- **Non-Standard Data and Data Format:** Research information frequently absence of standard and organization. They rely upon the orders and individual libraries. Despite the fact that a couple of controls may have made information models, because of a solid brought together information archive,

for example, political and social research, in many orders, there regularly don't exist information guidelines, especially for those examines which are individualized: for example every specialist characterizes the parameters which are imperative to the task. The information configuration is another issue. Analysts utilize them possess position for the information they gather. In any event, for the equivalent scientist, various information arrangements may be utilized for various ventures, which posture trouble to coordinate that information.

V. TRANSFORMATION OF DIGITAL LIBRARY IN BIG DATA

As indicated by OCLC's Information Context structure, administration transformation in advanced libraries in the big data time can be outlined from three principle viewpoints: the fundamental data condition, the conduct of data administration (OCLC, 2007). As per this thought, we demonstrate a generally speaking structure, as shown in figure 3.

We can portray the general capacity of an advanced library as a procedure of "information innovation administration client". This association is likewise near the four centre segments of the interior development of advanced libraries, i.e., asset development, stage development, new media administrations, and norms development (Han, 2016). Each progression of this process in a major information condition has its very own improvement heading also, change strategy.

- **Data:** in conventional advanced libraries essentially incorporate writing information, advanced asset accumulations, database assets, and different structures. In this manner, the development of computerized library assets dependent on huge information ought to underline two objectives. The first is to utilize huge information to improve the capacity and use of existing information assets, incorporate enormous information asset into existing advanced library asset frameworks, furthermore, enhance the current information size and type. The second is to incorporate recently produced information in new information organizes and related information on the web with the current information assets of advanced libraries. Such information assets give the plausibility of improving conventional administrations, and they can likewise give new assistance structures and techniques.
- **Technology:** is an essential piece of computerized libraries. The advancement of the computerized library includes the persistent utilization of data innovation. Customary innovation stages can be improved by innovation required for enormous information preparing, for example, information

obtaining, capacity, examination, and mining advances. New innovation arrangements, for example, dispersed systems, parallel registering, huge information, and man-made reasoning, will be an establishment of progressing computerized library development.

- **Service:** can be comprehended as a procedure in which an advanced library can give information assets legitimately or in a roundabout way to clients. It can likewise mirror the estimations of the utilization of innovation in a library. In the huge information time, it is conceivable to distinguish individual intrigue examples of clients with the end goal that administrations can be adjusted to the changing data necessities of clients. In this manner, a customary one-to-many help mode will bit by bit advance into a progressively customized coordinated assistance mode. Subsequently, every client will have their own advanced library, and the computerized library can give proactive administrations, for example, customized proposals as indicated by the client's advantages. At the equivalent time, we think about client access to multi-gadget terminals to improve and upgrade administration levels in all perspectives. Representation enables clients to get to advanced library benefits in a more natural and helpful way. In future, different innovations are expected to wind up accessible, for example, augmented reality and wearable gadgets.

Figure 3. Digital library in Big Data

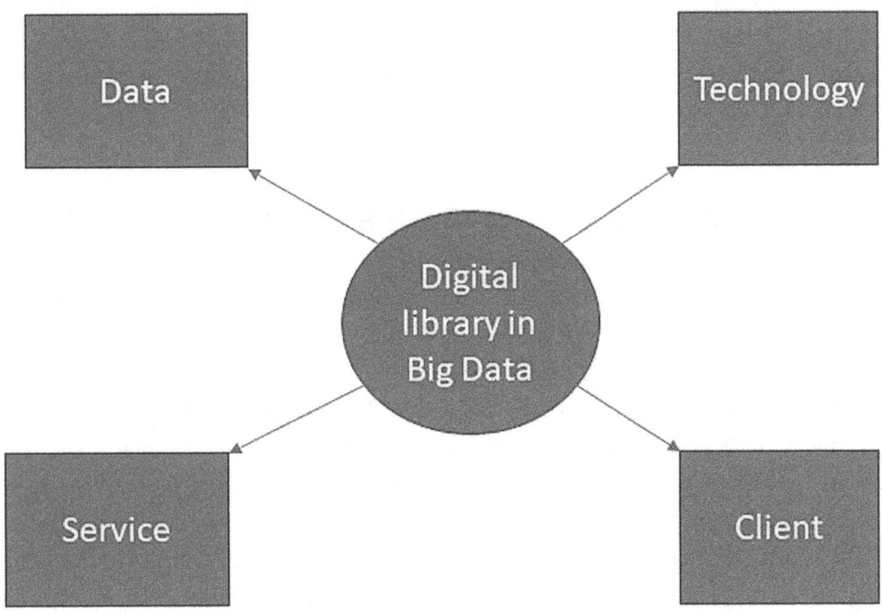

- **The client:** is the object of computerized library administrations. Be that as it may, the objective of a computerized library administration is to fulfil the client's data needs; in this manner, it is increasingly critical to think about current client prerequisites from the client's viewpoint to all the more successfully propose thoughts and techniques to improve existing administrations. Also, singular client necessities drive the advancement of computerized library administrations from asset sharing to client situated administrations (Wu, 2009). For instance, for general library clients, existing examinations have demonstrated that the data education of library clients has experienced extraordinary changes with the continuous advancement of data innovation. Logical scientists served by subject administrators have information asset and data processing abilities that administrators don't. Along these lines, the job of "helping clients" in a conventional library administration ought to be moved to "provoking clients" and "recommending to clients." However, McKinsey anticipated that about one-portion of information researcher employments in the United States will be empty in 2018 (Manyika et al., 2011) on the grounds that preparation information researchers brings about incredible expenses. Truth be told, this circumstance is the equivalent in the library field in light of the fact that, for bookkeepers to adjust to enormous information handling prerequisites, they should procure complex skill in related fields, for example, insights, software engineering, and data science. In any case, momentary fast preparing can't fulfil such prerequisites (De Mauro et al., 2016).

The client is the most significant objective of library administrations. Previously, we set forward the "client first;" notwithstanding, genuine activity isn't sufficient. Hence, to upgrade client fulfilment and improve existing administration procedures and techniques, the viewpoint must be an essential thought.

VI. SOLUTION FOR BIG DATA ISSUES AND CHALLENGES

In overseeing enormous information, there are mainly three components included which is individuals/ people, procedure and innovation as shown in figure 4.

Each association created and utilize huge measure of information and data in the association condition and the prerequisite of preparing, sharing, putting away, verifying and showing data offer accentuation to the fundamental job that data plays in making progress. Individuals or pioneer in the association have on exact, significant and auspicious data to make information driven choices in regards to the present and future objectives of the association. The way that data is undoubtedly isn't just an important corporate resource yet the distinction between an effective

Figure 4. Solutions for Big Data issues and challenges

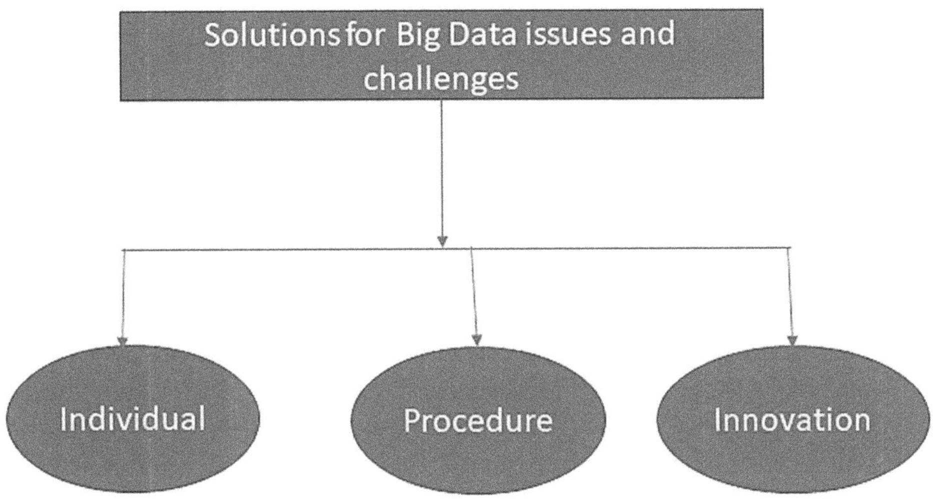

and ineffective association. Executing a fruitful answer for association the executives on data in the present condition requires a total comprehension of the association and the three component which is individuals/ people, procedure and innovation.

In this sense, these three components ought to be considered as the answer for requesting the executives of huge information in the association. To improve upper hand and basic leadership, an association must think about data as the crucial key to deal with the entire association. In the data and advanced period, data has turned into a benefit fundamental for business endurance. O'Brien and Marakas (2013) contend that there are three keys in data frameworks which are: 1) supporting procedures and activities, 2) supporting basic leadership by operators of the association, what's more, 3) supporting systems for upper hand. Essential prerequisites need to work together basic leadership and data frameworks, for example, the wellsprings of help given, recurrence and structure of data displayed, data configuration and technique utilized in handling the data. Enormous information is considered as a significant device to produce crucial contribution to basic leadership and upper hand. Each pioneer and chief in any association need the majority of their activity and choices depends on exact and exact data. In this manner, enormous information investigation is the best arrangement that distils terabytes of low-esteem information, changing them into a solitary piece of high-esteem information. Enormous information the board can produce data from a solitary piece of high-esteem information that present various structures. What's more, for as the answer for information the executives of enormous information, three components referenced before can help helps the earth where enormous information is distinguished. Subsequently,

- **Individuals component:** In huge information the executives, it is another pattern use in association, individuals included must be set up with new aptitudes to process the information. Along these lines, these individuals need to have ability to comprehend and to work with the enormous sum and diverse kind of information. The aptitude likewise not limited to the individuals who oversee information procedure related with enormous information innovation yet in addition to the individuals who act as the chief as they have to see those enormous measure of information to pick up the required data for settling on significant choices in the hierarchical and social changes. There are a couple of titles given to individuals committed with enormous information the executives and positions thusly Information Analyst, Data Architect, BI Manager and Data Scientist which is truly related with enormous information. The request on experts with the information wise skill to break down enormous information to make viable choices is truly elevated in the current worldwide innovation and business condition. Be that as it may, huge information capacity doesn't expel human factor. We know the most significant parts of enormous information is the result of reports on how choices are made and who are in control to make them. Thusly, the capacity of overseeing enormous information mechanically isn't relate with the capacity huge information provides for the chief. Individuals who oversee huge information in the association must be viewed as the significant component that give the association upper hand.
- **Procedure component:** Process identified with the activities performed in the mechanical condition. For example, some procedure in the mechanical condition utilize explicit instruments and methods to guarantee the business procedure work appropriately and it answerable to produce the information just as to utilize them unequivocally and precisely. In any case, in enormous information the board, procedure can be interrelated on the grounds that it is basic that they at the same time play out the exercises and procedure and specialized exercises identified with the business.
- **Innovation component:** A few advancements and systems are considered in enormous information the executives what's more, it is begun from gathering, putting away, preparing and dissecting information. After the pattern of enormous information existed in the innovative condition, numerous advancements and procedures have been created what's more, its capacity to the examination that is significant in enormous information execution. For instances of the methods utilized are as per the following:
    - Data mining – a method used to concentrate designs from a lot of information by combining factual strategies and AI information the board.

- Machine learning – a system utilized man-made brainpower standards and considers the improvement of calculations for perceiving complex examples in huge volumes of information and propose canny choices.

VII. TECHNOLOGY FOR HANDLING BIG DATA

Big Data revolutions are significant in giving increasingly precise investigation, which may prompt progressively solid basic leadership bringing about more prominent operational efficiencies, cost decreases, and diminished dangers for the business. To lead the intensity of enormous information, we require a framework that can supervise and process enormous volumes of organized and unstructured information continuously what's more, can ensure information protection and security. There are different advances in the market from various sellers including Amazon, IBM, Microsoft, and so on., to deal with enormous information. While looking into the technology and innovations that handle big data, we scrutinize the following two classes of innovation.

- **Operational Big Data:** This incorporates frameworks like MongoDB that give operational capacities for continuous, intuitive remaining tasks at hand where information is essentially caught and put away. No SQL Big Data frameworks are intended to exploit new distributed computing structures that have developed over the previous decade to permit immoral calculations to be run modestly and productively. This makes operational huge information remaining tasks at hand a lot simpler to oversee, less expensive, and quicker to execute.
- **Expository Big Data:** This incorporates frameworks like Massively Parallel Processing (MPP) database frameworks and MapReduce that give expository capacities for review and complex examination that may contact most or the majority of the information. MapReduce gives another strategy for examining information that is correlative to the abilities gave by SQL, and a framework dependent on MapReduce that can be scaled up from single servers to a large number of high and low-end machines. The Big Data taking care of systems and instruments incorporate Hadoop, Map Reduce, what's more, Big Table. Out of these, Hadoop is one of the most generally utilized advances.

HADOOP

Hadoop is an Apache open source system, written in java. High volumes of information, in any structure, are prepared by Hadoop. It permits conveyed capacity and disseminated preparing for exceptionally enormous informational collections. The complete framework of Hadoop can be categorized into 2 parts as:

1. Hadoop dispersed document framework (HDFS): HDFS is a versatile and dependable appropriated stockpiling framework that totals the capacity of each hub in a Hadoop bunch into a solitary worldwide document framework. HDFS stores individual records in enormous partitions, enabling it to proficiently store extremely huge or various documents over numerous machines and access individual lumps of information in parallel. Dependability is accomplished by recreating the information over various hosts, with each participant of information being put away, naturally, on three separate PCs.
2. MapReduce: It is a product structure for effectively composing applications which procedure enormous measures of information in-parallel on huge groups of item equipment in a solid, flaw tolerant way. The term MapReduce really alludes to the accompanying two distinct assignments that Hadoop programs perform:
3. Map Task: This is the primary assignment, which takes input information and changes over it into a lot of information, where individual components are separated into tuples (key/esteem sets).
4. Reduce Task: This assignment takes the yield from a guide task as information and joins those information tuples into a littler set of tuples. The diminish assignment is constantly performed after the guide task.

Regularly both the information and the yield are put away in a filesystem. The system deals with planning undertakings, observing them and re-executes the bombed assignments. The MapReduce system comprises of a solitary ace JobTracker and one slave TaskTracker per bunch hub. The ace is liable for asset the board, following asset utilization/accessibility and booking the employments segment errands on the slaves, checking them and re-executing the failed assignments. The slaves Task Tracker execute the undertakings as coordinated by the ace and give task-status data to the ace intermittently. The JobTracker is a solitary purpose of disappointment for the Hadoop MapReduce administration which means if Job Tracker goes down, all running employments are ended.

CONCLUSION

As there are colossal volumes of information that are delivered each day, so such huge size of information it turns out to be trying to accomplish successful handling utilizing the current conventional methods. Enormous information is information that surpasses the handling limit of regular database frameworks. In this chapter key ideas about Big Data are displayed. These ideas incorporate Huge Data attributes, apparatuses, methods and applications for taking care of enormous information.

REFERENCES

De Mauro, A., Greco, M., & Grimaldi, M. (2016). A formal definition of Big Data based on its essential features. *Library Review, 65*(3), 122–135. doi:10.1108/LR-06-2015-0061

Han, Y. J. (2016). *China library development report, rural library volume*. Chinese National Library Press.

Hurwitz, J., Nugent, A., Halper, F., & Kaufman, M. (2013). *Big data for dummies*. John Wiley & Sons, Inc.

Kaisler, S., Armour, F., Espinosa, J. A., & Money, W. (2013, January). Big data: Issues and challenges moving forward. In *2013 46th Hawaii International Conference on System Sciences* (pp. 995-1004). IEEE.

Manyika, J., Chui, M., Brown, B., Bughin, J., Dobbs, R., & Roxburgh, C. (2011). *Big data: The next frontier for innovation, competition, and productivity*. McKinsey Global Institute.

Noor, A. (2013). Putting big data to work. *Mechanical Engineering (New York, N.Y.), 135*(10), 32–37. doi:10.1115/1.2013-OCT-1

Salo, D. (2010). *Retooling libraries for the data challenge*. Academic Press.

Wani, M. A., & Jabin, S. (2018). Big Data: Issues, Challenges, and Techniques in Business Intelligence. In *Big Data Analytics* (pp. 613–628). Springer. doi:10.1007/978-981-10-6620-7_59

Wu, J. Z. (2009). On information need and service for digital library client. *Hebei Sci-Tech Library Journal, 22*(5), 59–61.

Zhang, X. L. (2005). From digital library to e-knowledge mechanism. *Journal of Library Science in China, 31*(4), 5–10.

Chapter 2
Awareness of Big Data Usage and Applications Among Librarians in Zimbabwe

Josiline Phiri Chigwada
https://orcid.org/0000-0003-0964-3582
Bindura University of Science Education, Zimbabwe

Justice Kasiroori
Bindura University of Science Education, Zimbabwe

ABSTRACT

The chapter showcases the awareness of big data usage among librarians in Zimbabwe. The concept of big data is new, and librarians are building capacity to move with the current trends in librarianship. This chapter assists in pointing areas where big data can be applied in libraries. It also documents the challenges that are faced when using big data applications and proffer solutions that can be applied to deal with those challenges. It answers the question of whether it is practical to utilise big data in any type of library. A qualitative study was done where an online questionnaire was administered to twenty librarians in research institutions in Zimbabwe. The findings revealed that librarians are aware of the big data concept but are not utilising the tools and techniques in data mining and analysis. The authors recommend that capacity building should be done to equip librarians with the requisite skills.

DOI: 10.4018/978-1-7998-3049-8.ch002

INTRODUCTION

Big data has become a buzzword and catchphrase in the technology industry and academia. With big data organisations have come to know more about their operations than before. The big data revolution transcends across all industries and academic institutions stand to benefit from it. Libraries were not spared from the use of big data applications although the concept is still new to librarians. Zhan and Widen (2017) point out that big data is used to refer to different things depending with the field of study and its characteristics are not the same in various subjects. The emergence of the library 4.0 due to the changes in information communication technologies led to the generation of a lot of data in libraries as stated by Noh (2015). This chapter documents the awareness among librarians of big data applications in Zimbabwe. The objectives of the study were:

1. To assess the knowledge of librarians about big data.
2. To examine the use of big data by librarians
3. To document the challenges faced by librarians when using big data applications.

The rest of the chapter has sections which documents the definitions of big data; big data applications in the library; use of big data by librarians; challenges of big data usage by librarians; methodology that was used for this study; findings; discussion; recommendations; areas of further study; conclusion; references; and definitions of key terms.

DEFINITIONS OF BIG DATA

Even though big data has become so pervasive in today's world, the term big data itself has been taken to mean a lot of things. Big data has instead evolved so quickly and disorderly that such a universally accepted formal statement denoting its meaning does not exist (De Mauro, Greco & Grimaldi 2015). Most researchers define big data in terms of its characteristics, the most common which are volume, velocity and variety (Zhan and Widen 2017). However, these definitions do not bring out the aspect that makes big data what it is, that is, the issue of the complexity of working with big data. The Method for an Integrated Knowledge Environment (MIKE2.0) project contends that complexity and not size is the dominant factor in defining and dealing with big data.

Zhan and Widen (2017) did a study on understanding big data in librarianship and provided a number of definitions for big data that were used by researchers. They found out that big data refers to the tools, processes, technologies or ideas for handling large amounts of data and the characteristics of such data which include volume, velocity, variety, value, and veracity. Some definitions included challenges, demand and benefits of big data in line with the changing technological landscape and what is needed in processing big data. Therefore, the definition that would be used in this study includes a mixture of the MIKE.2.0 definition and the characteristic based definition;

Big data is a term describing the storage and analysis of large and or complex data which exceed(s) the capacity or capability of current or conventional storage, computational methods and systems, has high volume, velocity and is composed of a variety of data types and sizes.

BIG DATA APPLICATIONS IN THE LIBRARY

Li et al. (2019) opine that few studies have been done relating libraries to big data. Therefore the question is, "Do libraries have big data at all?". Libraries have moved from the traditional setup where the only data generated by the Library Management System and resources were catalogued meticulously via a limited set of metadata. Nowadays, libraries now collect data from a variety of sources both structured and unstructured data and no longer focus on books, journals and catalogue data only (Ball, 2019). Library data sources include, LMS transactions, library social media applications, blogs, texts, metadata, images, audio files, videos, research data, 3D digital copies and software, chat facilities and user generated data (Ball, 2019; Zhan and Widén, 2017). A number of scholars have pointed out that libraries have lots of data which fits the definition that was adopted for this paper. Simovic (2018) is of the view that the complexity of data collected by libraries and the different types of formats and sources qualifies it to be categorised as big data.

The application of big data in libraries is varied but can be categorised into three broad categories as espoused by Ball (2019); data as sources, data analyses (i.e. collecting, cleaning up, integrating and processing) and data visualisation (presentation and communication). This view is shared by Li et al. (2019) who state that big data can be used for data mining, data management, data visualization analysis, auxiliary decision-making mechanisms, and reader behaviour analysis. The data can be used for research purposes by library staff so as to study the information seeking bahaviour of patrons, the information needs of the patrons and if there is need to improve on the collection. The data should be analysed for the librarians to be able to make correct decisions regarding collection development and maintenance, information literacy skills training or the need for a research seminar on college or changing any service that is available.

Libraries can use the data collected to benefit just like any other organisation especially for decision making purposes. For example, using data from analytics engines like Matomo or Google Analytics together with data from social media and library transactional data, libraries can find out interests, preferences and behaviours of their users and thus streamline their offerings and creating better user experience just like any other enterprise (Ball, 2019; Günther et al., 2017; Zhan and Widén, 2017). It is important to note that libraries have always done data analysis of the various data generated by the patrons and systems (Ahmad, JianMing and Rafi, 2019). This trend has changed now due to the emergence of big data whereby the traditional library systems are no longer able to process the data during analysis. Powerful tools and applications are now required to do data analysis so as to come up with better decisions and improve on the products and services that are provided by the library.

USE OF BIG DATA BY LIBRARIANS

Xu and Yang (2019) pointed out various types of big data which are admission data; data generated by the library management system such as borrowing data, reservation data, and book overdue data; digital library utilisation data such as library website traffic, number of views and downloads of digital resources, and special rooms utilisation data; reference services data such as online helpdesk, document delivery and interlibrary loan; and equipment utilisation data.

Libraries with access control systems where users use swipe cards to enter into the library provide library's admission data. This data is used to know the number of entrants to the library which can be used to determine use or non-use of the physical facility. This data would assist in determining whether there is need for expansion of the facility to ensure that all the patrons are accommodated or if there is a need to redesign the space. This data can also be used to assess the library reception of readers and to ensure that there is effective service response. It is easier to track the reading patterns and behaviours of clients by using such data since the same identification card would be used for entering and performing various services within the library such as self-check in and booking of materials such as computers and photocopiers.

Data generated by the library management system includes data from all the modules such as acquisitions, cataloguing, circulation, reports generation, online public access catalogue, course reserves, authorities, administration, and patrons records. Borrowing data includes the name of the patron, student/staff number, call number of the item, title of the item, publisher, year of publication, time when the item was borrowed and the library staff member who performed the transaction if there is no self-service in the library. This shows that it contains all the information of the patron and the item that has been borrowed. Xu and Yang (2019) posit that this data is used for value analysis and mining. The library would use it for analysing the reading behaviour of the patrons. Another facility is the service for putting items on hold and this assist the librarian in determining titles that need to be put on reserve or the purchase of extra copies to ensure that the items are enough to satisfy the needs of the patrons. Reservation data assist in purchasing resources for the library. Patrons can also suggest items for purchasing through the online public access catalogue (OPAC) and all this data is stored in the library.

Library website traffic statistics show visits that have been done to the library webpages. The data would assist the librarians in monitoring the time period, monthly visits as well as annual visits of patrons. This data would assist in improving the content of the website and in creating awareness to the patrons since patterns and features can be deduced from comparing such kind of data. The number of views and downloads from digital resources provide data to evaluate the use of electronic resources available in the library. This data would be analysed and used to determine subscription of digital resources or tailor making training sessions on how to use e-resources to create awareness of resources with low usage.

Besides using number of visits to the website libraries can also utilise log analysis methods to view which websites their patrons frequent and the type of information that is offered by the said websites. This will help libraries to tailor make and package information to the tastes of the users thereby making sure that the information is actually utilized. The use pattern would also assist in improving the website because some use patterns would point to webpages that are not used at all. The librarian would be in a position to find out why some pages are not used while some are receiving heavy usage. The landing pages would assist the librarians in knowing what is pointing the patrons to the library website and this data can assist in the management of library web pages.

Librarians are responsible for knowledge organisation, retrieval and dissemination of information and maintaining information systems. Li et al (2017) and Affelt (2015) pointed out that big data is reshaping how libraries carry out those duties which are indicated above. It has been indicated that big data is now used for evaluating service satisfaction of customers, decision making, and library collection data (Khan and Du 2018, Teets and Goldner 2013). This shows that librarians are using the big data that they collect to improve their services and products since there are so many competitors nowadays and some patrons do not see the value of visiting the library. The data that is collected through surveys can be used to enhance customer satisfaction by ensuring that the services and products provided meet the expectations of the patrons. Librarians would also be in a position to market their services and products so that the patrons are knowledgeable of what the library provides.

The library can extract and analyse large datasets and conduct data mining in order to identify the potential needs of library patrons as a way of attracting potential users and retaining the current users according to Li et al (2017). For example, the statistics that are provided by RemotexS, a software for enhancing remote access to e-resources are so detailed and it's easy to ascertain how users are using the resources provided by the library. These can assist in decision making especially when deciding which subscription to renew and which one to drop, or on databases which needs further training. This is supported by Provost and Fawcett (2013), and Narendra (2016). The statistics can be analysed up to patron level where the librarian can ascertain whether the patron has activated an account and the databases that he/she is using and the time that is spent during each search including the number of downloads. Reports from these statistics can be downloaded as large data sets which can be used and analysed when making renewal of subscriptions decisions.

The library is responsible for archiving datasets and making them available to researchers. It also uses data for establishing links between the library data and other datasets. As a result, the library is now regarded as a big data boomtown where there is facilitation of big data use, storage and referencing (Reinhalter and Wittmann 2014). Big data benefits the library through value creation and big data is generated in borrowing and lending transactions, user profiles, application of social media and mobile devices. Libraries are now developing and managing data repositories on top of the institutional repositories that were already available. This data is adding to the already available datasets and it is now easier to track the authors who would have submitted their data sets and also to track the citation of those data sets. This data is important since researchers are able to use such data to improve their marketing strategies after publishing their data sets.

Libraries can utilise Big Data to make data-driven decision, which can in turn help to provide more cost-effective, innovative decisions or recommendations that users wish to have (Al-Barashdi and Al-Karousi 2018). The ability to collect and analyze massive amounts of data will be a competitive advantage across all industries, including the library. The library is now able to visualise data to deduce user behaviours. Without big data analysis, it is difficult to find some patterns during library data visualisation.

CHALLENGES OF BIG DATA USAGE BY LIBRARIANS

The advent of big data brought about a number of challenges which include data privacy, data reduction and compression, data confidentiality and security, and big data processing and technology. (Li et al 2017, Wang et al. 2016, Cowan and Campbell 2016, Affelt 2015). This calls for capacity building amongst the librarians to ensure that they are able to offer the services in the big data era. Most librarians are not aware of how they can benefit from the big data era since they are failing to take advantage of the opportunities that are offered by big data due to these challenges.

The advancement of big data has caused privacy issues especially during use although the data sets are generated from actions of many people (Boyd and Crawford, 2012). Individual data can be accessed and this can negatively impact an individual in an unexpected way. (Narayanan and Shmatikov 2008) stated that this can be avoided by anonymization of the data sets thoroughly although the users of the dataset can attempt to deanonymise the data. As a result, librarians should be knowledgeable of this challenge to ensure that they protect the privacy of individuals when dealing with big data sets. In a library set up, patrons are free to access the type of information they want in any given situation as long as it is made available. Privacy issues can lead to deterioration in data security due to its openness which would result in easy accessibility to the data. Fuller (2015) added that it is not easy to store and manage big data as confidentiality issues might not be regarded to the personal information that is collected in library management systems. As a result, librarians must be able to respect the privacy of patrons when using such data sets.

There is a challenge of access to information especially concerning transactional data. Manovich (2011) noticed that social media data, for example, cannot be easily accessed. Large social data are available on social media applications such as Facebook, Twitter, YouTube, WhatsApp, Instagram, but only social media companies are able to access the data and can restrict who can access the information. This is also causing a division of information rich and information-lacking companies and countries leading to a new type of digital divide according to Boyd and Crawford (2012). There is need to promote policies that calls for free access to information so that those with the rights to access such data can do so without any restriction.

There is complexity in managing big data since formal dataset modeling processes cannot be used for big data (Daniel 2014). As a result, big data sets have no formal metadata and this is caused by the technical issues within the current technologies. This is coupled by infrastructure issues as the volume of big data is huge as compared to the current library databases (Hoy 2014). Some libraries are now resorting to the use of cloud computing to deal with storage, access, obsolescence and human resources costs. However, this can only be done by libraries which have the financial resources to pay for cloud computing services.

Affelt (2015) pointed out that librarians joined the big data usage late leading to lack of big data professionals in the library. Lack of skills in dealing with big data is another challenge that is experienced by librarians. This view is buttressed by Ahmad, JianMing and Rafi (2019) who conclude that there is strong correlation between the competencies and skills of librarians for the implementation of big data analytics in libraries. Expertise is needed to deal with big data applications and there is a need for capacity building so that people working with big data have the required skills (Pearson and Wegner 2013, McAfee et al 2012). Librarians should acquire skills to know how cloud computing works and how to deal with different formats of big data. They should also have knowledge of the FAIR (Findable, Accessible, Interoperable, Reusable) data principles. Librarians should have the skills of making the data findable by archiving it in good data repositories; and the correct metadata should be used to make it accessible using the metadata standards.

METHODOLOGY

An online questionnaire was administered to librarians in academic libraries and research institutions in Zimbabwe. Purposive sampling was used to select the population where librarians who handle the technology aspects of the libraries were chosen. Technology and System Librarians were chosen because they are the personnel that is responsible for information technology applications in the library. They are responsible for ensuring that the library is moving along with trending issues such as big data. A total of 20 librarians were selected from 18 academic institutions and two research institutions as the respondents of the study. These libraries have automated most of their transactions and utilize information technology in interacting with their clientele. The selection was on the assumption that libraries that are automated use big data applications.

FINDINGS

In terms of the knowledge of big data in libraries, all twenty (20) librarians stated that they are aware of the big data phenomenon and indicated that at one time or another they have researched into big data with the aim of adopting and using it in their libraries. However, only nine (9) of the librarians said they have offered the idea of utilizing big data to their institutions. All twenty (20) of the librarians agreed that the data that the libraries generate can be categorized as big data. It was also pointed out that most of the big data that the libraries generate is hosted by third parties like social media companies. This shows that the libraries are generating big data since they are automating their services and are resorting to use social media in their interactions with patrons.

The participants indicated that on the other hand only a few librarians who are not the IT people in the libraries are knowledgeable of big data and its basic concepts and how it works. The issue is usually left to the IT personnel or librarians conversant with technology. In terms of usage, none of the libraries that were represented are utilising any of the big data tools, techniques or methodology to mine, analyse and visualise the data that is generated by the libraries. The libraries utilize traditional methods of analytics and each library system is a standalone data source which in turn is analysed differently. For example, borrowing transactions are analysed separately from the computer usage data. This is linked to the lack of skills in the use of big data applications and the poor infrastructure that cannot process big data in research institutions.

In terms of the challenges in utilizing big data, the biggest challenge that was highlighted is that of the lack of awareness of the benefits that accrue to libraries when using big data against the traditional methods of data processing and analysis in libraries. This was indicated by sixteen (16) of the librarians, whereas one did not indicate that big data was well known at their institution. Three (3) participants indicated that at their institutions big data was moderately known and was not a major problem. This challenge is in addition from the challenges that were highlighted by the literature review. Only four (4) participants indicated that they have intermediate skills in data management including skills that can be utilized for big data management. The rest, 16, indicated that they lacked the expertise to manage or utilize big data, its tools and or applications. The lack of expertise is a challenge that was pointed out by various researchers (Li et al. 2017, Campbell and Cowan 2016, Affelt 2015, Pearson and Wegner 2013, McAffe et al. 2012).

Participants indicated that another challenge that they come across when offering to utilize big data for their libraries was the aspect of lack of funding from their institutions. All participants indicated that funding for big data applications and tools was not available. Funding would have been for purchase or lease of computing power, storage and other related costs. Participants indicated that none of the institutions provided or was willing to provide funding for big data endeavours. The challenge of funding was also pointed out by (Hoy, 2014) who stated that usage of big data comes with increased costs mainly in infrastructure. Another challenge that was raised by most of the participants, 17, was the perception that usage of big data is purely an IT concern and that other librarians who are not IT people have no role to play in the big data lifecycle. This perception cuts across all types of institutions. Only three participants indicated that their institutions acknowledged the library's role in spearheading big data adoption in their institutions. A challenge that is related to the issue of privacy is the fear of the lack of privacy that was indicated by 7 participants. Institutions were said to be afraid to commit to big data as they feared that institutional data may breach privacy laws. This can be dealt with by the use of institutional and national policies that would guide various institutions on how they can deal with big data problems.

DISCUSSION

The findings indicate that technology and systems librarians are well aware of big data and the areas where it is used in libraries. The findings also show that technology and systems librarians perform data analytics on various types of data that is collected by the libraries. This finding is similar to what Ahmad, JianMing and Rafi (2019) came up in their research. However, the analytics done by librarians is carried out per system or data source without aggregation of the different types of data. For example borrowing patterns are analysed in the Library Management System but this is not linked to any other data sources like social media platforms used by the libraries. By so doing librarians risk "the blind men and the elephant" scenario, that is, they will not get the whole picture but small pieces instead. Even though librarians are knowledgeable about big data, no library in the country is utilizing big data applications and or any of its tools. The reasons for this state are varied from lack of skills, lack of funding, negative perception amongst management and fellow workers and the complexity of the data that makes up big data. These findings reflect those by Daniel (2014), concerning the usage of complex data in libraries, and the findings by Hoy (2014) pertaining to the funding and technical aspect of using big data.

RECOMMENDATIONS

After dissecting the findings and going by the discussions in the preceding section, the following are the recommendations that were made by the authors. These recommendations should assist in the adoption of big data and its applications or tools in the Zimbabwean libraries landscape. There is a need to create awareness of the positive yields that come with usage of big data to the libraries. The awareness should not be limited to the librarians only but across the organisations, including all the stakeholders and management working together with the research office. There is also a need for capacity building for the librarians to be able to utilize big data and all its applications. Capacity building is also recommended by Ahmad, JianMing, Rafi (2019) in line with their research. This can be done by encouraging librarians to attend workshops, conferences, seminars, shout courses and webinars on the application of big data in libraries. One of the challenges that was highlighted, particularly from the academic librarians perspective is the absence of guiding policies for the establishment and or management of big data. Therefore, librarians should engage management or policy makers in order for policies to be enacted and enforced that enable utilization of big data in libraries. The issue of policies can also be tackled at a national level so that all institutions that want to utilise big data have guidance in place.

CONCLUSION

Libraries process a lot of complex data which can be categorised as big data. However, most libraries do not utilise this data as a whole and take a piecemeal approach to data management and analytics. It is important that libraries are given capacity to manage all the data that they process. This will in turn help the libraries make data driven decisions which enrich the services that libraries provide to their patrons. Librarians should acquire skills on how they can use big data applications and tools so as to benefit from this emerging issue in libraries. This would assist them in data mining, analysis and visualisation which in turn would lead to improved library services and products in the fourth industrial revolution.

AREAS FOR FURTHER STUDY

The tools that can be utilised by librarians and libraries to harness the power of big data is one of the areas that needs to be looked into. The analysis of competency gaps and the creation of effective teaching methods to fill them for both future and current managers and practitioners is a promising research area that has still much opportunity to grow. Library schools can also be studied to research on how they are revising the library and information science curriculum to cater for big data studies.

REFERENCES

Al-Barashdi, H., & Al-Karousi, R. (2018). Big Data in academic libraries: Literature review and future research directions. *Journal of Information Studies and Technology*, *2*(13), 2–16.

Ball, F. (2019). Big data and their impact on libraries. *American Journal of Information Science and Technology*, *3*(1), 1–9. doi:10.11648/j.ajist.20190301.11

Boyd, D., & Crawford, K. (2012). Critical questions for big data. *Information Communication and Society*, *15*(5), 662–679. doi:10.1080/1369118X.2012.678878

Cowan, S. R., & Campbell, D. G. (2016). The paradox of privacy: Revisiting a core library value in an age of big data and linked data. *Library Trends*, *64*(3), 492–511. doi:10.1353/lib.2016.0006

Daniel, B. (2014). Big data analytics in higher education: Opportunities and challenges. *British Journal of Educational Technology*, *46*(5), 1–10.

De Mauro, A., Greco, M., & Grimaldi, M. (2015). Article. *AIP Conference Proceedings*, *1644*, 97–104. doi:10.1063/1.4907823

Fuller, M. (2015). Big data: New science, new challenges, new dialogical opportunities. *Zygon*, *50*(3), 569–582. doi:10.1111/zygo.12187

Gunther, W. A., Mehrizi, M. H. R., Huysman, M., & Feldberg, F. (2017). Debating big data: A literature review on realising value from big data. *The Journal of Strategic Information Systems*, *26*(3), 191–209. doi:10.1016/j.jsis.2017.07.003

Hoy, M. B. (2014). Big data: An introduction for librarians. *Medical Reference Services Quarterly*, *33*(3), 320–326. doi:10.1080/02763869.2014.925709

Khan, H. R., & Du, Y. (2018). What is a data Librarian? A content analysis of job advertisements for data librarians in the United States Academic Libraries. IFLA WLIC 2018.

Li, J., Lu, M., Dou, G and Wang, S. (2017). Big data application framework and its feasibility analysis in library. *Information Discovery and Delivery*, *45*(4), 161-168.

Li, S., Jiao, F., Zhang, Y., & Xu, X. (2019). Problems and changes in digital libraries in the age of big data from the perspectives of user services. *Journal of Academic Librarianship*, *45*(1), 22–30. doi:10.1016/j.acalib.2018.11.012

Manovich, L. (2011). Debates Digit. *Humanit*,. 1.

McAfee, A., Brynjolfsson, E., Davenport, T. H., Patil, D., & Barton, D. (2012).. . *Harvard Business Review*, *90*, 61.

Narayanan, A., & Shmatikov, V. (2008). Article. *Proceedings of IEEE Symposium on Security and Privacy*, 111–125.

Narendra, A. P. (2016). Big Data, data analyst, and improving the competence of librarian. *Record and Library Journal*, *1*(2), 83–93. doi:10.20473/rlj.v1i2.1162

Noh, Y. (2015). Imagining library 4.0: Creating a model for future libraries. *Journal of Academic Librarianship*, *41*(6), 786–797. doi:10.1016/j.acalib.2015.08.020

Pearson, T and Wegener, R. (2013). *Big Data: The Organizational Challenge.* Bain & Company report.

Provost, F., & Fawcett, T. (2013). Data science and its relationship to big data and data-driven decision making. *Big Data*, *1*(1), 51–59. doi:10.1089/big.2013.1508

Reinhalter, L., & Wittmann, R. J. (2014). The library: Big data's boomtown. *The Serials Librarian*, *67*(4), 363–372. doi:10.1080/0361526X.2014.915605

Simovic, A. (2018). A big data smart library recommender system for an educational institution. *Library Hi Tech, 36*(3), 498–523. doi:10.1108/LHT-06-2017-0131

Teets, M., & Goldner, M. (2013). Libraries' role in curating and exposing big data. *Future Internet, 5*(3), 429–438. doi:10.3390/fi5030429

Wang, C., Xu, S., Chen, L., & Chen, X. (2016). Exposing library data with big data technology: A review. In *2016 IEEE/ACIS 15th International Conference on Computer and Information Science (ICIS),* 1-6). IEEE. 10.1109/ICIS.2016.7550937

Xu, R., & Yang, Y. (2019). Study of user behaviour data, mining and applications in university libraries: taking the Central China Normal University Library as an example. *Advances in Computer Science Research* Volume 87. *3rd International Conference on Mechatronics Engineering and Information Technology (ICMEIT 2019).* 10.2991/icmeit-19.2019.44

Zhan, M., & Widen, G. (2017). Understanding big data in librarianship. *Journal of Librarianship and Information Science, 51*(2), 561–576. doi:10.1177/0961000617742451

KEY TERMS AND DEFINITIONS

Big Data: Extremely large data sets that may be analysed computationally to reveal patterns, trends, and associations, especially relating to human behaviour and interactions.

Data Librarian: Librarian engaged in managing research data, using research data as a resource, or supporting researchers in these activities.

Digital Divide: The gulf between those who have ready access to computers and the Internet and those who do not have that facility.

Electronic Resources: Are materials in digital format accessible electronically using a computer which is connected to the internet.

Librarian: A person trained in library science and engaged in library service.

Library Management System: Enterprise resource planning system for a library, used to track items owned, orders made, bills paid, and patrons who have borrowed.

Chapter 3
Opportunities and Implementation of Big Data Management in Academic Libraries:
Strategic Approach and Discovering a Solution

Mahesh G. T.
Government First Grade College, Mysore, India

Nandeesha B.
All India Institute of Speech and Hearing, India

ABSTRACT

Data has changed the world in an unbelievable way and made an impact on our lifestyles at an exceptional rate. Big data is now the latest science of exploring and forecasting human-machine behavior dealing with a massive amount of associated data. The study is intended to understand the intensity and the competencies of librarians in implementing big data initiative project in academic libraries by the Government of Karnataka State. The study also tries to understand the application of big data in these libraries; 68 (87.17%) librarians completed the survey out of 78 respondents. The results of the study showed a strong association, that is, 72 (92.30%) respondents had the essential competencies and 58 (75.64%) librarians ability, intensity, readiness in implementing big data in academic libraries.

DOI: 10.4018/978-1-7998-3049-8.ch003

INTRODUCTION

Big data has been extensively conversed in the recent past, its varied impact and prospect have been known to all and proved pragmatically across the globe. Library professionals have always been good at organizing information and managing it, they do not need to become a software engineer but having a minimal knowledge of technological tools that can transform the huge amount of data in to Big Data and serve the user community.

In the ever changing vibrant digital environment, data, information, knowledge management systems are autonomously preserved and managed by all higher education institutions, explicit knowledge in the libraries are not easily accessible and not centralized. And within this context Big data is being created through digitally in the libraries and this has forced restrictions to academicians, researchers, information seekers and policy maker's work hard in humanizing and developing the excellence and competence. It would be a great challenge to all librarians in serving our chief stake holders merely with print books and journals that are available with their benefits. And this study addresses the strategic approach of fetching various information resources from a variety of academic and corporate sources at a single platform instantly in a real time.

The main objective is to reduce the instance that descends between probing the information and the actual reading. This is of vital importance in bridging the gap in accessing the information to those who have limited or no access to information and knowledge. Down the line large amount of information is collected from the chief stakeholders and other information baseline thus forming the big data to digitize the household and other information related tasks.

The expensive knowledge achieved from exploring substantial quantity of networked libraries data could endow with key insights in escalating the accessibility of information. This makes academicians, researchers and government policy maker's accomplishing strategic solutions without any difficulty and also making the information further accessible to the marginalized and underprivileged patrons. Application in instructive, academic analytics and data driven assessment is the utmost relevance of Big data as a source has been candid in the recent past. Pramod (2019) strongly recommended that this system plays a pivotal role in proposing appropriate information systems that are customer driven and helps in customer retention. Practically speaking Big data analytics could have an impact on academic libraries, because of the huge amount of information available, collection, and velocity of the information concerned, as a result the storage space and practice of the system are relatively irresistible, the techniques related to data analytics and algorithms are very complex, which makes Big Data analytics a technology a demanding assignment.

BACKGROUND

With the swift development in the social networks such as Facebook, Twitter, Google, LinkedIn, Instagram, What's App etc., many people across the world have one or the other accounts or a member of these social media. Registered and non-registered members may be for academic or non academic purpose of these networks are now impending these online platforms to investigate and make inquiries to accomplish their information needs and find a way of conventional library services. Higher education institution libraries coming under central Government and state governments have taken initiatives and policy measures in implementing these platforms well. Professional librarians coming under these hierarchies have involved exceptionally well and are competent to utilize big data. Big data gives intrinsic challenges of getting out through and updating both users and librarians. This confront has been coordinated by the incapability of many algorithms to execute healthy in searching and assessment settings, consequently they initiated their lapse in forecasting patron preference, awareness and modification in flavor. And in this situation big data should be no exemption, therefore the need for formal big data appliance in libraries that offers prognostic analytics of online information services and information seeking behaviour of their users resulting in better understanding the user's needs and necessities. As a result, big data is very much useful in forecasting and outlining of collection development, search history, user retention, reading habits, better usage of information systems and services for future library planning.

Department of Collegiate Education (DCE), Karnataka with its inception in the year 1960, has been striving to make quality higher education affordable and accessible to all sections of students. With a firm concern for the overall development of the students, the Department has been taking keen interest to see that students belonging to the most backward communities, women and rural students are not deprived of the accessibility to tertiary education. The Department manages planning, administration and funding of 430 government and 315 private aided colleges across the state.

Digitization initiatives, development in exploration and the social networks have shaped a situation where academic community is now gaining momentum to huge amount of data on an unparalleled scale, leading to innovation and research challenges in processing and curation. Funding initiatives from the DCE, Karnataka (2020) like ICT Infrastructure, Digitalization, MOOC, and Subscription to NLIST are now clearly cheering academicians to enhance their knowledge that leads to greater indulgence, utility, and applications of Big Data. With the efforts of Karnataka State College Librarians Association (KSCLA) in the month of March, 2020 our commissioner announced financial assistance of about 1.25 crore to the libraries where Big Data can be applied and also to enhance the efficiency of library and information services that can start using Big Data.

Library and Information Science is always been interdisciplinary and collaborative discipline, captivating the knowledge of numerous subject areas fetching the tools, techniques, and theories of information science to bear on subject-specific domains (Sugimoto, & Cronin, 2012). This understanding of engaging in interdisciplinary alliance have made libraries well situated to connect with such inventiveness such as the ICT, Digitalization, MOOC, and NList that give confidence and association for a more advanced thoughtful of the multifaceted challenges adjoining Big Data.

BIG DATA

Big data refers to swift growth in the quantity of structured, semi-structured and unstructured data and it's a huge database that is diverse and highly developed from the standard databases and stimulates from various sources and appear in several formats. The pace at which information is generating, there is a need to store, process and disseminate competently to the end user. Big Data is said to be the 'entire data', it can be depicted as data management, in terms of escalating high volume, velocity and variety of data that cannot be handled with conventional databases. Big data comes from all corners of the communication technologies such as electronic devices, digital sensors, audio-visual materials, all type of networks, log files and records, web applications and social networks, a large amount of these data are generated at a real time and in an extremely big scale.

Gartner Group Inc. (2001) defined Big Data as "high volume, high velocity, and high variety information resources that need new forms of processing to facilitate improved decision making, imminent discovery and process optimization."

According to International Data Corporation (IDC), "Big data technologies illustrate a new generation of technologies and architecture intended to economically extract value from very big volumes of an extensive diversity of data facilitating high velocity capture, discovery and analysis".

NEED OF BIG DATA IN LIBRARIES

It is observed from the literature that in the last two decades research data has mounted a lot and the information seekers wish to use collected works as an organised and data mining the information resourcefully. It is observed that there is an improper organization of data in terms of information available in the libraries such as books and journals are well organized since our users could use these varieties of information for what they need. Nevertheless, the circumstances are unusual for those scientific data accumulated in libraries. These research data in libraries seems to be unsystematic, less organised and described, and in unconventional formats which are poorly suited to preserve for long-term reuse. And there is no standardized data and data formats where research data may lack the standard and format. Generally it depends on the domain knowledge and institutional libraries.

The technologies that are implemented in library, big data might be dissimilar from that in other fields. In order to implement big data systems in library there are some considerations such as creating a centralized data repositories, wherein the data are stored, managed, cataloged and retrieved, common data standards and communities to maintain it having the analysis tool.

OPPORTUNITIES AND IMPLEMENTATION OF BIG DATA IN ACADEMIC LIBRARIES

Academic libraries in Karnataka state coming under the department of collegiate education encompasses a huge quantity of primary and secondary data with intellectual content. These contents could be networked and augmented with open data on the web and engender the advantage for our end users. This would comprise the user data and data of our library collection as well, and their dynamic content usage for the expansion of new information services, resulting in the technique and understanding of Big Data applications in libraries that are required. These significant value added services could be achieved with the help of these Big Data technology. This study furnishes the impression of the potentiality and probability of utilizing huge amounts of data in all academic libraries across the state. It is understood from the study that the Library professionals can occupy with a huge responsibility in handling Big Data as we have knowledge, skills and service attitude to facilitate higher education institutions, corporate and Government organizations.

WHY BIG DATA? GOVERNMENT OF KARNATAKA INITIATIVE

It is not that much clear that where this big data issue will lead us, as its utility would have a paramount impact not just when it comes to the management of data and electronic information, As far as the use of digital data is concerned, at present big data has the sturdy insinuation in its impact on the intellectual community.

When it comes to assessment part, we had only "minute data" which has scattered across the institutions that was accessible. And on the majority only books and journals have been catalogued and indexed. The main objective was to access the primary data electronically. Structured metadata was the only tool to achieve this.

The conventional cataloguing system was the only referencing technique for the entire collection and was the nucleus of reference services that are offered.

With the dawn of the data analytics the typical cataloguing form has reassigned to the digital media. As a result of this, digital data is made available in a wide range of forms and anywhere, anytime access. This digital content is even more being complemented with the huge data that are generously accessible on the internet that not only triggered modification in information behaviour creating incredible potential for academic libraries.

The methodological possibilities offered by big data and its analytics have changed the way of accessing the data by the users of current dynamic generation. We have a strong reason, as to why our libraries should look at the big data with more intent and objectively. This not only includes the leaving from the state of accurateness in conventional cataloguing, but also the prospect in dealing out the intellectual data and the linkage to free available data on the worldwide network. Nowadays, huge amount of data are created digitally in all Arts, Science, Commerce and Management disciplines. Teaching community has started recording and uploading the digital content and video lectures on the YouTube channel "*jnananidhi*" as a part of big data initiative

It has to be acknowledged that the vast amount of data is coming under single cloud platform in the form of e-Granthalaya as a part of application of big data initiative. It is understood from the data collected from professional association that majority of the government institution libraries coming under the common network and platform where users will have the access to wide range data irrespective of format such as full text data links, high streaming HD videos, networked and shared links. e-Granthalaya is a Digital Platform developed by National Informatics Centre, Ministry of Electronics and Information Technology, Government of India for Government Libraries. Under this platform, NIC provides comprehensive ICT solutions with integrated Library Management Software, Digital Library Module, Cloud hosting environment and a Library Portal (OPAC) with NICSI empanelled Roll-out Services support. e-Granthalaya is useful to transform traditional libraries to e-Library with Digital Library Services which includes, automation of in-house activities of libraries, digital library integration, and to provide various online member services using Single Window Access System. Latest version of e-Granthalaya i.e. Ver.4.0 is a 'Cloud Ready Application' and provides a Web-based solution in enterprise mode with a centralized database for cluster of libraries. The ICT solution is well compliance with International standards prevalent in Libraries with use of latest ICT technology and Cloud hosting. e-Granthalaya 4.0 uses PostgreSQL - an Open Source DBMS as back-end database solution and is made available in NIC National Cloud (Meghraj) for Government Libraries.

Earlier library collections were initially intended for its users only to search and access required chunks of information they needed. It is because of the state government initiative (2020) in building, networking the digital collections and library services where big data can be applied, to use other data analysis techniques it has made potential to research this library data completely or in phase for data mining.

If given the access over cloud umbrella, libraries just do not have to confine themselves to their own data collection. They are also capable of processing and analyzing peripheral data sources too. In the meantime, number of data sources from tertiary agents are made available to enable significant data services to remote and end users.

OBJECTIVES

Some of the main objectives of the present study are

1. To explore the intent of librarians in implementing Big Data initiative in academic libraries of Karnataka state.
2. To know the perceptions and competencies of library professionals towards the use of Big Data.

LITERATURE REVIEW

Big Data is the augmentation in volume and variety of data which can no longer be managed using the conventional databases with respect to its diverse data formats and volume. Big Data can be easily described using three V's, Volume, Velocity and Variety. Majority of the big data processing techniques emphasize high speed and competent use of huge amounts of data (Daniel, 2017). Shuqing, Fusen, Zhang and Xia (2019) stressed on the significance and use of big data in digital libraries in understanding its users reading habits and effectiveness of using the electronic information resources.

In their paper, Ferran, Mor, & Minguillon (2005), in their research paper depicted that libraries play a crucial role for communal societal information service systems. In continuing the satisfaction of library users, digital and virtual libraries must be continued to be a sign of changes in expertise, thereby using big data.

Li & Zhang (2013), in their study titled 'The problem of large data in the construction of digital library' renowned that digital libraries should focus more on their own data relatively than external data as it has uniqueness of big data and this would augment the efficient use of knowledge resources.

Gorman (2015) studied about the challenges and the opportunities for the libraries, he then projected a model for the accomplishment of Big Data analytics. It is also indispensable to assess the potential and limitations of the institutions to advance their products and services. He also stressed on the challenges and opportunities of the organizations, the execution of analytics that helps us to overcome these challenges.

RESEARCH METHODOLOGY

The study carried out an online survey through Google form to accomplish the said objectives, subsequently a methodical literature review was done and an investigation tool was derived to collect the data from the professional respondents. Study populations were the librarians working in government first grade colleges of Karnataka state and were selected through simple random sampling.

These colleges are affiliated to various Universities under University of Mysore, Bangalore University, Mangalore University, Karnatak University and Kuvempu University covering all the regions coming under the Department of Collegiate Education. Research data were received from 68 college librarians that were finally considered for the data analysis out of 78 respondents. The findings of the study showed a strong association of po0.005 between the tested values.

FINDINGS AND DISCUSSION

The study population of library professionals was a mixture of different age groups, education qualification and professional experience in different sectors such as universities, colleges, public libraries and corporate sectors of Karnataka state. Among these 68 respondent librarians, the number of males was 41 (60.29%) and the remaining 27 (39.70%) were female respondents. Respondents were of different age groups ranging between 30 to 60 years of age. The educational qualification of these respondents was Masters Degree in LIS with M.Phil and a doctoral degree, whereas 44 (64.70%) respondents were having PhD degree. Study respondents' professional experiences were categorized into three categories. 32 (47.05%) respondents were having the professional experience of 1–15 years, 24 (35.29%) were having the experience of 15-20 years and the remaining 12 (17.64%) respondents were having more than 20 years of experience.

The study investigated the practices, competencies and intent measures to extort the essential results in required formats in a varied library and information systems among the library professionals. Big data occupies in the different phases of data collection, processing and managing the quality of data, skill set of data about data, content development, preservation and conservation of data, finally data analysis and the application and implementation of Big Data in academic libraries. It also gave the approach to know the competency of librarians in the perspective and implementation of these skills in their working environment and performing in libraries. The study revealed that majority of the librarians i.e., 72 (92.30%) respondents were having explicit kind of expensive proficiency and the nature of work that have to make use of the different forms of data in the libraries. These results of the study also supports the study of Federer (2018) that librarians too have the expertise and required competencies in dealing with dynamic formats of data handling and these challenging work.

Librarians are already in the practice of collecting, processing, organizing, and disseminating data and information in their libraries, and it is found that 58 (75.64%) librarians showed the ability, intensity, readiness in implementing Big Data in academic libraries. The study findings reveal that librarians in academic libraries are having a good association between their skills of visualizing a data that depends on the culture and practices of parent organization keeping reputation and significance of data.

The study revealed the paradigm shift among the librarians and laid the basis for the dynamic growth and expansion in future in terms of Big Data works proficiency. The premeditated approach obtained from the research study and the Big Data initiative shows that, a scientific technique for any academic institution adjusted to transform its capabilities could be developed. Library professionals interested in research will have the wide range of opportunities to explore the underlying correlation between the innovation of Big Data initiatives and paradigm shift in the institutional necessities of academic libraries.

The available wide variety of data formats of Big Data skills is considerably associated with the acquisition, organization and management of data. Its interoperability, value, metadata skills, nature of institution, documentation, analysis, and also ethical issues were involved in the implementation of Big Data initiative in libraries. Thus, the pre-requisite skills of librarians are very much important for Big Data analytics in libraries. The study found that the knowledge about the superiority of data and knowledge is a very important skill for Big Data implementation.

This research study identified and addressed some of the issues that involved in Big Data, its implementation and academic indices that have been practiced in our academic libraries. A competency of the librarians has been considered as an essential requirement to contribute in the activities that are associated with Big Data initiative.

The study showed po0.005 level of significance that represents the considerable association among the variables of essential skill sets and competencies of librarians in implementing Big Data in academic libraries. This shows that there is an opportunity in developing the potentiality in the academic environment and also enhancing the attitude in meeting the research needs of academic community and other chief stakeholders by meeting the needs of dynamic users offering research based services. On the other hand as a result of swift growth and acquisition of huge volume of data few senior library professionals (having more than 20 years of experience who are not that much familiar with latest technology and advancement in information science) were unaware of the formats of Big Data. The study also revealed that libraries in urban areas have practiced the data analytics to some extent where they had the good financial support having good technology infrastructure.

The study also revealed that there is a bigger need, that librarians are to be acquainted with the Big Data technologies and enhance their skill sets participating in UGC sponsored Short Term Courses at state and central universities HRDC's, MOOC's and also through attending workshops/seminars/webinars etc. Data mining in libraries also needs some knowledge of programming that considerably enhances the Big Data in libraries significantly. These accessible library and information services are enhanced based on the library needs of the users to regulate the information need based effective library services and user studies.

The research also put forth the platform to library professionals for the advance research of vibrant skills of Big Data challenges from the strategic insight obtained from the Big Data initiatives, and a technique for any academic institution to regulate and transfer its potentials, also a research to determine the cost-effectiveness of big data in libraries and the benefits by analyzing the huge volume of data and social network contents in developing their library and information services.

CHALLENGES

Challenging issues seems to be the shortage of competent and skilled professionals, short of infrastructure, scientific challenges such as tools and data formats, safety and sustaining of overcoming the financial problems. Librarians have faced the challenges in Big Data analytics that focus on the lack of support from parent organizations. Lack of sufficient infrastructure to meet conservation needs and its initiatives, support for the provision of knowledge or literacy of data in libraries and information centers are some of the concerned areas (Thomas and Urban, 2018).

Big data and the libraries have the greater challenge of moving beyond the text having high definition audiovisual big data giving access & retrieval of full texts, documents with a long-term preservation of the data. Accessing the worldwide metadata and allied data sets through existing catalogues.

COMPETENCIES OF LIBRARIANS IN HANDLING BIG DATA

The current era of electronic environment offers opportunities for library professionals to indulge in data related activities. We the professionals should seek these skills and knowledge about the stipulation of possible data services. Librarians have taken the initiative in Big Data by acquiring newer skills such as enabling the data discovery and data (information) retrieval, maintenance of data quality through machine readable cataloguing, indexing & abstracting, archiving, preservation, management and demonstration. As a result we can make big data sets more significant, evident and accessible by generating taxonomies and folksonomies.

FIELDS OF APPLICATION FOR BIG DATA IN LIBRARIES

It offers the good platform to set up the big data era to our end users. It can be supportive for library and information science researchers to come up with innovative research topics and ascertain the prospective partnership, be advantageous for our information students to be well prepared themselves for potential and competent job markets. Big data technology could be helpful in data mining about the library holdings and also it is achievable to document and follow the track of our potential library user's activity and to accumulate that data in huge scale data storage, later on it would be helpful in conducting data analysis. The results of it could be then used to impending the overall user experience, and user satisfaction of library and information services. If we see some of the advantages of Big Data, here are some

- **Volume:** Volume is perhaps the well-known quality of big data. It is known that more than 90% of current data was created in the recent years.
- **Variety:** In terms of Big Data, we need to look the data in all formats like structured, semi-structured and unstructured data. We are receiving all varieties of data such as pdf, image, website, links, images HD audio-visuals etc.
- **Velocity:** It is the pace at which data is being created, processed, uploaded and accessed.
- **Variability:** The irregularity characteristics that the data has at times will slower down the upload or retrieval process every now and then depending on the connection.
- **Veracity:** It is confined to our data accurateness. How exact is our data and how significant it is to the data analytics.

It is observed from the literature that there are three major streams of relevance that can be illustrious for big data,

1. data as source
2. data analyses (planning, data collection, processing, refining, organization, synchronizing and storing) and
3. data visualization in terms of presentations and communications).

CONCLUSION

Applications of Big Data in libraries are very much composite and multifaceted and therefore in the recent past there is an increase in demand in resolving the information needs of our users. The main objective of this research is to present an impression of strategic approach in implementing of big data application in academic libraries and the competencies of librarians in meeting the dynamic needs of our users. The study indicates the Big Data applications in libraries resulting in the conception of newer knowledge that may use big data analytics more in creative and competent than ever. Tools and techniques of Big Data require a competent skill set that facilitates the enhanced performance in this ever changing dynamic world. The study presented here evidently demonstrates the huge prospective of big data application in academic libraries. The potential applications will enhance the individual library and information services creating newer dimensions in offering a value added services to its users by developing innovative data formats. The competencies and skill sets of librarians are basically important in offering excellent information services. Changing tendency in Big Data research is very much promising and to survive in this knowledge society, librarians should comprehend the significance of Big Data technologies and enhance their competencies to manage it accordingly.

REFERENCES

Collegiate Education. (n.d.). Retrieved on March 14, 2020 from http://www.dce.karnataka.nic.in

Daniel, K. B. (Ed.). (2017). *Big Data and Learning Analytics in Higher Education.* doi:10.1007/978-3-319-06520-5

E-granthalaya. (n.d.). Retrieved on April 5, 2020 from http://egranthalaya.nic.in

Ferran, N., Mor, E., & Minguillón, J. (2005). Towards personalization in digital libraries through ontologies. *Library Management, 26*(4/5), 206–217.

Gorman, M. (2015). *Our enduring values revisited: librarianship in an ever-changing world.* Available at: http://books.google.com/books

Khurshid, A. (2019). An analysis of academic librarians competencies and skills for implementation of Big Data analytics in libraries A correlational study. *Data Technologies and Applications, 53*(2), 201–216. doi:10.1108/DTA-09-2018-0085

Lariviere, V., Sugimoto, C. R., & Cronin, B. (2012). A bibliometric chronicling of Library and Information Science's first hundred years. *Journal of the American Society for Information Science and Technology, 63*(5), 997–1016. doi:10.1002/asi.22645

Li, B. Y., & Zhang, X. Y. (2013). The problem of large data in the construction of digital library. *Information Sciences, 11*, 26–29.

Li, S. (2019). Problems and Changes in Digital Libraries in the Age of Big Data from the Perspective of User Services. *The Journal of Academic Librarianship, 45*(2), 22-30.

Singh, P. (2019). *Recommender Systems: With Natural Language Processing and Recommender Systems.* . doi:10.1007/978-1-4842-4131-8_7

Thomas, C., & Urban, R. (2018). What do data librarians think of the MLIS? Professionals perceptions of knowledge transfer, trends, and challenges. *College & Research Libraries, 79*(3), 401–423. doi:10.5860/crl.79.3.401

Zhang, X. L. (2001). Mechanisms of digital library: Evolution of paradigms and its challenges. *Journal of the Library Science in China, 27*(6), 3–8.

Chapter 4
Application Framework of Big Data:
Its Challenge and Opportunity in Academic Libraries

Mahendra Kumar Sahu
Management Development Institute Murshidabad, India

ABSTRACT

The 21st century witnessed the development of every sector with the inclusion of big data application. Application of big data plays a pivotal role in academic research by providing information seamlessly. The advent of various technology, such as social networking, cloud computing, IoT, generates huge numbers of data. These data have the characteristics of high value large velocity, large volume, and great variety. The main objective of this chapter is to familiarize big data and its application, and the opportunity and challenges in an academic library. Further, the chapter examines the application framework of big data in academic library based on large scale analysis.

INTRODUCTION

Big Data emerged as an umbrella term of various requirements and development in information related to information and communication technology, (ICT) infrastructure, and very large data sets. These data sets are large enough to provide current software and hardware resources, and they need a new and innovative approach to effectively manage and use. Big Data is a set of collected a huge complex datasets,

DOI: 10.4018/978-1-7998-3049-8.ch004

and data volumes, which comprises enormous data, data management capabilities, social media analytics, and real-time data investigate. There is a short process to investigate huge amounts of data. It is about measuring volume of the data, and large data sets in the case of terabytes or petabytes. After the investigation of Big Data, the data is launched as Big Data Analytics. Nausher ..et al (2014) "Big Data has undoubtedly gained much attention within academia and the IT industry. In the current digital and computing world, information is generated and collected at an alarming rate that is rapidly exceeding storage capabilities". Around 4 billion people around the world are associated with Internet, and more than 5 billion people have mobile phones. Further over 3.39 people are using mobile internet. Numerous social networking platforms like WhatsApp, Facebook, Instagram, Twitter, etc, are the major source of production of indiscriminate of data. Further, there are a huge quantity of data being generated through IoT and Robotics devices such as sensors, actuators, etc. More than 50 billion device are expected to connect the web by 2020. At this time, estimated data production would be 44 times higher than 2010 [7] At this time, estimated data production will be 44 times higher than 2010. As a result of technological progress, millions of people are actually generating a tremendous amount of data through the increasing use of smart devices. Remote sensors, in particular, produce a large amount of continuous asymmetric data that can either be structured or unstructured. These data is known as Big Data.

WHAT IS BIG DATA?

Big data is a set of huge datasets that cannot be adequately processed through traditional processing techniques. It is not only a data that has become a full-fledged subject that includes various tools, techniques and structures. The Term Big Data describes the amount of data in a structured and unorganized manner in a day-to-day business environment. It is important that which organizations use them with important data. It also helps in making good decisions for the organization's development and analyzing deeper concepts for strategic. Further, Big Data is widely recognized by three aspects as follows:

1. The data is of a very high volume
2. The data generates, processes and preserves very firstly.
3. The data cannot be categorized into fixed relation databases.

Big Data: Its Big Sources

In the last few years, people have increased awareness on a Big Data. Good or bed, they also made more conscious on the big quantity of data generated by its possible utilizing for the activities includes social and scientific etc. It has augmented a series of new service in different field such as a computer system, machine learning and statistics, etc. However, the revolution of Big Data have deeply aware a range of segments such as Medical, Speech recognition, Wireless communication, finance and social networking. The concerned area and other, analysis of data yield Valuable information that deepens the understanding, Improve decision making, and enhances performance Prediction model. Let's have some quick view on some analysis on the core basis of data.[14]

- Social media: Every day, social media producing about 1,209,600, (1.2 million) new data.
- Twitter: Approximately 565 million tweets happen in each day!
- You Tube: Approximately, You Tube have been uploaded more than 4 million hours of content each day, and around 5.97 billion hours of You Tube video watching by its users per day.
- Instagram: Approximately 67, 305,600 (67.30 million) Instagram posts uploaded each day
- Facebook: More than 2 billion user added monthly in Face book in 2017 so far, as 1.44 billion from the begging of 2015 and around 1.65 billion at the start of 2016. On an average, as for as June 2017 concerned, around 1.32 billion users activate daily. Every day, 4.3 billion Face book message is posted. There are around 5.75 billion Face book likes every day.
- Mobile text messages: Around 22 billion text messages transactkon daily for either personal or commercial purpose.
- Google: Around 5.2 billion of daily Google searches has imitated in 2017
- IoT devices: It has a large data source, generates daily around 2.5 quintillion bytes in the form of mobile devices, smart TVs, airplanes, cars, etc. Hence, IoT generates a huge amount of data.

Big Data: Its Characteristics

Inderpal Bandar, Chief data officer in his presentation at the Big Data Innovation Summit in Boston noted that, Apart from 3Vs of big data, i.e Volume Variety and Velocity, there are additional Vs need to be concerned the data scientist of IT and business theses are as Value, and Veracity .[10]

- **Volume**: The Volume denotes the quantity of data generates and stores. It helps to determine the value and potential insights into it: Therefore, it assists us to aware whether a particular data set can be considered as Big Data or not.
- **Variety**: This property deals with the different types and nature of the data. This actually helps people who analyze the large data sets to effectively use the resulting insights obtained after analysis. If a specific set of data contains different varieties of data, then we can consider it is a Big data.
- **Velocity**: The speed of the data generation also plays a big role when we classify something as Big Data. The speed data is generated and further processed at to arrive at results that can be analyzed for further use is one of the major properties of Big Data.
- **Value**: Although the value is often shown as the fourth step of the Big Data Stool, the value does not separate big data from such a large data. It is the same as both large and small data that if we try to store and analyze it, then it should be considered as value.
- **Veracity**: The quality of the captured data can also vary a lot, which affects the accurate analysis of the large data sets. If the captured data's quality is not good enough to be analyzed then it needs to be processed before analysis.

BIG DATA IN ACADEMIC LIBRARY

The trends of data-fuel research are ubiquitous in all areas, creating opportunities for librarians to cooperate with other disciplines to fill the service gap. The library is well suited to provide information base, development of data resources and data literacy instructions through this development, the academic and research library has been most impressed; recently most of the federal research funding agency requires data management plans as a portion of application procedure. It is the main responsibility of librarian to create and supply data management service which happen to be the new grant description. Additionally, most of the libraries enters data lifecycle to provide data management plan. These work carried out from the data repository of student and faculty's research project by performing the work on the archiving of the data generated. Some libraries are managed to include special data department due to the emerging of data resources. According to Byron Heirdon "Libraries should become custodians of digital data in order to follow their main mission: to protect and spread information. Since, funding agency needs DMPs and data maintenance post research plan together.

Big Data Application Framework in Academic Library

With the advent of ICT, library and librarian have been offered a new way of techniques to collect and analysis data in the time of responsibility to legitimize their esteem and commitments. Gallagher, Bauer and Dollar (2005) in his paper analyzed the usage from all possible data sources and found that the user are preferred the electronic format of an article then the print format. After finding the usage report they are able to take the decision in subscription of e-journal. Many librarians are followings these data driven method to strengthen their library budget. The application of Big Data in an academic library is based on the method of large scale network analysis. This framework is associated with five major dimension: Human Resource, Literature resource, Technology support, Service Innovation and Infrastructure construction.

Human Resource

Big data is a cutting edge technology requires a couple of corresponding skills like, conversion of data skill, Compression of data reduction skills and depth analysis skills. Generally, most of the library professionals are lack of knowledge about these skills. Thus training is essential to the library professionals in order to adopt big data application in library. Various methodologies should be applied to train the library professional's i.e categorized the library professionals based on their expertise, who are keen on technology like IOT, Cloud computing, mobile technology, are required to train them in perspective of technology. Those are interest on marketing segment may train them in perspective of service. Irrespective of that a knowledgeable professional having good knowledge on this technology should be appointed as a librarian and data analysis in any academic library.

Literature Resource

With the evolution of ICT, access to print resources become decreases and most of the readers prefer e-resource rather than a print resource in the present era. Application of big data in the library is a complicated process to manage and utilize literature resource. Integration of print resource is most important. The library may utilize the sensor information to estimate the intention of the reader and integrate the print literature resource according to the user's needs. In addition to that library also can assess the usage report and then integrate the print resource. Digitization is important to convert the print resource into an electronic resource. The digital e-literature resource not only plays an important role to share or promote the literature, but it combines the traditional and digital library.

Technology Support

Data analysis, collection, and storage, are very difficult to encounter the needs of the present technology level of the library. The important of applying the big data application in library is how to upgrade and use the technology to advance the ability of intelligent decision making. Thinking about the heterogen0eity of information, NoSQL which is another way to say "Not only SQL" might be adopted (Pokorny, 2013). NoSQL may be utilized to preserve and process the semi-organized information and unstructured information, and advance data sharing and participation between libraries. Further, thinking about the information privacy and security, PKI which is another way to say "Open Key Infrastructure" can be received. PKI is a digital certificate and a new security innovation and it comprises of open key innovation. PKI is much help full for library to protect the privacy of users.

Service Innovation

In the digital era, the behavior and reading habits of a user have been changed. The library must be updated and innovative, while applying big data application in the library though, it does not suit to the traditional library. One of the service innovation of the big data application is personalized information push service. This service based on the personal portal platform helps to reciprocate the useful information timely to the user (yuehua, 2014). There are other innovations in library service, particularly in ILL segment, i.e., document delivery, express service, which promotes the document sharing in a cloud environment. Additionally, electronic resource do not meet the demand of disable readers. Hence, the library may initiate to learn from the express industry and provides the required resources to readers. Overall, with these innovative services of the library big data application run more productively.

Infrastructure Construction

Imperfect Infrastructure construction is a paramount aspect of big data and its application in the library. There is a huge obstacles in big data infrastructure construction due to the lack of funding. This needs to overcome as there are several suggestions that library would be obtained. The library can generate fund from the financial departments or some well-known sources. Apart from that, the library could change the business policy such as the library may run a coffee shop in the learning center to facilities its users in order to add some extra money in its fund. In the digital era, cooperation among each other is highly essential to overcome the difficulties form flawed infrastructure and resource sharing. (Oladokun, 2014).

Challenges of Big Data in Academic Library

Application of big data in academic library brings many challenges, the following are some of the example.

- **Data Accuracy**: In the big data environment archiving of accurate data is a major challenge. The library generates and capture a huge number of data both structure, semi structure, & unstructured daily (Feng, 2014). The nature of this data is different i.e structure, semantic etc. an appropriate procedure is most important to collect the data to ensure the accuracy to obtain meaningful information (zh, 2016). Inaccuracy of data leads to diminutions the original value of the information (Head, 2019).
- **Data reduction and compression**: Library generates high volume of data every day and some generated data is worthless (long, 2014). Compression and reduction of data is important to ensure that the value of useless data is not affected to the wroth data. Concurrently, data compression and reduction is much important to curtail the data analysis activities. . This activities is huge challenge for librarian as they don't have the skill of data redundant and compression. The librarian need to upgrade the skill to overcome the issue (law, 2005)
- **Data confidentiality and security:** Protecting data confidently is a major challenge in library. Most of the library depends up on the professional vendor for data acquiring and perform of data analysis activities in library. Because, the librarian are lack of technical skill to operate the big data technology, which may result as leakage of data and safety measure of data (chen et ..al, 2014).
- **Big data framework and Technology:** The current data management frameworks in library utilized are just connected to structured data. Henceforth, conventional data management frameworks can't gather and examine the big data and meet with the execution of performance (Lawton and Burns, 2015). The big data framework has appeared a special advantage in examining and processing the unstructured data (kitchin & Mcardile, 2016). Though, there are two problems associated with the big data framework i.e Cost for setting up big da framework and deficiency of trained librarian to run the big data framework. Hence, to setup a big data framework is a big challenge for library

Opportunity of Big Data in Academic Library

The traditional library becomes burgeoning towards digital library with the impact of information and communication technology and its application such as cloud, mobile,

IOT, etc. (Feng, 2014). Most of the reader prefer E-books, rather go to the library and find the relevant book. Because they easily acquires information by browsing internet. (Zhou, 2016) At present the library wants to extent their service and big data is one of the best medium to support the development process. It provides a new opportunity to extend library service as given below:

- Augment library database: Mainly the database of the traditional library is in the form of books, article, academic papers, magazine, newspaper, etc. In this digital era, huge number of data is being generating in different form i.e, audio, video, image, pdf etc. The library should augment the information to its own database.
- Enhancing librarian skills: In order to satisfy the end user's query timely, the librarian must be familiar with different search technique, search tools. At first librarian should gather the required information form the different sources of internet and then filtering the information according to the user. Conducting big data analysis is depends upon the skill of the librarian. Thus, in order to apply big data technology in library, the librarian should be enhancing the skill of big data technology.
- Promoting ILL service: The increasing demand of literature in library, the library budget becomes very costly. Most of the libraries have embraced, as the library budget is the less than the expenditure. It is very decisive to solve the difference between the shortage of literature and the user's demands. Due to the dissymmetry of information, most of the library procured the recommended literature, which have lack of essential component leads to wastage if money. This issue can be resolved with the application of big data. The application of big data assist the library sensibly to aware the user's demands and further supports to share the information on literature resource. Currently, Inter Library Loan is widely common literature resource service.
- Personalized knowledge service: The emerging of big data technology in the library, users behaviors becomes digitized. Library can be examined personalized characters of users such as, user behavior, user hobby, interest, etc, by using of the big data application. The application of big data helps the library to make a strategic framework of personalized service. Generally application of big data supports library to examine the structure and unstructured data. Further, the application benefits to aware the distribution services of the user thus take measure to observe the actual user. And helps to understand reading behavior of the potential user and take necessary steps to accommodate the user accordingly.

CONCLUSION

Big data application has a lot of potential in the academic library. The potentials of Big Data are being comprehended as its ability has drawn the attention of the library environment. The proliferation of information in academic research given an opportunity to build professionalism and provides the career opportunity to librarian. Apart from the others, librarian also escalating to the new challenge by obtaining the new technology and remain together with the recent development in research. In this article first narrated the concept of Big Data and its characteristics. Then emphasizes the application of big data in the academic library and try to provide a model framework of big data application. Further, the opportunities of applying big data in academic library augment the database, enhance the skill of the librarian and promoting various personalized service such as, ILL service, personalized knowledge Service. The paper provides a comprehensive summery to the user to aware and implementation of big data application in academic library.

REFERENCES

Big Data Commission. (2012). Demystifying Big Data: A practical guide to transforming the business of government, *Transportation Science*, *6*(1), 61–79. Available at: http://www.techamerica.org/Docs/techAmerica-BigDataReport-FINAL.pdf

Boland, M. V. (2016). Big Data, Big Challenges. *Ophthalmology*, *7–8*. doi:10.1016/j.ophtha.2015.08.041

Broome, M. E. (2016). Big data, data science, and big contributions. *Nursing Outlook*, *113–114*. doi:10.1016/j.outlook.2016.02.001

Data, B. I. G., & Big, M. A. (2011). *Big data makes a big impact*. NewBay Media.

Data, L. B. (2017). *Leveraging Big Data : Exploring the New Frontier in Construction*. Initiafy.

Ishwarappa & Anuradha. (2014). A Brief Introduction on Big Data 5Vs Characteristics and Hadoop Technology. *Procedia Computer Science*, *48*, 319–324. doi:10.1016/J.PROCS.2015.04.188

Jaakkola, T., & Analytics, B. D. (2014). *Big Data Analytics Machine Learning Tools*. Tackling The Challenges of Big Data.

Leyenaar, K., Big, P., & Engineer, D. (2016). Big Data Opportunities. *Express Computer*. Available at:http://search.ebscohost.com/login.aspx?direct=true&db=edsnbk&AN=14138C05E25EA138&site=eds-live

Li, C., Zhu, L., & Luo, Z. (2016). Big time-frequency domain data mining for underdetermined BSS using density component analysis, *2016 IEEE International Symposium on Signal Processing and Information Technology (ISSPIT)*, 188-192.

Luna, D. R. (2014). Challenges and potential solutions for big data implementations in developing countries. Yearbook of Medical Informatics, 9(1), 36–41.

Making, D. D. (2012). *Big data. Data Revolut. Big Data, Open Data, Data Infrastructures Their Consequences*. doi:10.1089/big.2013.0037.Published

Normandeau, K. (2013). *Variety and Velocity is the Issue of Big Data Veracity*. Available at https://insidebigdata.com/author/kevin/

Viceconti, M., Hunter, P., & Hose, R. (2015). Big Data, Big Knowledge: Big Data for Personalized Healthcare. *IEEE Journal of Biomedical and Health Informatics*, *19*(4), 1209–1215. doi:10.1109/JBHI.2015.2406883

Chapter 5
Application of Big Data Techniques for Efficient Web-Based Library Services Using Big Data: A Modern Approach

Amita S. Pradhan
Sinhgad Institutes, Pune, India

Swapnaja Rajesh Hiray
Sinhgad Institutes, Pune, India

ABSTRACT

Information communication technology is growing at a faster speed and diversified way. Cloud computing, internet of things, 5G, and such technologies are gearing-up and resulting in proliferation of data. Data is a raw information and it has created a big data. To handle such data, big data techniques are emerging. Library and information science is a big-way service profession that mediates between the data/information and the users, letting them be students, researchers, technocrats. Big data, mostly digital data, is being generated through multiple on-line surveys and repositories. Digital and social media is the main source of generating such data. Analyzing such data according to user needs is a huge task. This is the challenge now a days to organize the data explosion, specially the volume and variety of data. Big data analytics proves to be a major help in organizing and fetching data sets pertaining to user query. The authors, in this chapter, deal with four major services of libraries, wherein time efficiency can be achieved through big data analytics. Authors have focused on thrust areas of library and information science and indicate the benefits of big data analytics for service efficiency.

DOI: 10.4018/978-1-7998-3049-8.ch005

INTRODUCTION

World has observed many revolutions like Agricultural Revolution; Industrial Revolution and now the Information Media revolution. Since the evolution of mankind these stages of social development has given boost to record various data, information and convert it into knowledge as and when required. Libraries, since ages have been catering to the sharing of such information to the individual and the society at large. Libraries have Data in Physical as well as Electronic formats. Due to Multimedia information, managing libraries has become a tough task. The approach to Librarianship has undergone a paradigm shift from storage base to access base of information. Again, it matters when in the digital environment, the storage of information becomes important for easy and timely access. Specifically, technological innovations started taking place in post War era i.e.1950s. The Digital Era after 1970s marked with lot of research and development in computer, communication and reprographic technologies. There are many technology driven gadgets. Networked sensor chips are fitted into them to capture variety of Data, which can be analysed for future predictions. Library and Information Centres are the part and parcel of these innovations and storage of Library Data is done in various media and formats. The quantity of data and the variety of formats are making the data large, day by day. Also, all major projects in Government. Commerce and academic sector publish a huge research and statistical data. Fetching this data as per user requirement becomes a challenging tack. Much of the individual Data is still in isolation and unexplored from web. This requires sophisticated technique, which is more than simple Database management (DBMS) activity. This enormous data is tagged as "Big Data" Such Big data is required as a base of Social-political, Industrial, Economic and Academic Research. Library and Information Centres store such data and records for future use. There are many Data Banks, Repositories and Data Warehouses to complement Libraries for Data storage. They are based on Cloud Storage Technology.

Big Data technology is most suitable to cater the volume, variety and velocity of these records. The basic purpose or use of big data is that, it enhances the chances to improve predictions. It helps for accurate decision making in the fields like whether forecasting, finance and trade, Health care and Education. The Big data in Libraries serve, a very specific purpose by guiding researchers for identifying pin pointed research areas and guide them with various open avenues for Research. Big data understanding and processing in Libraries give the Library professional an insight to the new research topics in knowledge domain, and it would help them for anticipatory information storage. Libraries have to be proactive in Data collection, storage and retrieval. Library professionals need to adopt new skill sets to apply the big data techniques in Libraries. They need to capture data, analyse, classify, curate it, store it properly and retrieve with effective and efficient use of Technology, as per user demand.

There is a major threat of Data corruption and Hardware malfunction. This is an issue of concern for Big Data. It requires state of art Hardware which is always maintained and upgraded with Data security softwares. It also requires major backup facilities like cloud achieves and repositories.

WHAT IS BIG DATA?

Dictionary meaning of the term Big Data is "extremely large data sets that may be analysed computationally to reveal patterns, trends, and associations, especially relating to human behaviour and interactions." 'Big Data' is the application of specialized technological methods .to process large data sets. Traditional database systems are insufficient for processing these data for example web logs, phone call records, medical/ patient records, military surveillance, photography archives, video archives and large-scale e-commerce and trade analysis.

According to IBM, every day 2.5 quintillion (1018) bytes of Data is generated. 90% of such data has been created in 2013 to 2015, 2 years only. This data comes from everywhere as sensors used to gather climate information, posts on social media sites, digital images and videos, purchase transaction logs, cell phone GPS signals are some examples. This is big data.

REASONS OF BIG DATA CREATION

Big Data is generated every second. It can be generated through 3 mediums as:

1. Machine Generated: This data is sensor based information or satellite images, means any data directly captured by Machines.
2. Human Generated: It is the data specially referred to social media. Facebook, WhatsApp, Twitter, Instagram where one finds personal posts. This is semi-structured or no-structured data. It is through word, XML or ppt.
3. Organization Generated: Generally, organizations carry out projects and research, they public their results and share the statistics. This is formal data and structured one.

Main reasons of Big Data generation:

- **Technological Innovations:** All Engineering and technology fields are progressing with interdisciplinary parameters and new ideas, they are supported by generating enormous amount of Data. Cloud computing, Artificial Intelligence, Augmented Reality, 5G communication technology, interactive web are main features to generate Big Data.
- **Constant Developments in ICT:** Internet and communication technology is expanding its horizons in faster pace along with variety of hardware improvisations. Super computers and communication devices have made it easy and cost effective.
- **Diverse Application of Technology**: Internet of Things (IoT) and similar chip-based technologies boost in capturing variety of assorted data. Variety, Volume and Velocity are featured in Data handling.
- **Social Media Revolution:** Wikipedia statistics show that in 2019, 2.77 billion people around the world use social media for communication. After invention of interactive Web 2.0 around year 2015, social media speculations were more.

HISTORY OF BIG DATA CONCEPT (GANDOMI, 2015)

It is the last decade of 20th century, when the introduction of technology geared –up as Tim Burner-Lee British Computer Scientist invented WWW- World Wide Web around 1991 and this was followed by the hardware development of Super-Computer in 1995-96, which helped to process huge data in seconds. Theses technological developments, gave a boost to increased Data and Big Data concept came into being. This led to systematize the Data handling issues. Big data handles terabyte to peta byte data. It is mostly unstructured data like messages. The hardware and software technology available for storing and analysing big data is being cheaper and easily available for business and government purposes.

Brief Chronology of Development Concept of Big Data

The technology is new but the concept is traced back to olden days. World Economic Forum has given land marking years. Table 1 illustrates brief chronology for Big Data and Analytics.

Reinhalter and Wittmann(Kaladhar, 2018) mentioned that librarians could fill a service gap by enforcing standards and best practices in the big-data era because they could create trustworthy data repositories for researchers. Data and analysis of data for business decision making is a olden day concept, being evolved from 17th century, but the technological advents have made it is easy and reliable. Data mining, Indexing, Storage and retrieval are the major challenges for managing Big Data.

Table 1. Brief Chronology of Big Data Concept

Century	Data Storage – Highlights	Purpose
C 18,000 BCE	Humans storing and analyzing data with tally sticks The Ishango Bone discovered in 1960 in Uganda	Statistics keeping, Analysis
	Palaeolithic tribes marked notches into sticks or bones, to keep track of trading activity or supplies.	Compare sticks and notches to make predictions for food supplies to last.
C 2400 BCE	The abacus – was first devised for performing calculations – At Babylonian empire	The first libraries also appeared around this time for mass data storage.
300 BC – 48 AD	The Library of Alexandria the largest collection of data in the ancient world, housing up to perhaps half a million scrolls and covering everything	Unfortunately, in 48AD it is thought to have been destroyed by the invading Romans,
C 100 – 200 AD	The Antikythera Mechanism, the earliest discovered mechanical computer, is produced, by Greek scientists. It's "CPU" consists of 30 interlocking bronze gears.,	Designed for astrological purposes and tracking the cycle of Olympic Games.
The Emergence of Statistics		
1663	John Graunt carries out the first recorded experiment in statistical data analysis in London	Early warning system for the bubonic plague ravaging in Europe.
1865	Term "business intelligence" used by Richard Millar Devens, describing how the banker Henry Furnese achieved an advantage over competitors by collecting and analyzing information relevant to his business activities	This is thought to be the first study of a business putting data analysis to use for commercial purposes.
1880	In 1881 a young engineer– Herman Hollerith – produces what will become known as the Hollerith Tabulating Machine. Using punch cards, he reduces 10 years' work to three months and	Father of modern automated computation. The company Herman Hollerith founded is known as IBM
The Early Days of Modern Data Storage		
1928	Fritz Pfleumer, German-Austrian engineer, invented method of storing information magnetically on tape.	Data analysis
1944	Fremont Rider, Librarian at Wesleyan University, US, published a paper 'The Scholar and the Future of the Research Library' In one of the earliest attempts to quantify the amount of information being produced,	He observes that in order to store all the academic and popular works of value being produced, American libraries would have to double their capacity every 16 years.
The Start of Large Data Centers		
1965	The US Government planed the world's first data center.	Stored 742 million tax returns and 175 million sets of fingerprints on magnetic tape.
1970	IBM mathematician Edgar F Codd presented his framework for a "relational database". The model provides the framework that many modern data services use today,	To store information in a hierarchical format, to be accessed by anyone who knows what they are looking for.
1989	Possibly the first use of term Big Data. Erik Larson wrote article for Harpers Magazine on the origin of the junk mail he received He wrote, "The keepers of big data say they are doing it for the consumer's benefit.	Data is used for Business Intelligence- with newly emerging software and systems for analyzing commercial and operational performance.
The Emergence of the Internet		
1991	Computer scientist Tim Berners-Lee announced the birth of the Internet He gave specifications for a worldwide, interconnected web	Data was accessible to anyone from anywhere.
1996	R J T Morris, B J Truskowski in their 2003 book 'The Evolution of Storage Systems' proposed Digital Storage	This is the point where digital storage became more cost effective.

continues on following page

Table 1. Continued

Century	Data Storage – Highlights	Purpose
1997	Michael Lesk publishes his paper 'How Much Information is there in the World?' Theorizing that the existence of 12,000 petabytes is "perhaps not an unreasonable guess". The web is increasing in size 10-fold each year..	Google Search deviced for searching the internet for data.
Early Ideas of Big Data		
1999	The term Big Data appeared in 'Visually Exploring Gigabyte Datasets in Real Time', published by the Association for Computing Machinery. Internet of Things to describe the growing number of devices online	The potential to communicate with each other via machine, without a human "middle man".
2001	Doug Laney, analyst at Gartner, wrote paper '3D Data Management: Controlling Data Volume, Velocity and Variety'	Defined three to be the commonly-accepted characteristics of Big Data-Volume, Variety, Velocity
2005	Birth of "Web 2.0" – the user-generated web where the majority of content are provided by users of services, rather than the service providers themselves.	This is achieved through integration of traditional HTML-style web pages with vast back-end databases built on SQL.
	Facebook was launched a year earlier. 5.5 million people were already using Facebook	To upload and share own data with friends.
	Creation of Hadoop – the open source framework for Big Data	Specially, created for storage and analysis of Big Data sets.

RECENT TECHNOLOGIES RESPONSIBLE FOR GENERATION OF BIG DATA (BALL, 2019)

The exponential growth in data has created a challenge in Database Management system, including the Library Data. Big data cannot be processed by usual computer applications, like Microsoft Access or Excel. Here one needs to understand the recently developed technologies, which are responsible for creating the Big Data.

- **Could computing:** Cloud computing is depending on shared computing resources than having own local servers to handle data applications. As per the Webopedia, Cloud computing enables cloud services to move outside the organization's firewall. All services are delivered and used over the Internet and are paid for, by the cloud customer on as subscription or pay-per-use business model. Cloud is a technology of Distributed data processing the goal of cloud computing is to provide easy, scalable access to Data resources and IT services. Cloud computing is basically an extended mega storage technology on remote place facilitated by cloud operators. Cloud providers offer three primary services as:(Gervais, 2019) 1) Infrastructure as a Service (IAAS) - provider offers entire infrastructure along with the maintenance related tasks.2) Platform as a Service (PAAS):Cloud provider offers resources like object storage, runtime, queuing, databases, but the responsibility of configuration and implementation related tasks depend on the client.3) Software as a Service (SAAS): This provides all the necessary settings and software for the platform and infrastructure.

- **Artificial Intelligence, Machine Learning and Deep Learning:** Artificial intelligence is a core subject of computer science which helps to create intelligent machines. Such machines are used, especially in industry. The core area of artificial intelligence include programming computers for features as: Knowledge access, Reasoning, Problem solving, Perception, Learning, Planning, and Ability to manipulate and move objects. By adding these AI parameters to any device, it automatically captures and creates type of huge data, which can be called a big data.
- **Internet of Things (IoT):** The internet of things (IoT) is a recent computing concept date back to 2011.With the help of IoT, everyday physical objects are connected to the internet and they are able to identify themselves to other devices. The term relates to RFID as the method of communication, although it also may include other sensor technologies, wireless technologies, and Bluetooth or QR codes. Embedded computing or Pervasive computing are basic subjects for IoT It generates Machine readable data automatically.
- **Data Mining, data warehousing: Data mining:** Data Mining is a technology used to explore hidden, valid, and potentially useful patterns in huge data sets. Data Mining discovers previously unknown relationships amongst the data sets. It is a multi-disciplinary skill that uses machine learning and statistics. Whereas, Data Warehousing is a technique for collecting and managing data from varied sources to provide meaningful business insights. It is a process of transforming data into information and making it available to users for analysis. Data mining helps Data warehousing to cater to the business needs.

Above mentioned all technologies have boosted the creation and use of Big Data for industry based application and decision making. In libraries also, User transaction logs, Resource utilization records, Various Reference Services are examples of Big Data. Big analytics gives insight to user behavior patterns and needs analysis to make collection development which anticipatory decision making.

TYPES OF DATA (JHAROTIA, N.D.)

Data is generated from various sources, so it is not standard and structured always. It is most of the time raw and non- processed, Data sets can be classified as under, shown in Figure 1.

Figure 1. Types of Big data

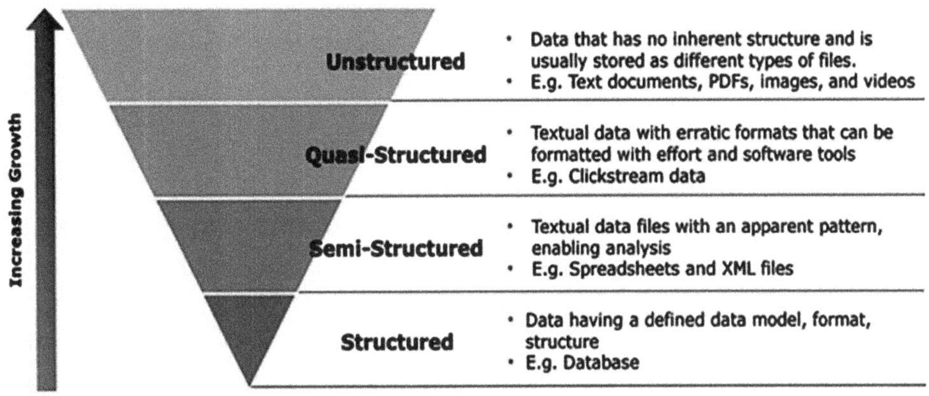

1. **Unstructured Data:** It is casual data and does not have any fixed pattern or format. It is inconsistent data. It comes in different forms as emails, social media messages, text, images, audio, video,. Most of it is unexplored and unimportant. Complicated to sort and organize.
2. **Quaci/ semi Structured Data:** It is textual data apparently formatted but need to be structured and can be formatted with help of software. Examples are web logs, trade transactions. In libraries, it is records of searching patterns by users.
3. **Structured Data:** Data having specific repetitive patterns. Sorting and processing becomes easier. This data is organized, predefined, fixed fields for data entry. Example Govt online records. Library user data or book data and Metadata.

BENEFITS OF BIG DATA

- Using the information mentioned in the social networks like Facebook, the marketing agencies are learning about the response for their advertisements, campaigns, promotions, **Consumer Market research** is carried out by using this big data. .
- Using the information in the social media like preferences and product perception of their consumers, companies and retail organizations are **planning their production**.
- Using the data regarding the previous medical history of patients, hospitals are providing better and quick service. Enhanced and effective **Medical services** are made available.

- Big data technologies are important in providing more accurate analysis, which may lead to more concrete decision-making resulting in greater operational efficiencies, cost reductions, and **reduced risks for the business**.

CHARACTERISTICS OF BIG DATA (JHAROTIA, N.D.)

Big data handles torrent of data, which is structured, semi-structured and unstructured data to store and process it for data analysis. There are five aspects of Big Data which are described through 5Vs. Volume, Variety and Velocity are 3 devised by Doug Laney (2001), 2 more were added as Veracity and value. Some people write about Visualization of Data and Variability of Data, also as characteristics to make 7 Vs of Big Data.

- Volume – the amount of data
- Variety – different types of data
- Velocity – data flow rate in the system
- Veracity – data confidentiality and availability
- Value – the value of data based on the information contained within

Volume: Volume refers to the incredible amounts of data generated each second from social media, cell phones, credit cards, trade transactions, etc. The vast amounts of data is so large that one cannot be able to store and analyze it using traditional database technology. For Bg Data distributed systems are used, where parts of the data is stored in different locations and brought together by software for [processing. Collecting and analyzing this data is indeed an engineering challenge of immensely vast proportions.

Variety: Variety is defined as the different types of data. There are data sets in text, audio, video, images, emoticons. It is casual, structured and non-structured. Data looks very different than data from the past. Most of the data is unstructured. Big data technology facilitates structured and unstructured data to be harvested, stored, and used simultaneously.

Velocity: Velocity refers to the speed at which vast amounts of data are being generated, collected and analysed. The data is ever increasing due to technology and sharing. The speed of transmission from device to device, and access to the data at distant locations is instantaneous. The technology allows real-time access to website, credit card verification and instant messaging. Big data facilitates to analyse the data while it is being generated, before recording in databases.

Veracity: Veracity is the quality or trustworthiness of huge data. Even if, it is unstructured, the data has to be authentic. The data content should be reliable and accurate.

Value: Worth or usefulness of the data being extracted is important. The value is in two aspects one is usefulness of the Data and second is usage of Big Data for monitory gains out of it.

VARIOUS BIG DATA METHODS / TECHNIQUES APPLICABLE IN LIBRARY DATA (KALADHAR, 2018)

Big Data has certain challenges for data management due to its volume and variety, velocity. major amongst them are a) Data Capturing b) Curation of Data c) Storage of huge data d) Searching for data in huge data storage e) Sharing the data with end user f) Transfer of data in various file formats g) Sorting and Analysis of data h) Presentation of Big Data to the client.

To sort out with these challenges, some special techniques are used, they are called Big Data Methods or Techniques, as:

- **Classification:** Various classification methods make the unstructured data turn into organized data so that users can access the required data easily. These classification techniques can be applied over big transactional databases to provide data services to users from large volume data sets. This classification can be algorithm based and can processed unstructured or non-structured data also. Classification is basically a Library Science Technique.
- **Clustering:** Clustering is a Machine Learning technique that involves the grouping of data sets. One can use a clustering algorithm to classify each data point into a specific group of alike data. Clustering is a common technique for statistical data analysis used in many fields. Clusters are data sets of similar attribution.
- **Metadata and tagging:** eXtensible Markup Language (XML) is a technique for presenting unstructured text files with meaningful tags which are called Meta-tags and form Metadata similar to library catalogue record. Metadata is data about data. Metadata is defined as a set of data that describes and gives information about other data the organizations can completely explore the Big Data when it is assigned with Meta tag. Through machine learning, deep learning and artificial intelligence Big Data with a metadata can be utilized more effectively for Business Intelligence.

- **Cataloguing:** The size of data is exponentially growing with increasing every day. Big data consists of heterogeneous datasets, both structured and unstructured. They are diverse data and various file formats. It is very difficult to locate and retrieve the relevant information in real time from the universe of semi structured big data. Cataloguing is the most effective technique that Librarians can contribute to manage Big Data.
- **Sandboxes:** As per Technopedia, "A data sandbox, in the context of big data, is a scalable and developmental platform used to explore, organization's rich information sets through interaction and collaboration." A data sandbox is a platform for stand-alone, analytic data cluster. It is a logical partition in organization's data warehouse/ Data mart. Data sandbox is a set of alike data grouped together which has the facility to interact across the Sand Boxes.
- **Map Reduce:** MapReduce technique divides the huge data into small parts and assigns them to many computers. MapReduce is very useful for performing large-scale data analysis using multiple machines. MapReduce is a programming model or algorhythm suitable for processing of huge data. It works in two phases i.e. Mapping data and reducing it. The whole process of MapReduce goes through four phases of execution namely a) splitting and mapping by frequency of occurrences, b) shuffling by consolidating through relevance by data aggregation, c) reducing by elimination of duplication and d) summarizing data finally.
- **Hadoop and R:** In Big Data, Hadoop is used to develop applications that could perform complete statistical analysis on huge amounts of data on multiple machine with the use of Map Reduce algorithm. It is supported with languages like JAVA, RUBY, Python and C++.

Hadoop is an Apache open source framework written in java that allows distributed processing of large datasets across clusters of computers using simple programming models.

R is open source software and having a variety of built in statistical commands, which is widely used tool by statisticians and Data analysts now-a-days. There are a lot of new packages being developed and old packages constantly updated in R to support and handle Big Data. The advantage is that, R users don't have to migrate to other platforms to handle their huge volumes of data.

- **Dspace software:** Dura Space a US Based NGO has created Dspace software. DSpace is open source software package for creating repositories focused on delivering digital content to end users. DSpace was originally developed by MIT Libraries and Hewlett-Packard (HP) Labs. DSpace became a DuraSpace project in 2009 when the Fedora Commons and DSpace organizations merged to form DuraSpace. It is rated as best Data management and retrieval software for Institutional Repositories. Since, it is on open platform, it can handle Big Data.

PROBLEMS WITH BIG DATA (KORALJKA, 2017)

Challenges in Big Data analysis include data inconsistency and incompleteness, scalability, timeliness and data security. These are big challenge to purpose efficient representation, access, and analysis of unstructured or semi-structured data in Big Data handling. Therefore, a number of data preprocessing techniques, including data cleaning and data integration, data transformation and date reduction, can be applied to remove noise data and correct inconsistencies.

- **Big Data and Libraries:(Koraljka, 2017)**_Big Data handling is a big task for Service Industry. Big Data is user created data, people participation is recorded everywhere. The data generated though Emails, Blogs, Facebook, Twitter, Instagram, WhatsApp chats, various mobile Apps is called Big Data. Controlling such a huge amount of data generated daily and hourly is really a difficult task. Big Data implications cover all major industries and important for Business purposes. With the use of "Mining" and "Analytics" techniques one can draw inferences with Big Data, which are helpful for decision making and further actions.

New technologies have offered libraries and librarians' new ways and methods to collect and organize data in the era of accountability. Many library professionals recommend data-driven library management to strengthen and specify library budget proposals, especially in case of Journal and e Resources procurement. Libraries are the store houses of knowledge, information and data. They process the data to cater to the users as Academicians, scientists and researchers, Govt. employees. Big Data examples in library operations are as Book Inventory, User Records, transaction logs, electronic databases and its usage hits, email and message service etc. Large scale libraries generate Big Data. Library and Information centres are service organizations and they generate huge amount of user data which is mainly termed as Big Data. Due to the changes in technology and the usage requirements of Library Data, following main services are added to Library domain that specifically need various Big Data Techniques.

Here, four such Library services are discussed namely – 1. Digital Storage and Retrieval of Data, 2. Intellectual Property Right (IPR) and Data privacy, 3 .Plagiarism Detection - similarity checking. 4. Open Access Recourses and their Indexing

- **Digital storage and Retrieval of Data**:(Liu & Shen, 2018) This is one of the major services offered to the users by the Library and Information Centre. Digital Storage and retrieval means capturing the data or information and preserve it in such a way that it can be retrieved by the user or for the user as and when required. Digital Libraries have become the inseparable part of any traditional library, may it be Academic, Research or Public library. Because of constant changes technology, more space is available to store data process data. Maximum Data is stored and processed every day. To store this data, it requires specialized preparation of Sandboxes. In the sandboxes majorly a distributed or classified data is stored. Specialized distributed file system is used. Along with the text, audio books and videos are also part of digital library. Various Digitization projects(Ball, 2019) add more data to Digital Achieves and Repositories. Such a huge and heterogeneous data set forces us to use different innovative techniques such as development of specialized Sandboxes for library. A Sandbox in layman language is a group alike data stored on a cloud or in a cloud based repository. A data Sandbox includes massive parallel central processing units, high-end memory, high-capacity storage and input, output capacity. Sandbox technique is useful to separate data for further process in data warehouses. Sandbox technique is adopted for big data processing in Digital Libraries.

Data or information Retrieval means to locate or identify data and extract it against the user demand or query. In short, Digital storage and retrieval means input and output process of data as per user demands in digital environment. Due to the digital media speculation, lot of formal and informal records are generated. Libraries generally deal with formal records. Library and Information centre are always indulged in circulation of information to the end users.

PROBLEMS FACED WHILE STORAGE AND RETRIEVAL OF DIGITAL RECORDS: (WANG, 2016)

- **Data Standardization:** In digital storage the records are stored with metadata, tagging or RSS feed in MARK Format, in any repository. Data formats are one major problem considered during data storage and retrieval. For example, Govt. research projects generate a lot of statistical records and descriptions useful for library users but these records are generated in various formats. Standardizing such formats for huge data storage is a herculean task.
- **Data Sorting and classification:** Another problem for Library data managers is the sorting of Data. Classification of records is a challenge as user demands

are specific. Due to the variety of data, noise data or non-required data may be processed which leads to wastage of time and efforts. Sorting or classification of data and finally storage of useful data is important.

- **Data Retrieval:** (Zhan & Akademi, n.d.) Libraries are involved into "Resource Sharing". For this activity storage and retrieval of Data in given time at given locations, plays an important Role. Retrieval of Data is the other side of Storage of data. The proper the storage the effective is the retrieval of data. Data retrieval tools or algorithms should also be flawless. Proper Database Management System should be selected for effective and efficient retrieval of Data. The problem in digital storage and retrieval, in user's perspective is that they need user friendly interface and data should be easy to locate and ease to access. IP based access is important. Users are more satisfied when they get remote access facility at their workplace.

To solve problems in Digital Storage and Retrieval, Big Data technology plays an important role. Sandbox technique is beneficial, wherein alike data is stored by sorting and cross matching is possible. Classification is used for storage of data. Streaming of real time high velocity data is done in case of Digital Data. It works for faster retrieval. Hadoop File system and MapReduce technique are used for Digital information storage and retrieval.

In this way, big data makes the Digital Storage and Retrieval service of Digital Library, effective for the users.

INTELLECTUAL PROPERTY RIGHT (IPR) AND DATA PRIVACY (RAMESH & MAHESH, 2012)

This is the recently added service for Libraries to help their Users in view of data and Information Security. The Definition of IPR (https://stats.oecd.org/glossary/detail.asp?ID=3236) according to the glossary of statistical terms is as "Intellectual property rights refer to the assignment of property rights through patents, copyrights and trademarks. These property rights allow the holder to exercise a monopoly on the use of the item for a specified period." The term "intellectual property" began to be used in the 19th century. The main purpose of intellectual property law is to encourage the creation of a wide variety of intellectual property, it is national asset. These are ownership materials. They have access limitation. Restricted pattern of access as copy right, IPR for Print material. One cannot photocopy it completely, duplication is not permitted. No digitization is permissible. It cannot be converted it in other media or format. There are four types of IPR generally, Libraries are concerned with them. They are Copyrights, Patents, Trade Secrets, Trade Marks,

Libraries can play a duel role as fetching out information regarding previously registered IPR, by scanning through the Patent Repositories as well as assisting the scholar to register for new patent or copyrights.

LIBRARY HOLDINGS AND IPR (GERVAIS, 2019)

Libraries hold various types of Print Resources as well as Electronic Resources. They can be categorized as:

1. Text books: - They are published for Academic help to students and are according to prescribed syllabus.
2. Reference Books: They are designed for additional aid to students and for reference purpose.
3. E-Books: These are titles available online on internet, which are full text and indexed with mata-data. They are generally in .pdf format.
4. Printed Periodicals/ Journals: Serially published primary source document.
5. On-line Periodicals and journals: electronic journals and databases
6. Audio-Visual Material: Educational CD-DVDs, online MOOCs (Massive Open Online Courses), Educational Videos of reputed Institutions like IITs, NITs, IIMs
7. Institutional Memberships: Libraries are members of renewed Libraries and Library Networks, they have their holdings which are copyright protected.

Above mentioned material is possess by the Library and Information Centers. These materials are restricted for use with IPR. For example. In case of electronic resources IP authentication is important for data privacy. Subscribed Online resources are available only through IP rang or restricted by "User Name" and "Pass word" based access. Many times libraries form policies for usage of Digital Content. Systematic Downloading is prohibited. There are agreements with publishers and violating any rule for access is punishable by law. Data privacy in Big Data environment faces these challenges as Increased Potential for Large scale Theft or Breach of Data is possible. Data integrity is expected in case of Structured Data and Library Data is a structured data.

Big data goes through three phases as 1. Data generation, 2 data storage and 3. Data processing. At all stages IPR and Data integrity and Data privacy is required. Access Restriction is main method of Data privacy for Big Data environment, in this model the personal information is not revealed or modified by the analyst or made available publiclly. The analyst does not have any access to the information directly .It has a privacy guard. In general, Capchas and OTPs work as privacy Guards.

- **Plagiarism Detection - Similarity checking across Documents and Records: (Dwivedi & Abhigyan, 2017)** Due to internet technology, the literature is flourishing day by day on Open as well as Closed Platform. This enormous growth in research and literature has come up with its pros and cons. Research is required for growth in the society. Pure and applied research is increased in Academic as well as Industry sector. The research output is recorded in the form of Project Report, Journal Paper, Dissertation and Thesis. With this publication of research reports, problem of Plagiarism or coping of previous text has been identified. Plagiarism is a Latin word indicating the meaning as "kidnapping". The concept dates back to 17th century. The term "Plagiarism" basically means claiming others works as one's own. The ideas, writings are deliberately repeated. It is a conscious copy of others literature. In this act of copying, many a time's credit is not given to the original author. Due to internet and sharing technology, evidences of copying are many. To identify and avoid this detection of plagiarism is a must. There are softwares for plagiarism detection by cross matching the content across cloud based Repositories and finding the similarities. All plagiarism detection softwares have their own repositories. There is on one common standard repository, so they have different reports and credibility is in doubts.

The main Big Data technique used in plagiarism detection is pattern matching, similarity detection. Word similarity percentage and sorting method is used for plagiarism detection. The software is programmed to match the documents by counting consecutive similar words Clustering, classification and cross matching is done within the Sandboxes created in the cloud Repositories. Plagiarism checker tools/ softwares can help illicit copied content and content theft which is displayed in percentage. Examples: Turnitin and Urkund are proprietary plagiarism checker softwares. There are many open source softwares available on internet like Viper, Duplichecker, and copyleak, to name the few. Due to emergence of Big Data, lot of web pages daily occur and it is difficult to manage and keep vigilance on copying. Library professionals can help the users to identify the similarities and guide them to avoid such writing.

- **Types of Plagiarism:** Mainly, Intentional and Unintentional plagiarism, are two categories of plagiarism. Intentional is purposeful content theft, in which material is consciously copied. Unintentional plagiarism occurs when the writer is unaware of the fact that the content is copied from already existing resources. Some types of plagiarism are known as:
    - Word to word copy: This is direct plagiarism, without quoting reference to someone else's work.

 - Self Plagiarism: In this, the author submits his own writing or part of writing again without consent of guide or publishing authority.
 - Mosaic Plagiarism: Author steels smaller contents from many sources and writes it as his own without reference. Like a mosaic it is copy pasted from different sources.
 - Accidental Plagiarism: Negligence in citing proper sources. This is unintentional but the works are not cited properly so the text is interpreted as plagiarism.

- **Open Access Recourses and their Indexing:** Now a days, with the initiative of Ministry of Human Resource Development (MHRD), Gov. of India, a lot of Open source Literature is being published and circulated through Internet in huge quantity. This called Open Access Initiative (OAI). Open Access Resources are available in various forms and types as e- journals, e-books, Databases, Electronic Theses & Dissertations, Directories, e-print archives, Digital repositories, Open Education resources, Search engines and Blogs etc. All these e-resources are scholarly and useful to support the academics and research. Most of these resources are free, can be accessed without any restrictions. They are only governed by Creative Common (4) license which permits to copy with reference, for the users. The outcomes of government funded research projects, which are national and international are published in public domain and are accessible to all.

Other than these official recourses many social media literature is added to the gamut of open source literature. They cover Websites, Blogs, Tweeter, Face Book, Research Gate publishing. Mobile communications as WhatsApp logs, Video logs, Web series, Different media advertising. e- Newspapers, RSS feeds. These pieces of literature create a huge data and indexing this data is a big challenge. Open electronic resources are mushrooming with social media support. They have different access patterns as Green Access and Golden Access. It is open for all with no restriction on use and duplication. It is a Big Data and is indexed in Open cloud-based Repositories. Indexing them is big task. Sorting, patterning and fetching them on demand is a major task.

Library and Information Centres possess lot of open material like ebooks and e journals, video links. They are easily available for their users. Library professionals can explore on the web and cater to the users with readily indexed web resources, then can create a Selective Dissemination service (SDI) for that. Library can keep those resources by selecting and downloading as per the user requirements. The quality and authenticity of open resources is only to be judged before keep them for user purpose or research citation purpose. Library professionals can manage this task.

USE OF BIG DATA ANALYTICS IN LIBRARIANSHIP

The Data is proliferating and available in tremendous quantity. One can add quality parameter to it. The data which is usable is a quality data. It can be analysed with the help of analytics. The data which is of no use is a noise data. One can apply various parameters to the usable data and derive inferences for further organizational decision making. In case of Big Data, there are special techniques applied for data analysis and inferences are gathered, that is called "Big data Analytics" This analysis of big data gives answers to many questions of market survey, and user behaviour analysis. Below mentioned are the applications of Big Data Analytics in Libraries:

- **User Needs Analysis,(Lia et al., 2019)** - Analytics help to account user needs and library holding are planned accordingly. Which subject areas to prefer or which format is preferred, is decided accordingly.
- **User behaviour pattern understanding:** Behaviour pattern of Library users is analysed through Analytics tools, it can help to decide the Library Layout is designed. If the users are connected through W—Fi they would get updates on cell phones. The resources are planned for them accordingly. They may be given the Remote Access for 24/7 Library Access.
- **Collection Development Warrant areas,** -Big Data Analytics helps Libraries to identify the warrant area to develop print and electronic collection. The collection can be developed in recent and required subject disciplines, as per analysis of the user demand.
- **Elimination of noise collection:** Noise collection is outdated or unused collection in Libraries. Data analytics may help to identify such collections in library, so that organization can take weeding out decisions. This also saves space constraints.
- **Data integration with ERP:** Library Data is been generated daily, that can be integrated with Enterprise Resource Planning (ERP) programme of the parent organization this will facilitate to justify Library Budgets and infrastructure requirements.

CONCLUSION

Big data is gaining importance in the Smart world of today. Libraries are not away from it. Digital or Web resources are growing. Data sets are increasing, professionals need to convert them in information and Knowledge. Analytics plays an important role in big data environment. Cloud computing, Artificial Intelligence, Augmented Technologies are governing the Data world. Library and Information professionals cannot remain in isolation. Big Data is a big challenge before us which we need to handle with mastering over recent technological tools. Libraries may not use card catalogues anymore, but they can use a blend of old and new methods like metadata to master over the ever increasing electronic data and data demands to serve patrons. Big data can become another major tool for librarians. Library is a growing organism and needs adapt technological changes every now and then. Libraries and Knowledge Centres continue to be a key part of a learned society and big data can help to serve those communities even more.

The library services, explained in the present chapter are the outcomes of the new technologies and data generated because of them. Library professional must have deep understanding about these services to cater to users effectively and efficiently.

REFERENCES

A Brief History of Big Data Every Should Read. (n.d.). https://www.weforum.org/agenda/2015/02/a-brief-history-of-big-data-everyone-should-read/

Ball, R. (2019). Big Data and Their Impact on Libraries. *American Journal of Information Science and Technology*, *3*(1), 1–9. doi:10.11648/j.ajist.20190301.11

Dwivedi, J., & Abhigyan, T. (2017). Plagiarism detection on bigdata using modified map-reduced based SCAM algorithm. In *International Conference on Innovative Mechanisms for Industry Applications (ICIMIA)*. Banglore: IEEE. 10.1109/ICIMIA.2017.7975533

Gandomi, A. M. H. (2015). Beyond the hype: Big data concepts, methods, and analytics. *International Journal of Information Management, 35*, 137–144. www.elsevier.com/locate/ijinfomgt

Gervais, D. (2019). Exploring the Interfaces Between Big Data and Intellectual Property Law. *Journal of Intellectual Property, Information Technology and Electronic Commerce Law*, *10*(3). www.jipitec.eu

Jharotia, A. K. (n.d.). *Big Data Technology: Big Opportunity for Librarians.* GGSIP University.

Kaladhar, A. (2018). Application of Big Data Technology to Library data; A review. *International Journal of Library and Information Studies, 8*(2)

Koraljka, G. (2017). (Big) Data in Library and Information Science:A Brief Overview of Some Important Problem Areas. *Journal of Universal Computer Science*, *23*(11), 1098–1108.

Lia, Jiaoa, & Zhanga. (2019). Problems and Changes in Digital Libraries in the Age of Big Data From the Perspective of User Services. *The Journal of Academic Librarianship, 45*, 22–30. www.elsevier.com/locate/jacalib

Liu & Shen. (2018). Library management and innovation in the Big Data Era. *Library Hi Tech, 36*(3), 374-377. 8 doi:10.1108/LHT-09-2018-272

Ramesh & Mahesh. (2012). Managing Intellectual Property Rights (IPR) In Libraries: A Practical Approach And Solution. *International Journal of Digital Library Services, 2*(3). www.ijodls.in

Wang, C. (2016). Exposing Library Data with Big Data Technology: A Review. In *ICIS 2016*. IEEE. 10.1109/ICIS.2016.7550937

Zhan & Akademi. (n.d.). Understanding big data in librarianship. *Journal of Librarianship and Information Science*, 1–16. DOI: doi:10.1177/0961000617742451

Chapter 6
Big Data Concept Information Literacy Perspectives and Applications in Academic Environments

Vandana Ravindra Shelar
MES Abasaheb Garware College, India

Pravin R. Dusane
MES Abasaheb Garware College, India

ABSTRACT

The investigators have brought out the history of big data, its meaning, its different types such as web data, text data, location and time data, social network data, etc. The characteristics of big data such as volume, velocity, variety, and complexity are discussed. Application of big data in various fields in everyday life is discussed in different fields such detection of fraud, application in agriculture field, banking implication, healthcare implication. Entertainment and media industry is also using it effectively. Big data is also used in weather forecasting, transportation industry, education industry, and sports sector. Future of big data is bright. More data on everything is available today. One needs to analyse everything today in order to implement policies. Software is available to process such voluminous data. The chapter also discusses the influence of big data on Indian governance, digitalization in India, finance and banking sector. In conclusion, one can say there is bright future of big data in various private and public sectors. Today's problem is information overload. One has to be very dexterous in disseminating using information with

DOI: 10.4018/978-1-7998-3049-8.ch006

the help of web tools and software one can use. The investigators also discuss the perspectives and applications in academic. Voluminous data available in the academic environment requires proper accumulation, assembly, access, curation, retrieval, and dissemination. Dexterous skills are required for handling this situation. Information literacy deals with accessing, evaluating, and ethically using information.

INTRODUCTION

"Big data is a broad term used for data sets which are complex and large whose analysis is not possible with traditional data processing applications. Challenges are search, storage, visualization, capture, analysis, curation, sharing, transfer and privacy of information. The term often refers simply to the use of certain advanced methods to extract value from particular size of data set and then analyse it."

HISTORY

Application of big data and its use is something that has been in existence for quite a long time. According to records, the application of data to control and analyse business activities isas far back as 7,000 years. In 1889 whena computing system was invented by Herman Hollerith to organize census data was the starting point of modern data.After his input, the next important data development happened in 1937 under presidential administration of Franklin D. Roosevelt's in the United States. The UnitedStates government was required to keep track of millions of their citizen after the United States congress passed the Social Security Act. The government made contract with IBM to develop a punch card-reading system which can be applied in this targeted data project.In order to decipher Nazi codes in World War II, 1943 British developed first data-processing machine named Colossus. The work that would take weeks was reduced to just a few hours with the help of this machine which worked at a record rate of five thousand characters per second.United State government built first data centre in 1965 for storing millions of tax returns and fingerprints sets, which was achieved through transferring every record onto magnetic tapesand it was starting point of electronic big storage. A BritishComputer scientist Tim Berners-Lee invented the World Wide Web in 1989 to enable the sharing of information by hypertext system.

Sin, K., and Loganathan Muthu (2015) describes about Big Data Concept its application in Education, Data Mining and Learning Analytics. The term Big Data was first used by Roger Mougalas back in 2005.In this year itself Yahoo created the open-source Hadoopfor indexing the entire World Wide Web. This is now used by huge number of businesses to go through large number of data. Social networks were rapidly increasing during this period and large amount of data were being created daily. Various organizations have come up over the past number of years in an attempt to deal with this big data generated. Day by day more businesses are accepting the importance of big data.

WHAT IS BIG DATA?

Generally big data is the term used to refer to technologies which contains data which is too vast, fast evolving and too diverse for ordinary technologies and skills to address exhaustively. Big data involves various processes like creation of huge amount of data, its storage, it's retentively and finally its analysis. Various examples of big data are:

- **Web data:** Searches, reading reviews, page views, website views can be collected to enhance the performance in areas such as next modelling, best offers and focused advertisement.
- **Text data:** It contains Facebook feeds, emails, documents etc. The main focus is typically to extract key facts from such form of text data as an inputs to analytic processes.
- **Location and time data:** Wi-Fi connections and GPS gives time and location information. Lots of interesting applications are emerging because of location and time data. But as this data is very sensitive it should be treated with great precaution.
- **Social network data:** Analysis of social networking sites can give insights into users' interest. Also interest of their friend circle and colleagues can be figured out.
- **Sensor data:** Sensor data can be collected from vehicles, various instruments, etc. This data provide important information about performance of respected machinery. Through this data diagnosis of any problem can be easier.

Big data is high-volume, high-velocity and is with great variety of information which demands innovative and effective information processing to enhance insight for decision making. Big data means not just referring of data volume alone, but it also means at what speed it is coming and in which format it is coming from various sources. Important factors for growth of big data are: Availability of data, increase in the storage capacities, and increase of processing power. There are various tools used in big data out of which Hadoop and NoSQL are popularly used tools. Advances in the technology are allowing businesses to draw value from big data even though it is complex. It may be fair to assume that in the future, the success of businesses will lie who uses big data to their greatest advantage and make plans accordingly.

CHARACTERISTICS OF BIG DATA:

Kalra, S. (2014) describes application of big data in education and highlights characteristic as follows

- **Volume:** The size of big data in terms of storage and access. Big data contains datasets with sizes of terabytes to zettabyte. For example unstructured data from social media like Facebook, Instagram in form of video, audio and posts, etc. The tremendous use of smartphones and internet results in the generation of billions of terabytes of data from diverse fields.
- **Velocity:** defines speed of incoming data and the time required to process that data.
- **Variety:** Big data come from both internal and external data sources. Also, data can be structured, such as database table which is pre-formatted data collected over the time period, semi-structured data like XML data, unstructured data such as text, video streams, images, audios, email, etc.
- **Complexity:** Big data management and analysis is very complex process, especially when large volume of data comes from variable sources with high speed.

APPLICATION OF BIG DATA IN VARIOUS FIELDS:

Eynon (2013) mentions about usages of Bigdata into education, technology and other sectors.

1. **Detection of fraud**: Fraud detection is compelling application for all the businesses involving claims and transactions. Generally, fraud is detected long time after the damage and only thing left is to implement the policies to prevent it from happening in future again. Big data can analyse the anomalous behaviour from users which can bring change in the frauddetection field.
2. **Social media analytics**: With the help of insights of social media one can analyse how the market is responding to campaigns and products, which can be useful for promotion, campaign and adjustment of pricing of products. In

order to derive some intelligent and valuable results from big data some pre-processing needs tobe done.

3. **Agriculture**: Sensor data to optimize crop efficiency can be used in a biotechnology firm. Test crops can be planted and how plants react to various changes in condition can be studied through running simulations.These test crops consistently adjust to changes in temperature, soil composition, water level and this data can be collectedto optimize the environment conditions for givengene type.
4. **Banking:** Sensitive personal information can be revealed through big data which raises privacy issues particularly in banking section. Outsourcing of data analysis activities increases privacy issues like customers' earnings, savings, and insurance policies may ended up in the wrong hands which can lead to misuse ofcredit/debit cards, money laundering. Such incidents prevent customers from sharing personal information in exchange for customized offers.Big data study can help detect any and all illegal activities that are beingcarried out.
5. **Healthcare:** Healthcare is yet another industry which generates a huge amount of data. Big data has contributed to healthcare sector also. Big data can reduce the costs of treatment because there are less chances of having to perform unnecessary diagnosis. It helpsto predict outbreaks of epidemics and also in deciding what preventive measures could be taken. It is helpful to avoid preventable diseases by detecting them in early stages which in turn makes their treatment effective and easy. After doing research on past medical results patients can be provided with evidence-based medicine.Sensors and wearable devices have been introduced in this industry whichprovides real-time feedback to the electronic health record of a patient. Good example of such technology is from Apple who has come up with AppleCare kit, Health Kit and Research Kit. Pharmaceutical industry exportsand providers are also now beginning to use and analyse big data.
6. **Government sector:** Government of any country have to keep track of various records and databases of their citizens, their growth, geographical surveys and energy resources. The proper study and analysis of this data can help governments in many ways. Some of them are a) Cyber security: to catch tax evaders b) Welfare schemes: to make fast and informed decisions related to various political programs, to identify areas who needs immediate attention, to overcome challenges like terrorism, unemployment, exploration of energy sources.
7. **Entertainment and media Industry:** Some benefits can betaken from big data in the entertainment and media industry like prediction of interests of audiences, getting interesting ideas from customer's reviews, optimization of scheduling of media streams in various digital media distribution platforms,

on-demand music providing collects data from all its users around the globe to use thatanalysed data to give music suggestions and recommendations to individual user. For example, Amazon Prime that offers, videos, music, and also Kindle books is using big data.

8. **Weather forecasting:** A huge amount of data is collected from weather sensors and satellites and this collected data contribute to big data which can be used in many ways such as to study warming, to understand the pattern of natural calamities, in weather forecasting, to make necessary preparations in the case of natural disasters, for prediction of the available usable water around the globe.
9. **Transportation industry:** Big data is used in variety of ways to make transportation easier and more efficient. Big data contributes to transportation in following ways: a) Planning of route: Utilize route planning to avoid wastage of time b) Traffic control: To estimate traffic pattern. C) Safety: To identify and avoid accident-prone areas. For example, Uber is generating and using a huge amount of data of drivers, their vehicles, every trip from every vehicle, location etc. This data is used to predict demand, supply and fares for trip.
10. **Education Industry:** Education industry is generating huge amount of data related to students, faculty, results and courses. Education industry that has been transformed by big data analysis in following fields: a) customized learning programs: To benefit every student on bases of individual student's learning history to improve results. b) Grading systems: For proper analysis of student learning ability.c) reframing of course material: Real time monitoring of the content of the course which will be beneficial for the students. d) Career prediction: Suggesting suitable career path for each student by understanding each student's interests, weaknessand strengths.
11. **Sports:** In sports industry a huge amount of information is being collected. Athletes are constantly monitored by variety of tools these numbers can be insight for coaches, trainers, administrators, athletes and players. This data can be analysed for better understanding of critical factors affecting performance and success. Also, which players and athletes need additional training and guidance can be understood easily through big data statistics.

FUTURE OF BIG DATA IN INDIA

Indian analytics industry is predicted to reach $16 billion mark by 2025 according to a study by NASSCOM which means India will have 32% of the global market. 90,000 analytics professionals are currently working in various Indian companies but still there is shortage of skilled professionals. Fresh and the experienced candidates are getting trained by number of analytics institutes in India. In NCR and Bangalore, the state of art training facilities is available.

- **Influence of big data on Indian governance:** The Indian administrative body is keen enough to use power of big data for good cause.How the Indian electorate is responding to government action, as well as ideas for policy augmentation is being analysed by Indian governmentthrough study of available big data.
- **Digitalisation in India:** India is next to USA in Internet usage. Very soon India will become highest internet using as well as the highest smart-phone using country.
- **Finance and banking sector:** Most of Indianfinance-based companies and banks are keeping a database of taxpayers and borrowers. Through analysis historical data they can ensure safe returns of customer's money. So, finance-based companies' corps is happier after implementing big data analytics.
- **Bright future of Healthcare in India:** We know India is still struggling to provide fast and efficient rural health support across the whole country so withthe help of big data health care service can make remarkable improvement.Some of the examples of use of big data in healthcare industry are: some start-ups are using clinical data to improve patient care, predictive analysis in diagnosis and prescription.

Big Data in Education

In education field various opportunities for educators to reach out students in whole new ways is offered by big data. Big data can give them a great understanding of student's education experience which helps them to evaluate the current state of the education system.

- **To improve student's result:** The main purpose of using big data in education system is to improve the student results. Conventional way of measuring the performance of the students is mainly exams. It is possible to monitor student's actions like which sources they are using for preparation of exam, how long they take to answer a particular question etc. by using big data in the education sector.
- **Personalized programs:** For each individual student customized programs can be created. Which will give students the freedom to take the classes of their interest so that they can work at their own pace with guidance of professors. For example, MOOC

- **To reduce dropouts:** Student's results can be improved by using big data in the education field which will definitely reduce the dropout rates in the schools and colleges.
- **Recruitment:** How students are performing their respective jobs after graduation from college can be monitored by big data. Accordingly, institutions can modify their recruitment strategies also it will help the future students to choose the right course and college.

BIG DATA AND LIBRARY SERVICES

Library deals with the voluminous data. **Data** is fact, figure, symbol, figure and stimuli. It is pleural of datum. It is crude, unorganized facts which need to be processed. It can be something simple and seemingly random and useless until it is organized and communicated properly. When **data** is processed, organized, structured or presented in a given context revealing meaning it is called **information,** the voluminous data needs to be clustered, classified, predicted, associated and correlated, analysed and characterized. If it is done appropriately then decisions and policies becomes appropriate. In today's increasingly complex and dynamic world information plays very important and vital role for human and society.

Today too much information is generated via social media. The problem is information obesity. Voluminous information is generated in various social platform in one click. Social media platform is used for sharing personal photographs, vacation clicks and informing about your likes, dislikes happenings in the family and views on current events not only this But it is today used to make buying decisions, to develop new relationships, to get updates and to be in society both personal and professional level. Expectations of library users have changed. They expect libraries to engage them with online personalized services and conversations. Libraries has only option but to go digital and reach out to their user community

Open resources on the other hand also provide information about academic and research out comes. Libraries need to implement technologies for offering its Service. Like any other technology it too has strengths and weaknesses. Technologies are tools and they are not the finished products like Hence, it is important to understand the technology in accordance to clients, audience, decide which services to be to use in providing service to offered and implemented in library.

BIG DATA AND INFORMATION LITERACY

In today's voluminous information driven society information literacy is the prime competency enabling information seeker of all ages, to prosper by acquiring, handing and using information creatively and improve economic status and quality of life of individual. Libraries serve as the source of information for users of all categories like students, researchers and faculty members. Consequently the information science professional's role demands to guide individual to go beyond any one information source boundaries for seeking information. This higher level of skills and competencies in contemporary environment of rapid technological change is need of an hour. The individual must be dexterous possessing reading skills, technology skills and in addition to these they should have information awareness, knowing the way in which information is organized. Thus information literacy is the basic skill required for an individual in the environment of big data.

INFORMATION LITERACY: DEFINITION

American Library Association (1989) in presidential committee defines information Literacy as follows

"Information literacy is set of abilities requiring individuals to recognize as when information is needed and to have the abilities to locate, evaluate, and use effectively the needed information."

Thus IL is prime competences required in the age of information.

Association of College and Research Libraries (ACRL) Board of Directors gave following six fundamental characteristics of information literate Individual as a person who can:

1. Determine the extent of information needed
2. Access the needed information effectively and efficiently
3. Evaluate information and its sources critically
4. Incorporate selected information into one's knowledge base
5. Use information effectively to accomplish a specific purpose
6. Understand the economic, legal, and social issues surrounding the access and use of information ethically and legally (ACRL, 2005)

ELEMENTS OF INFORMATION LITERACY

Eisenberg has given seven elements of IL for individual in context of today's environment these components are applicable for effective utilization of big data.

1. **Library Literacy:** These are basic library skill focuses on helping individual to understand how to use various resources from the library like from basic encyclopaedia to the online catalogue.
2. **Computer Literacy:** Computer Literacy is to describe a general understanding of electronic computing. The skill needed to be considered 'computer literate change with each new development in the technology.
3. **Information Technology (IT) Literacy:** It is ability to evaluate critically the benefits and costs of information technologies, may also have carried with it an initial connotation of somewhat broader perspective than computer literacy.
4. **Network Literacy:** It is ability to locate access and use information from the globally networked information resources and environment. These skills based literacy are all emerged to meet the needs of a more complex information environment, with new technologies, and a wider variety of media and services.
5. **Digital Literacy:** Haendel, M. A., Vasilevsky, N. A., & Wirz, J. A. (2012) describes about the data and data management literacy as it is the ability to understand and use the information when available in digital format. The broad range of resources are today are accessible online and underscores the importance of looking at each of these resources with a critical eye is needed. A digitally literate person will consider the author of the information a clue to the accuracy and bias of the information.
6. **Media Literacy:** The term is used to imply critical thinking in assessing information gained from the mass media: television, radio, newspapers and magazines, and also increasingly through the Internet.

Carlson, Jake, Nelson, M. S., Johnston, L. R., & Koshoffer, A. (2015). Designed Media Literacy programme working with Undergraduate, Graduate and Faculty in science discipline

7. **Data literacy** is the ability to read, work with, analyze, and argue with **data**... Much like **literacy** as a general concept, **data literacy** focuses on the competencies involved in working with **data**.

Data literacy is important because it allows individual to understand numbers, charts, and graphs created by others. Carlson, Jacob, Fosmire, M., Miller, C. C.,

& Nelson, M. S. (2011). Determined data and Information Literacy need amongst researcher Gives everyone access to data helping individual for following aspects

1. Empower people to use data. ...
2. Offer training Data literacy comes with a learning curve. ...
3. It is lead by example.

MacMillan, D. (2015).designed two Information Literacy workshop for Scaffold Student learning guided through the discovery and analysis of life science. All these skills are implicit in information literacy.

CONCLUSION

Big data is achieved lot of importance in the today world. Libraries are also vital part of it. Digital resources are exponentially growing. Data sets are increasing on one hand and individuals need be dexterous to convert them in information and knowledge. Information Literacy plays a vital role in big data environment. Internet of things (IOT), Artificial Intelligence, Augmented Technologies are prevailing the information world. Educationalist and consequently Library and Information professionals cannot be deprived of it. Big Data is challenge and one needs to handle it skilfully by adapting lifelong learning approach and mastering over recent technological tools. Libraries need to metamorphose its function by adapting recent technologies over.

The concept explained in the present chapter are the outcomes of the emerging technologies and data generated because of them. Library professional needs to revamp their skills to cater to diversified need of users.

REFERENCES

American Library Association (ALA). (1989). *ALA Presidential Committee on Information Literacy Final Report*. American Library Association ALA.

Association of College and Research Libraries (ACRL). (2005). *Information Literacy Competency Standards for Higher Education*. Chicago: ACRL. Retrieved from http://www.ala.org/acrl/ilcomstan.html

Carlson, J., Fosmire, M., Miller, C. C., & Nelson, M. S. (2011). Determining Data Information Literacy Needs: A Study of Students and Research Faculty. *Portal (Baltimore, Md.)*, *11*(2), 629–657. doi:10.1353/pla.2011.0022

Carlson, J., Nelson, M. S., Johnston, L. R., & Koshoffer, A. (2015). Developing Data Literacy Programs: Working with Faculty, Graduate Students and Undergraduates. *Bulletin of the Association for Information Science and Technology*, *41*(6), 14–17. doi:10.1002/bult.2015.1720410608

Eynon, R. (2013). The rise of Big Data: What does it mean for education, technology, and media research? *Learning, Media and Technology*, *38*(3), 237–240. doi:10.1080/17439884.2013.771783

Haendel, M. A., Vasilevsky, N. A., & Wirz, J. A. (2012). Dealing with Data: A Case Study on Information and Data Management Literacy. *PLoS Biology*, *10*(5), e1001339. doi:10.1371/journal.pbio.1001339

Kalra, S. (2014). *Applications of big Data: Current Status and Future Scope*. Academic Press.

MacMillan, D. (2015). Developing data literacy competencies to enhance faculty collaborations. *LIBER Quarterly*, *24*(3), 140. doi:10.18352/lq.9868

Sin, K., & Muthu, L. (2015). Application Of Big Data In Education Data Mining And Learning Analytics – A Literature Review. *ICTACT Journal on Soft Computing*, *5*(4), 1035–1049. doi:10.21917/ijsc.2015.0145

Chapter 7
Big Data and Knowledge Resource Centre

Sukhada Dinesh Pandkar
Modern College of Arts, Science, and Commerce, Pune, India

Soochitra Dhananjay Paatil
Dr. D. Y. Patil Institute of Management Studies, India

ABSTRACT

The explosion of information has transformed libraries into knowledge resource centres. Explosion of information is in many forms, and it can be explored in terms of "big data". Library professionals should be aware that using big data in resource management is a need of today's era. Management of big data in knowledge resource centre is a big challenge of librarianship. Knowledge resource centre includes information in multiple formats. Handling this information is sort of handling big data in knowledge resource centres. In this chapter, the authors discuss arrangement of big data to fulfill requirements of users effectively. The different segments of library including big data are explored. It discusses the various problems, challenges, and issues involved in big data of knowledge resource centres.

INTRODUCTION

Half a century after computers entered mainstream society, the data has begun to accumulate to the point where something new and special is taking place. Not only is the world awash with the information is growing faster. The change of scale has led to change of state. The quantitative change has led to qualitative one. The sciences

DOI: 10.4018/978-1-7998-3049-8.ch007

like astronomy and genomics, which first experienced the explosion in the 2000s, coined the term "big data". The concept is now migration to all areas of human life.

Quite a few data technologies have been developed specifically to handle the big data. One of them is "Data Mining" or "Knowledge Discovery in Database" software tool. It facilitates deeper analysis to unearth something extraordinary from a big data collection. It combines statistical analysis, genetic algorithms, machine learning and database management technologies. Data mining typically looks for an association between two or more objects located anywhere in the data base, determines chronological path of events, culls of underlying patterns, classifies similar objects and prediction with associated probabilities. For instance, an online commercial vendor like Amazon subjects its worldwide customer database to data mining and based on the profile and past porches record of its given customer, it regularly alerts him or her about similar new products and related information automatically and expands its business in turn. A branch of knowledge called "Data Science" has grown rapidly to process the big data stored in the date ware house o extract novel information and knowledge.

Knowledge Resource centre/Library science is also surrounded by big data. Discovery services of library allows to search across hundreds of millions of items. Individual publisher platforms can add million more. Beyond traditional journal, articles and eBooks, libraries house non textual materials. Datasets created by researchers in the academic and corporate environment contribute petabytes more to librarians' big data world. Videos, photographs, artwork and other types of images further adds to the amount of data that information professionals struggle to make discoverable.

BIG DATA

Defining Big Data

Big data is a hot concept in recent years. Big data is an abstract term and there are different definitions for different researchers due to different concerns. According to McKinsey, big data is used to refer to datasets whose size is large and exceed the capability of existing data analytics tools to mine, collect, store, process and analyze within a specific amount of time. Gantz and Reinsel (2011)defined big data as big data technologies which describe a new generation of technologies and architectures, designed to economically extract value from very large volumes of a wide variety of data, by enabling high-velocity capture, discovery and analysis. Chenet al. (2014) noted that big data is used to describe an unprecedented amount of data and it includes masses of unstructured data and semi-structured data that need to spend more real-time to conduct the analysis. Chen and Zhang (2014) indicated that big data is a bundle of huge data sets that come from different sources and with various formats so that it is difficult to use the traditional data analytical systems, tools and techniques to conduct big data processing and analysis. Pawar (2016) noted that big data is typically a data with large volume and it is difficult to mine, collect, maintain and manage by analysis tools or techniques. Roughly speaking big data typically refers to more or too much data than what by conventional means as a basis for useful information or reliable knowledge. The adjective big in *Big Data* implies a dynamic and shifting meaning, depending on possibly highly individual circumstances, advancing technology available storage capacity, processing and other cultural or historical contingencies.

Characteristics of Big Data

Based on the definitions, characteristics of big data can be summarized as three V's., namely, Volume, Variety and Velocity (Pawar, 2016). Volume means the data keep growing rapidly and the size of data is so big that it could reach exabytes, zettabytes and even more. Velocity means data are generated very fast and the data collection, data mining and data analysis should be conducted as soon as possible in a tolerable time so as to exploit the potential value of these data (Chenet al, 2014). Variety means the data are obtained from different sources and presented in different formats.

The Formats of big data not only include traditional structural data but also semi-structural data and unstructured data, such as video, audio, image and webpage. To some extent, the volume of semi-structural data and unstructured data are much larger than traditional structural data in the big data era. Most of the data we faced are semi-structured data and unstructured data. Furthermore, some researchers also extended the characteristics of big data by adding a V, namely, Value (Pawar, 2016). Value means that mining and analyzing the big data are beneficial to users.

At its core, big data is about predictions. Though it is described as part of the branch of computer science called artificial intelligence and more specially, an area called machine learning, this characterization is misleading. Big data is not about trying to "teach" a computer to "think" like humans. Instead, it's about applying math to huge quantities of data in order to infer probabilities. Big data is all about seeing and understanding the relations within and among pieces of information that, until very recently, we struggled to fully grasp.

KNOWLEDGE RESOURCE CENTRE

Traditionally speaking, libraries have always been a storehouse of information representing and providing valuable guidance to convert the same into useful knowledge for the benefit of mankind. With the evolution of computer and communication technologies, libraries are getting transformed into knowledge centres going beyond the traditional printed matter in the form of books, journals, etc. Libraries can support networking of knowledge and people to the maximum extent if the desired content and the requirements of users are available with them in machine readable form. This ensures best use of resources of knowledge available. The information and knowledge combined with technology not only helps in matching user's needs with knowledge resources, but also helps in taking decisions in the wide perspectives of global importance. Keeping this in view we are using the term knowledge resource centre instead of library.

The sources of information are continuously growing at a faster pace in quantity, variety and complexity. Even unpublished sources are becoming increasingly important especially in university and college libraries wherein the information is required by user without precondition about the form of document. Effective use of library presupposes a good grasp of the organization of library collection and its content. It is essential that the user should acquaint thoroughly with the library, the location of varied facilities and the regulation governing the use of various information sources and services and circulation matters.

When we talk of knowledge centres, we talk of organized knowledge, may be explicit or tacit, which can be accessed by public or researchers at these centres. What goes behind the science is not what common users is bothered about. The user is interested in 'knowing' and this 'knowing' has six aspects. "know-who" and these six aspects are compared to the six dimensions such as:

1. Know-What – The Asset Dimension.
2. Know-Why – The Reasoning Dimension.
3. Know-When –The Time Dimension.
4. Know-How – The Mechanics Dimension.
5. Know-Where –The Geography Dimension.
6. Know-Who –The Living Being Dimension".
7. Utilization of Knowledge

As libraries are meant for promoting the intellectual and economic welfare of people, there is a strong case in favor of establishing them as knowledge centres. The barriers will begin to vanish and every individual will have his share of knowledge resource available within his vicinity. The knowledge will begin to be treated as an essential commodity. The creations of the knowledge and the utilization of knowledge are interrelated.

BIG DATA AND KNOWLEDGE RESOURCE CENTRE

Data are nothing new to LIS. One thing that distinguishes this discipline from most others is, however, that data is seen not just as the result of empirical work or the raw material for statistical analysis, but as a research object in its own right. In [Rowley 2007] it is placed in a data-information-knowledge-wisdom hierarchy, where information is defined as data structured in a way that is helpful for analysis and understanding of a certain phenomenon.

Big Data refers to things one can do at a large scale that cannot be done at a smaller one to extract new insights or create new forms of value in ways that change markets, organization, the relationship between citizens and government and more. While information is growing fast, so is knowledge. Knowledge can be used for the transformation of a society. And for that purpose use of knowledge becomes essential. So does its management. Our objectives in libraries and information center are to achieve quality management of knowledge. A branch of knowledge called data science has grown rapidly to process the big data stored in the data warehouse to extract novel information and knowledge.

In traditional libraries, the library database is mainly full of paper literature resources, such as books, articles, newspapers, academic papers and research reports. However, in the big data era, lots of data are produced and presented in different forms, such as image, video, sound, audio and figure. These digital data can enrich the library database.

Big data makes the knowledge resource centre service more wonderful but also makes the knowledge resource centre suffer the service and the attraction crisis. Big data can be applied in various areas of knowledge resource centre such as Human Resource, Literature sources, Technology, Service, Infrastructure.

Human Resource

Big data is about major shifts of mindset that are interlinked and hence reinforce one another. The first is the ability to analyze vast amount of data about topic rather than be forced to settle for smaller sets. The second is willing ness to embrace data's real world messiness rather than privilege exactitude. The third is growing respect for correlations rather than a continuing quest for elusive causality. The users of big data need to own corresponding skills, such as data collection skills, data conversion skills, data reduction and compression skills and data depth analysis skills. However,

Figure 1. Big Data in KRC

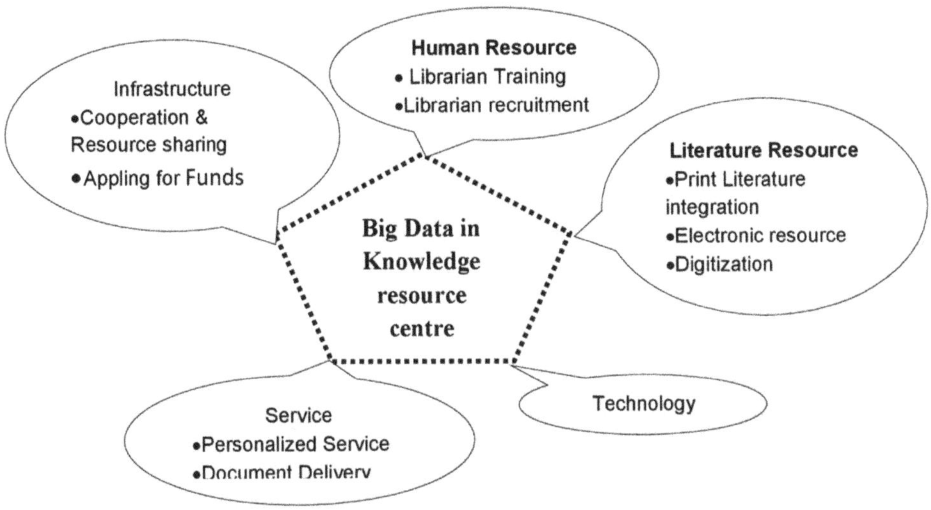

most KRC lack these skilled librarians. Hence, training librarians is vital to apply big data in libraries. There are several measures that can be adopted. For example, the librarians can be classified into different categories based on their majors and expertise and trained from different perspectives. Librarians who are good at cloud computing, internet of things, mobile internet and information science can be trained from a technological perspective. Librarians who are good at psychology, marketing and management can be trained from a service perspective. KRC can also recruit some excellent big data talents as librarians from universities and data analysis organizations

Literature Resource

In the big data era, readers prefer electronic literature resource rather than paper literature resource. In National Library of China, the click rate of electronic literature resource is more than 7 million times while the borrow rate of paper literature resource is dropped from 200,000 to 80,000 times per year (Feng, 2014). How to manage and utilize literature resource is a tricky problem to apply big data in libraries.

For print literature resource, integration is important. Libraries can use the sensor data to predict which paper literature resources are most liked by readers and then integrate and arrange these paper literature resources in an easily accessible place. Other paper literature resources can be arranged in compact stacks or taken away from the bookshelves (Xu and Shi, 2014). In addition, libraries can analyze the borrow rate to obtain the use rate and then integrate the paper literature resource.

The purpose of integrating paper literature resource is to meet the readers' needs. For electronic literature resource, digitization is important. The digitization of electronic literature resource not only needs to combine traditional library and digital library, paper literature resource and electronic literature resource but also needs to promote the electronic literature resource sharing.

Technology

Data collection, data shortage and data analysis is difficult in current states of technology in KRC. It is necessary to update and upgrade technology and use of technology to improve the intelligent decision making ability which is indispensible for application of big data in KRC.

Considering the heterogeneity of the data, NoSQL, which is short for "Not Only SQL", can be adopted (Pokorny, 2013). NoSQL can be used to store and process the semi-structured data and unstructured data, and promote information sharing and cooperation between libraries. Considering the data confidentiality and security, PKI, which is short for "Public Key Infrastructure", can be adopted. PKI is a new security technology and it consists of public key technology and its security strategy, digital certificate and certificate authority (Kumar*et al.*, 2015). Adopting PKI is beneficial for libraries to protect readers' privacy. In addition, other technologies can also be upgraded and adopted, such as HNC (Hierarchical Network of Concepts) which is an advanced information retrieval technology (Pei, 2014). These technologies are all useful to apply big data in libraries.

Service

Readers' reading behavior and reading methods have changed in the big data era, and the traditional services of libraries cannot meet the requirements of applying big data. Hence, to apply big data, libraries should be repositioned and the service must be innovated. Personalized information push service based on personal portal platform is one of the service innovations. With the help of personal portal platform, libraries can gather the useful information. Personalized information push services such as literature reservation service, e-mail document delivery service and consulting service can also be provided by personal portal platform.

Document delivery and express service is anotherinnovation of library service in the big data era (Bakti and Sumaedi, 2013). Document delivery is a special form of inter library loan service and it can promote document sharing. In addition, in some cases, electronic literature resource may not be able to meet some special readers' demands, such as disabled readers. Thus, libraries can learn from express industry and deliver these literature resources to these readers. With the support of these innovative services, big data application in libraries will be more smooth and productive.

Infrastructure

Infrastructure construction is important to big data application in KRC. Lack of funding for infrastructure construction is a huge obstacle which needs to be overcome. There are several suggestions that libraries can be used. On the one hand, libraries can apply for funds from financial departments or some well-known enterprises. On the other hand, libraries can change their business philosophy. For example, coffee bars can be set up in KRC to make some extra money and regard the coffee bar as a learning, leisure and even business negotiation place. In addition, libraries can cooperate with each other. In the big data era, to overcome the obstacles of imperfect library infrastructure, cooperation and resource sharing (e.g. technology, information and human resource) between libraries are indispensable

A library has to identify its core materials and core competencies in its specialized disciplines/s. While this affects ordering books, subscribing to journals, online publications and library networks, it also means such a particular subject and gain competency in that field.

The methods of offering high quality reliable and user-friendly library services will be different in different types of libraries. Library services conducted in the past such as selecting, acquiring, managing/processing and disseminating information are still valid today in the digitized environment. Today we need to package information in a more selective manner because the digital resources are vast and diverse in nature. The digital resources can include any type of document including the networked resources, multimedia resources etc. Therefore it is the evaluation of information that is important before packaging it and once delivered it should prove to be useful and productive to the user.

The management of quality library service in libraries changes from one type of library to another. It would be important to oversee the present conditions of our libraries and the demands of their users, especially in case of public and academic libraries.

Today the greatest dilemma is created by the undependable quality of the Web resource. On one hand, they may be subjective in nature, unreliable and mostly self published, on the other, they do contain useful information. To sift through the Web resources for quality information is increasingly becoming difficult and there has to be a global effort made to identify quality content in these sources for research and reference.

e-Content Sources and Strategies

Web Resources

The web resources that we access through the search engines are estimated to be less than 10% of digital resources accessible through the Web. The remaining e-content which is called the 'Hidden Web' is a very important resource for reading, research and reference. The basic point is that what strategies librarians should adopt to access this resource which is considered of vital importance. Many of the websites holding that content are controlled by passwords and are mostly subscription based. The issue is how do librarians make access to these resources possible, cheaper and reliable? They are not indexed by search engines. The information environment is evolving. Librarians will have to remain learning the advances taking place, conduct research and innovate or adopt latest technologies to use deep web resources, while maintaining the copyright concerns of publishers and authors. Also the deep web is used by anti-social elements, drugs peddlers, pornographic agencies, weapon dealers etc, for their own nefarious activities. There is a need for librarians to identify good sites and the bad ones, and learn how to use them or stop their use.

e-Journals

Publishing of e-journals has shifted the ownership concepts of holding print copies of journals to having online access of e-journals. Libraries cannot afford to maintain print copies when access to them is available through the web. But there are users who prefer to use print copies while at the same time some users prefer to access online copies only. In some libraries, preference is given to maintaining both the editions until the use of e-journals becomes more dependable. Within these constraints print-on-demand is considered desirable. Some publishers and distributors have begun offering such a service. Keeping in view the escalating costs of e-journals, lack of archiving facilities with libraries, limitations of consortia et.al the following issues need to be considered in future so far as access to non-open-source e-journals are concerned.

1. Print on demand with online preview of content may be an option for libraries.
2. Back files of all journals need to get digitized and becoming available online if they are not already available online.
3. The consortia managers will have to negotiate proper pricing for access to back files of journals.
4. The reliability of archiving back files of journals by publishers is an issue that needs to be tackled at the national level in each country and a policy defined.

e-Books

In the past, in print format, an author would write a manuscript and the publisher would get it edited and publish it for distribution. In the eBook format there are several other actors who play different roles. These include hardware manufacturers, software producers, digital market places, aggregators, vendors and others who handle e-content on that subject and those who are interested in the use of eBooks. The Digital Content and Libraries Working Group (DGWG) recommend three basic attributes that should be looked into while selecting eBooks:

"Inclusion of all titles: All eBooks titles available for sale to the public should also be available to the libraries.

Enduring rights: Libraries should have the option to effectively own the eBooks they purchase, including the right to transfer them to another delivery platform and to continue to lend them indefinitely.

"Integration: Libraries need access to metadata and management tools provided by publishers to enhance the discovery of eBooks."

It may be noted that whichever content is recommended for student to read may not be available in e-book form. In India, eBooks are slowly becoming available in languages other than English. But, their number and rate of conversion into e-book form is much too small. Librarians will have to look into the standardizations issues as the formats of e-books remain changing. Proprietary formats such as Adobe PDF, PostScript, Microsoft Reader and DAISY Digital Book are equipped with Digital Rights.

The libraries have to look into the licensing models. The libraries should the able to offer e-books to unlimited number of users with the permissions of printing the necessary texts. Database models which allow simultaneous access to e-book contents could be preferred. The report of the EBook Strategy Working Group of the University of Guelph Library has made useful recommendations. On the basis of the report the following recommendations may help in establishing proper management strategies.

1. Keep a watch on the e-book market and identify the new business models regularly;
2. Prefer a model with unlimited simultaneous user access;
3. Avoided accepting as far as possible, digital rights management (DRM) restrictions;

4. Get accurate and detailed MARC records with e-books;
5. Prefer to have collaboration on collection development of e-books;
6. A checklist of licensing requirements be prepared;
7. Archiving of e-book content be explored;
8. Acquisition of e-book should be demand driven;
9. Gaps in essential e-book resources be identified and acquired in due course of time;
10. Open access e-books need to be selected for future use. Collaborate with library networks like DELENT in getting the best open access resources;
11. Interlibrary Loan (ILL) facility should be got introduced in the e-book license agreements;
12. Short term loan options are discussed with vendors to avoid unnecessary subscriptions to large packages.

E-book hardware also needs to be looked into. The use of e-readers is necessary and that necessitates that the quality of e-readers be better and affordable. There are several portable e-books devices, e-book reader software for as Adobe Frame Maker, Adobe, page Maker, Adobe Design, Adobe Acrobat, Adobe Capture etc.

The report of the EBook Strategy Working Group of the University of Guelph Library makes further recommendations on technology issues:

1. Information about new platforms and changes in the existing ones be regularly monitored and reviewed:
2. Downloadable PDF format be preferred.
3. Availability of discovery features with seamless access be referred;
4. Navigation tools within eBook ecosystem for users and library staff be created or selected with the packages.

Digital Textbook Adoption

Of late digital textbooks are beginning to be used a students are becoming familiar with reading e-content at ease. These text books serve as alternative texts to printed text books. Some text books over the internet are available free of charge and some specifically covering the course of the students could be available at a lower cost than the printed book. While students would prefer printed texts, however, those students interested in the latest additions to the text books can get them through online text books. Another advantage of digital textbooks is that they can have multimedia content and interactive features. There is a great need for educational institutions and libraries to get associated with publishers in developing advanced text books which could be much more useful for student. For instance in India CBSE textbooks from class I to class XII are available from NCERT (National Council of Educational Research and Training and can be downloaded, printed and used by students free of charge.

Libraries and the institutions interested in the use of textbooks by students have to into the quality of textbooks. The content need to be authentic and should get upgraded and updated from time to time. This does not happen always. Libraries, however, will have to get associated with the textbook managements in schools and colleges to streamline issues of content and technology.

Flipbooks

The multimedia and ICT applications are being used in developing more advanced interactive e-books called flipbooks. The programs and services are available to develop flipping-page-style publications. This technology is also used in producing online magazines, catalogues, brochures etc. "Digital flipbooks provide an interactive, dynamic and visually attractive format for text, graphics, audio, links and other elements to coalesce into a more engaging and entertaining experience for users." [9] Librarians can use open source and customized software to convert PDF based eBooks into flipbooks.

Open Access Content

Open access initiatives have been gaining ground since the inception of the Web. Directory of Open Access journals (DOAJ) increased by over 21,000 in the first quarter of 2014; the Directory of Open Access Books (DIAB) added 293 open access monographs in the same quarter for an 18% growth rate (annual equivalent 72%) and a total of 1,912 books as of march 31,2014;

The Budapest Open Access initiative is one of them. Open access content is available either free of charge or with some additional usage rights. The authors contribute to open access either by self-archiving which is called 'green' open access or by publishing in an open access journals which is called 'gold' open access.

Libraries have to look into the specific strategies that need to be adopted and encouraged. Open access strategies should also cover national policies for open access content created within the country and policies for using open access content that is available through the Web from different global sources. The Berlin Declaration on Open Access to knowledge in the Sciences and Humanities (2003) advocates the promotion of a new open access paradigm as per the following guidelines:

- "Encouraging our researchers/grant recipients to publish their work according to the principals of the open access paradigm.

- "Encouraging the holders of cultural heritage to support open access by providing their resources on the internet.
- "Developing means and ways to evaluate open access contribution and online-journals in order to maintain the standards of quality assurance and good scientific practice.
- "Advocating that open access publications be recognized in promotion and tenure evaluation.
- "Advocating the intrinsic merit of contributions to an open access infrastructure by software tool development, content provisional, metadata creation, or the publication of individual articles."

I give below the strategies that need to be adopted in giving a push to the open access movement.

Government Policies

1. All content and data created with public funding should be openly accessible for study, research and reference free of charge through Web.
2. Government agencies and institutions creating and using content should participate in international efforts on OA.
3. Policies be framed to invite teaching and research community to publish in open access journals while maintaining standards through peer-reviewing;
4. Publicity is given to public rights to open access.
5. Support Green and gold open access initiatives of authors.
6. Support is given for infrastructure and institutional repository development.
7. National strategies for long term preservation of open access content are framed.

Institutions and Libraries

1. Associate research staff with library professionals for selecting quality content. The content should not only be of high quality but should be relevant to the institution.
2. Discovery and aggregation of appropriate content be achieved through Library Networks and through specialized agencies and associations. This should be from various sources including open access and open content born-digital resources. The use of indexing of local OA resources discovery tools etc. would be essential.
3. The library professionals have to be trained in acquiring and archiving open access content.

They should be able to handle technical issues concerning interoperability, Open Archives Initiative, protocol for Metadata Harvesting (OAI-PMH)[13] compliance, metadata creation etc.

4. Long term preservation strategies for open access content would have to be part of the library activity wherever manageable for otherwise cloud services are also available for this purpose.

Institutional Repositories

Institutional repositories can greatly help in making knowledge accessible to users and general public without any barriers or payment of fees, if institutions and educationists coordinate and cooperate in this regard. There are step-by-step guides available for developing institutional repositories and a variety of softwares are also available for the purpose. DELNET also offers supports for this work.

With regard to copyright issues, it may be mentioned that a number of journal editors allow author to deposit a copy in the institutional repository of its institution where the author has worked on the paper. A number of countries are appreciating the importance of institutional repositories and therefore support the cause. The Canadian creative commons (CCCA) issue licenses to attach them to their contributions. In any case authors should negotiate with the editors of commercial journals to allow them to let a copy of the paper be made available through an institutional repository. The Canadian association of research libraries supports archiving by institutional repositories of Canadian academic organizations.

UNESCO has come out with the guidelines for comparing institutional repository software, keeping in view the major platforms that present software for this purpose. The five softwares mostly adopted for developing IRs such as Digital Commons, Dspace, Eprints, Fedora, and Islandora have been compared. Jean-Gabriel Bankier, Kenneth Glason and Devika Madalli have contributed the text of the recommendations.

E-Content Strategies by the Universities

Following examples will give an overview of the management strategies adopted by the University Libraries in this regard:

1. The University of Massachusetts, Amherst Libraries follow the following strategies:
    a. A Digital strategies Group is established and the Group provides direction and offers strategic planning. The Group also coordinates the digital activities.

b. The University has established Working Groups for looking into metadata creation, digital creation and preservation and data management.

2. University of California, Riverside campus has adopted, among various strategies, the following strategies for digital content:
   a. "Curate digital research data in order to preserve and disseminate the unique research findings of UCR faculty and students with the world and to enable new forms of academic inquiry and to enable new forms of academic inquiry and discovery through creative and dynamic use and reuse of the digital assets of the university.
   b. "Curate distinctive collection of purchased, licensed, and unique content supporting diverse research and teaching initiatives on campus.
   c. "Support researchers in developing and producing new knowledge products."
3. University of Virginia Library
   a. Acquisitions Services that work for acquiring resources from different parts of the world;
   b. Cataloguing and metadata services that help in accessing that content;
   c. Digitization services, that digitize important and rare collections; and
   d. Digital stewardship services that include long time preservation and curation of digital collections.

CONCLUSION

Apart from massive volume, variety, volatility and veracity the distinguishing feature of big data is that it involves dynamic manipulation of the data to support intelligence based decision-making and extracting a value that is not otherwise apparent. Big data is resource and a tool. It is meant to inform, rather than explain; it points us toward understanding, but it can still lead to misunderstanding, depending on how well or poorly it is wielded. And however dazzling we find the power of big data to be, we must never let its seductive glimmer blind us to its inherent imperfections. We must use this tool with generous degree of humility and humanity.

The librarian, either in team or alone in corporate libraries, is often required to work on a big data to provide a wide range of information for the management and operational staff as per the demand. Identifying leads to new business through big data analysis is also expected. Even in the academic libraries use of big data analysis to provide most relevant information with some amount of processing and links in very limited time can serve the community of researchers and academicians gainfully. It would be a typical scaling of big data analysis techniques to work on the medium or lower size data in some cases. So, even in the dataset is limited the new insights and direction for research, services organization and library management cam emerge by their application. Generating the knowledge and ideas from the unstructured content would be quite enriching.

REFERENCES

Acker, F., & Saunders, S. (2017). Approaching big data: harnessing app information in social marketing. In *Formative Research in Social Marketing* (pp. 33–52). Springer. doi:10.1007/978-981-10-1829-9_3

Alotaibi, N. M., & Abdullah, M. A. (2016). Big data mining: a classification perspective. *Communication, Management and Information Technology, Proceedings of the International Conference on Communication, Management and Information Technology*, 687-696.

Armstrong, J. S., & Overton, T. S. (1977). Estimating nonresponse bias in mail surveys. *JMR, Journal of Marketing Research, 14*(3), 396–402. doi:10.1177/002224377701400320

Bakti, I. G. M. Y., & Sumaedi, S. (2013). An analysis of library customer loyalty: The role of service quality and customer satisfaction, a case study in Indonesia. *Library Management, 34*(6/7), 397–414. doi:10.1108/LM-05-2012-0025

Bello-Orgaz, G., Jung, J. J., & Camacho, D. (2016). Social big data: Recent achievements and new challenges. *Information Fusion, 28*, 45–59. doi:10.1016/j.inffus.2015.08.005

Chen, C. P., & Zhang, C. Y. (2014). Data-intensive applications, challenges, techniques and technologies: A survey on Big Data. *Information Sciences, 275*(10), 314–347. doi:10.1016/j.ins.2014.01.015

Chen, M., Mao, S., & Liu, Y. (2014). Big data: A survey. *Mobile Networks and Applications, 19*(2), 171–209. doi:10.100711036-013-0489-0

Fagan, J. C. (2014). The dimensions of library service quality: A confirmatory factor analysis of the LibQUAL instrument. *Library & Information Science Research, 36*(1), 36–48. doi:10.1016/j.lisr.2013.10.003

Feng, J. A. (2014). A scheme to improve the international inter-library loan service in the National Library of China. *Interlending & Document Supply, 42*(2), 88–91. doi:10.1108/ILDS-01-2014-0005

Gantz, J., & Reinsel, D. (2011). Extracting value from chaos. *IDC iView, 1142*, 1-12.

Hashem, I. A. T., Yaqoob, I., Anuar, N. B., Mokhtar, S., Gani, A., & Khan, S. U. (2015). The rise of 'big data' on cloud computing: Review and open research issues. *Information Systems*, *47*, 98–115. doi:10.1016/j.is.2014.07.006

Head, S. R., Komori, H. K., LaMere, S. A., Whisenant, T., Van Nieuwerburgh, F., Salomon, D. R., & Ordoukhanian, P. (2014). Library construction for next-generation sequencing: Overviews and challenges. *BioTechniques*, *56*(2), 61.

Hu, C. P., Hu, J. M., Deng, S. L., & Liu, Y. (2013). A co-word analysis of library and information science in China. *Scientometrics*, *97*(2), 369–382.

James, M., Michael, C., Brad, B., Jacques, B., Richard, D., Charles, R., & Angela, H. (2011). Big Data: The Next Frontier for Innovation, Competition, and Productivity. McKinsey Global Institute.

Kaul, H. K. (2013). Library Networks: The Futuristic Trends and the Emerging Roles and Responsibilities. In *Knowledge, Library and Information Networking: NACLIN 2013. Papers of sixteenth National Convention on Knowledge, Library and information Networking (NACLIN 2013).* Delhi: DELNET – Developing Library Network.

Chapter 8
Opportunities and Challenges of Using Big Data Applications in Institutions of Higher Learning Libraries and Research Institutions

Josiline Phiri Chigwada
https://orcid.org/0000-0003-0964-3582
Bindura University of Science Education, Zimbabwe

ABSTRACT

The chapter documents opportunities and challenges experienced when using big data applications in libraries. The objective of the study was to examine the big data applications that are used in libraries. The big data concept is new, and some librarians are not aware of it while others do not have the knowledge and skills of using big data applications. A structured literature review was done to examine how libraries use big data. The search terms that were used were "big data AND libraries." The findings revealed that libraries are generating big data. The challenges that are experienced include data accuracy, data confidentiality and security, lack of skills to deal with data reduction and compression, and the unavailability of big data processing systems and technology in libraries. The author recommends the up skilling of librarians so that they are able to deal with the challenges of working with big data applications.

DOI: 10.4018/978-1-7998-3049-8.ch008

INTRODUCTION

The development of information communication technologies (ICTs), digital information techniques, internet technology, internet of things and cloud computing have caused an increase in data generation and use (Alotaibi and Abdullah 2016). Institutions of higher learning and research institutions produce a lot of data in their day to day operations and their libraries are busy due to high usage be it on or off campus. Libraries have a virtual presence and users are able to use the information resources regardless of location and time. The data is coming from various sources such as sensors, smart devices, social networking interactions, web pages, videos, images, personal browsing history, and online transactions among other things (Wu et al 2014, Alotaibi and Abdullah 2016). As a result, the data is presented as structured, unstructured and semi structured (Bello-Orgaz et al 2016, Zaharia et al 2016). The literature indicates that the big data concept was started in 2001 by Laney in his research notes. Laney believes that an important feature of big data is that it cannot be processed effectively by traditional data management tools (Laney, 2001). Most big data-processing methods emphasize high-speed and efficient use of large amounts of data (Li et al 2019). It is also stated that big data is a collection of datasets so large and complex that it is difficult to use on-hand database management tools, or traditional data processing applications, for their processing that includes capturing, storage, search, sharing, transfer, analysis, and visualization (Li et al 2019).

The trend towards having and dealing with larger data sets produced by different actors is also due to the additional information derivable from the analysis of a single large set of related data, as compared to separate smaller sets with the same total amount of data, allowing correlations to be found to spot business trends, determine quality of research, prevent diseases, link legal citations, combat crime, and determine real-time roadway traffic conditions. (Lu 2014). Zhan and Widen (2019) indicated that big data is data oriented and ability oriented. Data oriented shows that the data or information has certain features such as large volume and increasing rapidly while ability oriented highlights the need for technology to handle the data. In this study, a definition that was provided by Zhan and Widen (2019) was adopted. They stated that big data is "data with large size, fast growing speed, and various types which can complicate data handling techniques but also boost the creation of technological solutions. Value is generated by the proper operation and use of big data" (Zhan and Widen 2019: 563). It is in light of this background that the chapter seeks to address the following objectives:

1. To examine the big data applications that can be used by libraries in institutions of higher learning.

2. To document the opportunities of using big data applications in libraries in institutions of higher learning.
3. To discuss the challenges faced when using big data applications in libraries in institutions of higher learning.

PROBLEM STATEMENT

The use of big data applications in libraries is a new field where research is limited as stated by Hashem et al (2015) and Kim and Choi (2016). There is also insufficient emphasis on the practical application of big data in libraries as stated by Li et al (2019) and Lu (2014). Zhan and Widen (2019) concluded that big data are rare in librarianship. As a result, the problem statement for this study is how libraries in research institutions and institutions of higher learning can take advantage of the opportunities and challenges that are offered by big data. A structured literature review and content analysis was employed to unpack the opportunities and challenges of using big data applications in institutions of higher learning and research institutions. Big data AND libraries were the search terms that were used to retrieve electronic information resources from academic databases that documents the application of big data in libraries. Content analysis was used to analyse the collected information which was presented in themes according to the objectives of the study.

CHARACTERISTICS OF BIG DATA

The growth of the volume of data and statistics led to the development of big data due to the increase in datasets available to researchers in research institutions and institutions of higher learning. Pawar (2016), Gandomi and Haider (2015) and Jules (2013) indicated that big data has three Vs namely volume, velocity and variety. Federer (2016), Pawar (2016), Joshi (2015), Xu et al (2015) and Katal (2013) added value to make them 4 Vs. An additional V, veracity, was also added leading to the 5 Vs of big data which is regarded as the five model proposed by Fosso Wamba et al (2015) as pointed out by Bello-Organz, Jung, and Camacho (2016), Emani (2015) and Jin et al (2015). Volume, velocity and variety describe the characteristics of the data involved while specific technology and analytical methods clarify the unique requirements to use the data (Pawar 2016).

Volume deals with the growth of data where it keeps growing rapidly and the size of the data is huge. The scale of the data and the datasets are large making it difficult to use traditional data processing and storage techniques (Federer 2016). For example, parallel and distributed computing involves the use of many computers and a single processor cannot handle the big dataset. **Velocity** is the speed at which the data is generated. Chen et al (2014) pointed out that data are generated fast and data collection, mining, analysis and visualisation should be done within a specified time to exploit the value of the data. The data is generated all the times at a big rate. **Variety** refers to the different types of data that form a dataset. The data is obtained from different sources and presented in different formats. Data can be structured, semi structured or unstructured such as videos, image, audio, and webpages. A single data set can have all these different formats. **Value** of the data would be seen after data mining and analysis and this is beneficial to both the users and the library. **Veracity** emphasises the need to ensure reliability and integrity of big data to deal with accountability and transparency in research. This helps in maintaining and using error free and accurate data.

USE OF BIG DATA IN LIBRARIES

The information from the retrieved articles revealed that libraries are generating big data, and librarians are assisting researchers in using big data. Big data is generated from library management system transactions such as borrowing, cataloguing, reports, patron data and administrative data, websites, and electronic resources usage among others (Xu and Yang 2019). Libraries are also offering online reference services which generate huge amounts of data such as live chat facilities and the use of social media platforms such as Facebook, Twitter, YouTube, Skype, and WhatsApp (Affelt 2015, Teets and Goldner 2013). The data is available in various formats such as images, text, audio, videos and audio visual. The library website is also generating big data whereby traffic and usage statistics would be available for analysis and this can be used for decision making and improving the web pages and other library services. Number of views and downloads of electronic information resources assist the library in knowing the usage of the resources that are available and this assist librarians in subscription decisions. In all these areas, a librarian has a major role to play in the big data era.

ROLE OF LIBRARIANS IN THE BIG DATA ERA

Chigwada (2020) pointed out that librarians have a big role to play in the research data life cycle. Library and information professionals offer assistance to researchers who need guidance in working with data since they are experienced in knowledge management. They also manage and archive data in institutional repositories and must train researchers how to access and use such data. Some researchers might also be interested in archiving their own research data and the library should create awareness on the available data repositories. This calls for research data management skills in order to be able to assist researchers in managing and organising data in the big data era (Federer 2016).

In the big data era, librarians provide access to big data and maintain data lifecycles (Knapp 2013). Hoy (2014) added that librarians provide guidance to patrons who want to use big data by helping individuals to find and use library resources. This shows that the librarians should offer referencing, indexing and abstracting services in the big data era. The librarian is also regarded as a curator who determines where data should be obtained and then cleans and archives that data. The librarian also use big data at the management level to deal with privacy issues in the era of cloud computing, security and governance issues of big data applications.

COMPETENCIES OF A DATA LIBRARIAN

Due to the advent of big data, librarians are taking new job titles such as data librarian, data services librarian, data curation librarian, and research data management librarian (Khan and Du 2018). Data Librarians are responsible for acting as facilitators in the research life cycle as they provide services and products that are used in data management and curation. Semeler et al (2017) stated that data librarians disseminate findings relating to the research through gathering data from different sources then organise and clean the data. Therefore, librarians should possess skills that are taught in data science. Semeler et al (2017) pointed out that data librarians have their origin in the social sciences while Kellam and Peter (2011) stated that data librarians come from many disciplines. Kellam and Thompson (2016) added that the field of data librarianship is varied and the roles overlap in providing access to, documenting and preserving data.

Data librarians should possess the following skills: data information literacy, knowledge of data sources, research assistance, outreach, teaching, knowledge of statistical software packages such as R, SPSS, Stata, SAS, Python, NVIVO, Visualisation, knowledge of standard-based metadata schema, qualitative and quantitative data analysis, critical thinking and problem solving (Zhan and Widen 2019, Khan and Du 2018, Semeler et al 2017, Federer 2016, Kellam and Thompson 2016, Kellam and Peter 2011). Smith et al (2012) pointed out that education for LIS professionals should include information policy and ethics, process of information transfer, information generation and use, information resources management, research, analysis and interpretation of information, assessing information needs and designing responsive services, ICT applications in libraries, knowledge management, evaluation of libraries and information use, information agency management, and awareness of indigenous knowledge paradigms.

OPPORTUNITIES OF USING BIG DATA IN LIBRARIES

With the continuous development of information technologies, libraries have been evolving constantly, and this has greatly expanded library services and improved their efficiency and effectiveness (Li et al 2019). This led to the development of digital libraries which have huge amounts of data which cannot be easily processed and analysed using traditional processing systems and technology. Khan and Du (2018) posits that librarians have been using big data from a long time in the form of scrolls and printed books. The growth of information communication technologies (ICTs) has led to the introduction of electronic resources. Li et al (2017) added that the digital age has changed the way data is produced and consumed. There is also increasing demands from funding agencies and research institutions leading to the creation and support of data intensive research.

The development of the library 4.0 which is an intelligent library for analysing information and presenting findings to users shows that libraries are now handling huge amounts of data (Zhan and Widen 2019, Noh 2015). This proliferation of data calls for skills development and upgrade in order to deal with big data as stated by Gordon-Murname (2012), Hoy (2014) and Reinhalter and Wittmann (2014). The International Federation of Library Associations and Institutions (IFLA) trend reports pointed out that artificial intelligence would greatly affect the future of libraries by introducing next generation browsers that do not only deal with keyword searches and semantic web content analysis but also integrated speech recognition and machine translation, and identification of cloud services for web content (IFLA 2018).

Digital devices are now affordable and they are now being used in libraries in research institutions and institutions of higher learning. There is an increase in the amount of digital resource types and this led to the development of advanced technologies in collecting, recording, analysing and aggregating data. Federer (2016) stated that because of these new technologies, data can now be gathered quickly and cheaply leading to an increase in born digital data. For example, the adoption of electronic health records in hospitals led to easy accessibility to patient data since it is no longer kept in hand written files which are filed in the clinician's office. This data can now be used in research although there is an issue of patient's privacy. These developments have enabled the spread of data utilisation and enhanced library services to attract more readers. In America, for example, libraries launched programmes that utilise large data sets to promote the use of government resources (Marvin 2014).

Libraries are changing their products and services in the big data era taking advantage of the opportunities such as enriching the library database, enhancing the skills of librarians, promoting interlibrary loan services, and providing personalised loan services (Li et al 2017). Data that is produced and stored in different formats enrich the library database due to the huge amounts of resources that can be stored, unlike in the traditional library with a database full of books, articles, newspapers, academic papers in print format (Long and Harvey 2014). The application of big data in libraries is an avenue for librarians to upgrade their skills to have knowledge of search tools and search strategies. The skills would also be used for collecting data and conducting big data analysis (Lawton and Burns 2015). Big data applications assist libraries in understanding the needs of users and resource sharing. Feng (2014) stated that ILL service is the common resource sharing activity around the world. Big data also enables the digitisation of readers' activities and reading behaviour. This data assist in making decisions that help to keep the current users and attract potential users. Hu et al (2013) added that the information is used to understand the needs of patrons and to adjust the strategies for offering services.

CHALLENGES OF BIG DATA IN LIBRARIES

Feng (2014) and Li et al (2017) pointed out that challenges are caused by information and internet technologies due to the advent of mobile devices and cloud computing. Federer (2016) added that lack of infrastructure, gaps in training for librarians, lack of standards, data security problems, need for new software and IT solutions for handling big data are some of the challenges that are experienced by librarians when using big data. In a library set up, most of the readers are now interested in using electronic resources which are accessible via remote locations as compared to print sources (Zhou 2016). Use of resources off campus may negatively affect the statistics of library visitors to the physical building.

The challenges that are presented by the big data include data accuracy, data reduction and compression, big data processing system and technology, and data confidentiality and security (Li et al 2017, Li et al 2019). A lot of data is being generated in libraries according to Feng (2014). There is need to maintain the accuracy of the data in different types and structures to get meaningful results (Zhou 2016). If the data is not accurate, the value of the data decreases and there is too much work during data analysis. The issue of data reduction and compression should be dealt with since most of the data is not useful (Long and Harvey 2014). This would help in ensuring that the useful data is not affected by the useless data and the efficiency of data analysis is improved. Lawton and Burns (2015) pointed out that librarians do not have skills to reduce and compress the data and should be trained. The two authors added that the systems used in traditional libraries cannot collect and analyse big data effectively except for structured data only. Semi-structured and unstructured data can be analysed with big data processing system and technology as stated by Kitchin and McArdle (2016). In order to successfully work with these processing systems and technology, there is need to meet the cost of acquiring them and the skills needed to operate them. Libraries, however, do not have the financial resources and skilled librarians to work with these big data processing systems and technology. Chen et al (2014) pointed out that since most librarians do not possess skills to work with big data, professional data analysts are hired to process and analyse library data which is a security risk as confidential data might leak. The browsing history of a patron, for example, might reflect one reading habits and the information is sensitive according to Wang et al (2016). Librarians who outsource data processing and analysis should take measures to ensure data confidentiality and security. In order to deal with such challenges, the framework for big data applications can be utilised in implementing the use of big data.

FRAMEWORK FOR BIG DATA APPLICATIONS

Kim and Choi (2016) and Fagan (2014) view the application of big data in libraries as a two edged sword where it enhances library services at the same time suffering from attraction crisis. This framework was proposed as a way of avoiding weaknesses of big data to enjoy the advantages that big data offers. Li et al (2017) posit that the framework is considered from five dimensions which are human resources, literature resources, technology support, service innovation and infrastructure construction.

Human Resources

This calls for the need for the necessary skills to deal with big data applications. These skills involve "data collection skills, data conversion skills, data reduction and compressions skills and data depth analysis skills" (Li et al 2017: 164). It has been noted that not all the librarians possess these skills and therefore there is need to offer training to ensure that librarians are able to deal with big data issues. The human resources component is vital for the successful application of big data in libraries. Librarians can be trained according to what they are good at doing, for example, those who have strength and expertise in the technical issues such as cloud computing, internet of things, mobile internet and information science can be separated from those with marketing and management strengths. The former would be trained from a technological perspective while the latter is trained from a service perspective (Li et al 2017). Another avenue that can be used is the employment of big data experts to deal with the issues in libraries.

Literature Resources

The advent of big data led to a shift from a preference of print resources to electronic resources (Li et al 2017). Feng (2014) pointed out that the usage of electronic resources in National Library of China has been increasing everyday while the borrowing rate of print resources is dropping. Big data applications can be used to manage and utilise resources that are available in libraries. Li et al (2017) stated that sensor data can be used for predicting print resources that are used by patrons and make them easily accessible. Libraries can also utilise the data from borrowing to determine the usage of the collection.

Technology Support

Long and Harvey (2014) pointed out that libraries do not have the required technology for data collection, storage and analysis. In order to apply big data in libraries, there is need to upgrade the technology so that it can be used for decision making. In light of this, Pokorny (2013) recommended the adoption of NoSQL (Not Only SQL) for the storage and processing of semi structured data and the promotion of information sharing and cooperation between libraries. To deal with data security and confidentiality, Kumar et al (2015) stated that the PKI (Public Key Infrastructure) can be adopted since it contains security strategy, and digital certificate authority. This would help to deal with privacy issues by protecting the patrons.

Service Innovation

There have been some changes in the way that readers look for information due to the advent of big data. There has to be some innovations within the libraries to reposition traditional services which cannot meet the requirements of big data applications. For example, libraries can introduce personalised information push service to gather information based on personal portal platform (Yuehua 2014). The personal portal platform can also be used to provide personalised information push services such as literature reservation service, e-mail document delivery service and consultation service. Bakti and Sumaedi (2013) added that document delivery and express service such as interlibrary loan services can be used to promote resource sharing. The innovative services would assist in determining the needs of different patrons within the library such as patrons with special needs.

Infrastructure Construction

Infrastructure construction has been hampered by lack of funding. This can be overcome by applying for funds and the application of fund raising initiatives to raise funds for the library. Fund raising projects can also be introduced in libraries to ensure that enough funds are available, for example introducing coffee bars, tuck-shops, and gardens within the library as a way of fund raising. Oladokun (2014) stressed the importance of resource sharing to deal with the challenge of not so perfect library infrastructure. Resources such as technology, information and human resources can be shared in the big data era.

RECOMMENDATIONS

Capacity building should be done among librarians to develop skills that suit the new roles and responsibilities of big data. Academic librarians should develop their skills to meet the demands of big data through continuous professional development. This can be done by holding workshops where experts can train the librarians on the emerging issues of big data. The librarians can also attend webinars, conferences, massive open online courses (MOOCs), and formal education such as short courses to upskill and upgrade themselves.

There is need to introduce big data courses in the library and information science (LIS) curriculum in order to develop and implement pedagogy that would help the needs of data librarians and develop skills that are needed in the new job title. This means that lecturers in the LIS schools should also upgrade themselves so that they are able to teach the learners to know how to deal with big data applications.

There is need to develop a framework of core competencies for data librarians to educate the LIS educators and curriculum developers so that students are well prepared for the new title. This would assist in pointing out who should lead in tackling big data issues in the library. Librarians can be actively involved since they have knowledge of organisation of knowledge, open access, privacy rights, meeting the needs of patrons, ensuring the accuracy of information and preserving information. There is also need to apply the framework of big data applications in libraries to ensure that all the necessary requirements are available.

FURTHER RESEARCH DIRECTIONS

Since this was a web content analysis, there is need for doing an actual field study on how librarians are taking advantage of opportunities offered by big data and how they are dealing with the challenges that they face. This would help to point out the actual use of big data applications in libraries in institutions of higher learning and research institutions. There is also need to investigate how LIS educators and curriculum development officers are incorporating the big data issues in library schools in the big data era to have learners who are skilled.

CONCLUSION

Big data is important in libraries and a number of factors caused its development such as new technologies leading to the increase of born digital data. The librarian has a major role to play to ensure that the value of big data is enjoyed by both the library and the patrons. The opportunities that are offered by big data include the process of enriching the library database, enhancing the skills of the librarians, promoting inter-library loan services and providing personalised knowledge services. However, the chapter showed that there are some challenges that are experienced in the big data era which include lack of big data skills, data accuracy, deterioration of data security, infrastructure issues, and the technical demands of big data. It was noted that librarians should upgrade themselves so that they know how to store, manage and use different formats of data and cloud computing. The framework for big data applications in libraries can be used when introducing big data in libraries to ensure that the resources are available in order to enjoy the advantages of big data.

REFERENCES

Affelt, A. (2015). *The Accidental Data Scientist: Big Data Applications and Opportunities for librarians and information professionals*. Information Today.

Alotaibi, N. M., & Abdullah, M. A. (2016). Big data mining: a classification perspective. *Communication, Management and Information Technology, Proceedings of the International Conference on Communication, Management and Information Technology*, 687-696.

Bakti, I. G. M. Y., & Sumaedi, S. (2013). An analysis of library customer loyalty: The role of service quality and customer satisfaction, a case study in Indonesia. *Library Management, 34*(6/7), 397–414. doi:10.1108/LM-05-2012-0025

Bello-Orgaz, G., Jung, J. J., & Camacho, D. (2016). Social big data: recent achievements and new challenges. *Information fusion, 28*(March), 45-59.

Chen, M., Mao, S., & Liu, Y. (2014). Big data: A survey. *Mobile Networks and Applications*, *19*(2), 171–209. doi:10.100711036-013-0489-0

Chigwada, J. P. (2020). The Role of the Librarian in the Research Life Cycle: Research Collaboration Among the Library and Faculty. In C. Chisita (Ed.), *Cooperation and Collaboration Initiatives for Libraries and Related Institutions* (pp. 335–346). IGI Global. doi:10.4018/978-1-7998-0043-9.ch017

Emani, C. K., Cullot, N., & Nicolle, C. (2015). Understandable big data: A survey. *Computer Science Review*, *17*(August), 70–81. doi:10.1016/j.cosrev.2015.05.002

Fagan, J. C. (2014). The dimensions of library service quality: A confirmatory factor analysis of the LibQUAL_instrument. *Library & Information Science Research*, *36*(1), 36–48. doi:10.1016/j.lisr.2013.10.003

Federer, L. (2016). Research data management in the age of big data: Roles and opportunities for librarians. *Information Services & Use*, *36*(1/2), 35–43. doi:10.3233/ISU-160797

Feng, J. A. (2014). A scheme to improve the international inter-library loan service in the National Library of China. *Interlending & Document Supply*, *42*(2), 88–91. doi:10.1108/ILDS-01-2014-0005

Fosso Wamba, S., Akter, S., Edwards, A., Chopin, G., & Gnanzou, D. (2015). How big data can make big impact: Findings from a systematic review and a longitudinal case study. *International Journal of Production Economics*, *165*(July), 234–246. doi:10.1016/j.ijpe.2014.12.031

Gandomi, A., & Haider, M. (2015). Beyond the hype: Big data concepts, methods, and analytics. *International Journal of Information Management*, *35*(2), 137–144. doi:10.1016/j.ijinfomgt.2014.10.007

Gordon-Murname, L. (2012). Big data: A big opportunity for librarians. *Online (Bergheim)*, *36*(5), 30–34.

Hashem, I. A. T., Yaqoob, I., Anuar, N. B., Mokhtar, S., Gani, A., & Khan, S. U. (2015). The rise of 'big data' on cloud computing: Review and open research issues. *Information Systems*, *47*, 98–115. doi:10.1016/j.is.2014.07.006

Hoy, M. B. (2014). Big data: An introduction for librarians. *Medical Reference Services Quarterly*, *33*(3), 320–326. doi:10.1080/02763869.2014.925709

Hu, C. P., Hu, J. M., Deng, S. L., & Liu, Y. (2013). A co-word analysis of library and information science in China. *Scientometrics*, *97*(2), 369–382. doi:10.100711192-013-1076-7

IFLA. (2018). *IFLA trend report 2018 update.* https://trends.ifla.org/update-2018

Jin, X., Wah, B.W., & Cheng, X. (2015). Significance and challenges of big data research. *Big Data Research, 2*(2), 59-64.

Joshi, P. (2015). Analysing big data tools and development platforms. *International Journal of Multidisciplinary Approach and Studies, 2*(2), 45–56.

Jules, J. (2013). Simple but powerful big data techniques, principles of big data. In *Principles of big data. Burlinton* (pp. 99–127). Morgan Kaufmann.

Katal, A., Wazid, M., & Goudar, R. H. (2013). Big data: issues, challenges, tools and good practices. In *Contemporary computing (IC3), 2013 Sixth International Conference.* IEEE. 10.1109/IC3.2013.6612229

Kellam, L., & Peter, K. (2011). *Numeric data services and sources for the general reference librarian.* Elsevier. doi:10.1533/9781780632599

Kellam, L. M., & Thompson, K. (2016). *Datalibrarianship: the academic data librarian in theory and in practice.* ALA.

Khan, H. R., & Du, Y. (2018). What is a data Librarian? A content analysis of job advertisements for data librarians in the United States Academic Libraries. IFLA WLIC 2018.

Kim, S., & Choi, M. S. (2016). Study on data center and data librarian role for reuse of research data. *Knowledge and Smart Technology (KST), 2016 8th International Conference on IEEE,* 303-308. 10.1109/KST.2016.7440517

Kitchin, R., & McArdle, G. (2016). What makes Big Data, Big Data? Exploring the ontological characteristics of 26 datasets. *Big Data and Society, 3*(1), 1–10. doi:10.1177/2053951716631130

Knapp, M. (2013). Big data. *Journal of Electronic Resources in Medical Libraries, 10*(4), 215–222. doi:10.1080/15424065.2013.847713

Kumar, N., Iqbal, R., Misra, S., & Rodrigues, J. J. (2015). An intelligent approach for building a secure decentralized public key infrastructure in VANET. *Journal of Computer and System Sciences, 81*(6), 1042–1058. doi:10.1016/j.jcss.2014.12.016

Laney, D. (2001). *3D Data Management: Controlling Data Volume, Velocity and Variety.* META Group Research Note, 6.

Lawton, A., & Burns, J. (2015). A review of competencies needed for health librarians-a comparison of Irish and international practice. *Health Information and Libraries Journal, 32*(2), 84–94. doi:10.1111/hir.12093

Li, J., Lu, M., Dou, G., & Wang, S. (2017). Big data application framework and its feasibility analysis in library. *Information Discovery and Delivery*, *45*(4), 161-168.

Li, S., Jiao, F., Zhang, Y., & Xu, X. (2019). Problems and changes in digital libraries in the age of big data from the perspectives of user services. *Journal of Academic Librarianship*, *45*(1), 22–30. doi:10.1016/j.acalib.2018.11.012

Long, R., & Harvey, P. (2014). Technologies for Libraries. *The ANZTLA EJournal*, *10*(10), 2–9. doi:10.31046/anztla.vi10.242

Lu, J. (2014). The evaluation and prospects of big data research in library in China. *Library Journal*, *33*(1), 20–25.

Marvin, H. (2014). Big data in Libraries: Content and policies for librarians. *Government Information Quarterly*, *31*(4), 681.

Noh, Y. (2015). Imagining library 4.0: Creating a model for future libraries. *Journal of Academic Librarianship*, *41*(6), 786–797. doi:10.1016/j.acalib.2015.08.020

Oladokun, O. (2014). Library cooperation and resource sharing: Some lessons from the University of Botswana. *African Journal of Library Archives and Information Science*, *24*(2), 187–193.

Pawar, A. M. (2016). Big Data mining: Challenges, technologies, tools and applications. *Database Systems Journal*, *7*(2), 28–33.

Pokorny, J. (2013). NoSQL databases: A step to database scalability in web environment. *International Journal of Web Information Systems*, *9*(1), 69–82. doi:10.1108/17440081311316398

Reinhalter, L., & Wittmann, R. J. (2014). The library: Big data's boomtown. *The Serials Librarian*, *67*(4), 363–372. doi:10.1080/0361526X.2014.915605

Semeler, A. R., Pinto, A. L., & Rozados, H. B. F. (2017). Data science in data librarianship: Core competencies of a data Librarian. *Journal of Librarianship and Information Science*, *51*(3), 771–780. doi:10.1177/0961000617742465

Smith, K., Hallam, G., & Ghosh, S. B. (2012). *Guidelines for professional library / Information Educational Programs-2012*. http://www.ifla.org/publications

Teets, M., & Goldner, M. (2013). Libraries' role in curating and exposing big data. *Future Internet*, *5*(3), 429–438. doi:10.3390/fi5030429

Wang, C., Xu, S., Chen, L., & Chen, X. (2016). Exposing library data with big data technology: A review. In *2016 IEEE/ACIS 15th International Conference on Computer and Information Science (ICIS),* 1-6). IEEE. 10.1109/ICIS.2016.7550937

Wu, J., Zhang, Y., & Mu, Z. (2014). Predicting nucleosome positioning based on geometrically transformed Tsallis entopy. *PLoS One*, *9*(11), e109395. doi:10.1371/journal.pone.0109395

Xu, R., & Yang, Y. (2019). Study of user behaviour data, mining and applications in university libraries: taking the Central China Normal University Library as an example. *Advances in Computer Science Research* 87. 10.2991/icmeit-19.2019.44

Xu, Z., Liu, Y., Mei, L., Hu, C., & Chen, L. (2015). Semantic based representing and organising surveillance big data using video structural description technology. *Journal of Systems and Software*, *102*(April), 217–225. doi:10.1016/j.jss.2014.07.024

Yuehua, F. (2014). Library personalized information push service based on Smartphone APP. *Journal of Library Science*, *3*, 116–118.

Zaharia, M., Xin, R. S., Wendell, P., Das, T., Armbrust, M., Dave, A., & Ghodsi, A. (2016). Apache spark: A unified engine for big data processing. *Communications of the ACM*, *59*(11), 56–65. doi:10.1145/2934664

Zhan, M., & Widen, G. (2019). Understanding big data in librarianship. *Journal of Librarianship and Information Science*, *51*(2), 561–576. doi:10.1177/0961000617742451

Zhou, Q. (2016). eBook Service in Shanghai Library. *International Journal of Librarianship*, *1*(1), 66–73. doi:10.23974/ijol.2016.vol1.1.16

KEY TERMS AND DEFINITIONS

Artificial Intelligence: Development of computer systems that perform tasks normally requiring human intelligence, for example, speech recognition, decision making, visual perception and translations.

Big Data: Large data sets that cannot be processed and analysed using traditional processing systems.

Cloud computing: Using remote servers hosted on the Internet to store, manage, and process data.

Curation: The process of selecting, organising, and looking after online content in a collection.

Data Librarian: An information professional responsible for developing technical expertise on practical solutions of data management, archiving and dissemination and on data mining and visualisation.

Digital Library: A collection of information resources in digital formats and accessible by computers.

Machine Learning: An application of artificial intelligence that provides systems the ability to automatically learn and improve from experience without being explicitly programmed.

Research Data Life Cycle: It identifies the steps that are taken at the different stages of the research process to ensure successful data curation and preservation such as data creation, data processing, data analysis, data preservation, data access, and data reuse.

Research Data Management: The organisation, storage, preservation, and sharing of data collected and used in a research project.

Visualisation: The representation of an object, situation, or set of information as a chart or other image.

Chapter 9
Is Twitter an Unexploited Potential in Indian Academic Libraries?
Case Study Based on Select Academic Library Tweets

Swapan Kumar Patra
https://orcid.org/0000-0002-0825-7973
Tshwane University of Technology, South Africa

ABSTRACT

Social media have revolutionized today's globalized world including all spheres of modern human being. Among many social networking sites (SNSs), Twitter is one of the most popular. Librarians all over the globe are increasingly using Twitter in their daily routine activities as well as promotion of their systems and services. This study is an attempt to map the Indian libraries' Twitter activity, taking academic libraries as case study. Selected Indian academic library tweets have collected form the Twitter using R programming language. The study further compares few develop countries' academic library tweets. The study observed that Indian academic libraries are very limited activities in Twitter. The sentiment analysis shows that library Tweets are more positive. The study recommends more Twitter activity for Indian academic libraries to attract their users. With the more Twitter activities, library's image will be more friendly and acceptable to the young users particularly the college and university students.

DOI: 10.4018/978-1-7998-3049-8.ch009

INTRODUCTION

In the present day, with the development of latest Information and Communication Technology (ICT), particularly with the advancement of many Web Technologies, the human life has been transformed in an unprecedent way. Today, social media and its effects are all pervasive. There are many Social Networking Sites (SNSs) which have become inseparable for modern human being. Libraries are not immune to this recent ICT effect, rather libraries all over the globe are the primary adopter of ICT systems and services. The use of social media tools like microblogs (e.g. Twitter) has gained wide acceptance in libraries and among librarians globally (Munigal 2014). Library and Information Science (LIS) professionals are always forerunners in adoption and utilization of the latest ICT tools and techniques for disseminating information to their users. Libraries have adopted various ICT tools in their routine housekeeping activities, marketing their systems and services. In the recent years, many of the routine library activities are getting new dimensions with the popular social media. For example, the networking sites, like Facebook and Twitter are getting popularity in libraries and librarians for promoting their library services. Among all the SNS, Twitter is the most popular microblog where anyone can open an account and post textual, video, images and other contents. However, its users can post very limited text. It is freely available and become common in all strata of public life.

Librarians have struggled hard to dispel their stereotype image in information processing and management. The people's perception of libraries and librarians is gradually changing with the ICT tools to deliver services innovatively. Twitter is one of those innovative ways that librarians have added to existing communication channels (Patra 2019). Many big and famous libraries around the world use Twitter for their various services for example, content alerts, Selective Dissemination of Information (SDI), Current Awareness Service (CAS) and so on services (Munigal 2014).

Because of its handy and inexpensive characters, librarians worldwide are using it as an effective communication tool. The greatest advantage of Twitter is its direct and two-way communication with its users. In Twitter librarians can interact with their users and can get direct feedback.

In this context, it is an exploratory study of Indian academic libraries' activities in Twitter. Indian Libraries are one of the early adapters of ICT tools in their libraries among the developing Asian countries. However, how the Indian libraries are in social media network is the main objectives of this study. To fulfil this objective this study has selected academic libraries as case study. Some selected libraries are chosen and their Tweets are collected from the Twitter handle. The study will further examine the most frequently occurring keywords and the sentiments are derived from the tweets.

Literature Review

Information and Communication Technology (ICT) have revolutionized every aspect of modern human being. Along with the ICT revolution, the emergence of social media has added a new dimension to the modern human life. Today, Social networking sites (SNSs) have gradually acquired important share of time and space in people's daily routines. Several SNS have emerged in the last decade, such as Twitter, Facebook, LinkedIn and so on (Vassilakaki & Garoufallou 2015).

Among all these social media, Twitter is one of the most important as well as popular instant messaging platform (Sakas & Sarlis 2016). It is a microblogging social networking service where a user can post very limited text. With this limited text, it can offer news services, share information, and can interact with their users. Moreover, it also offers additional functions, for example, sharing of pictures, audio and videos messages. Beside this, Twitter's Application Programming Interface (API), gives users the opportunity to build various applications for different devices and diverse platforms (Stuart 2010).

Twitter provides 140-character microblogging service, is very popular among the LIS professionals (Stuart 2010). It is popular among LIS professional because of it inexpensive and quick means of reaching users (Shulman, Yep and Tomé 2015; Fields, 2010). It is an important tool for promoting their services (Vassilakaki and Garoufallou 2015). Twitter can also act as a marketing tool for librarians (Carscaddon and Chapman 2013). As a continuous stream of user's post in various different format, it generates a constant stream of unstructured data. This massive source of data is considered a huge source of information. These unstructured data can generate very meaningful information, if it is processed in ordered way (Thelwall, Buckley and Paltoglou 2011). An analysis of Twitter may therefore, give insights into the peoples' opinion in a particular subject or events. It may be used as a strong feedback mechanism of any event or organisation. Hence, Twitter offers an unprecedented opportunity to public utility or benefit organizations like libraries to promote their services and build a powerful digital information exchange community (Sakas and Sarlis 2016). So, it is very interesting to examine this phenomenon in different kinds of Indian libraries (Aharony 2010).

Twitter and Libraries

As it is already discussed in the previous section, that Twitter is becoming increasingly popular since the last few years. Microblogging SNSs like Twitter is a relatively a recent development in online social networking. Libraries all over the globe use the potential of Twitter in their daily routine activities. Along with the growth and popularity of this SNSs its various facets have been investigated from different developed countries perspective (Verishagen and Hank 2014; Del Bosque, Leif and Skarl 2012; Palmer 2014).

Empirical studies have observed that, librarians use of Twitter is context dependent. Its use depends on the nature of the library, for example, there are differences of Tweets between public and academic libraries. The variations may include the number of Tweets, linguistic differences, and content. However, the library and librarian's use of twitter is mainly to disseminate and share information about their activities, opinions, status, and professional interests (Aharony 2010).

There is no general trend of who control twitter handle of an academic institution's library. However, it is observed that academic libraries' Twitter accounts associated directly with the institutions get more attention. In many cases it is found that some of the individual related to library activity, university faculty, staff, or students, are regulating or maintaining Twitter accounts. However, that types of accounts get less attention (followers). So, according to this observation academic library's Twitter networks must be directly handled by the responsible persons of the library rather than the other individuals. Furthermore, the library, as an institutional account itself, is also influential entity to the broader Twitter community of its parent institution. So, it can be said that library is a vital organization and in a key position to propagate information from the parent institute's accounts (Shulman,Yep and Tomé 2015).

Academic libraries use Twitter as a multifaceted tool. Academic libraries and librarians are using Twitter more efficiently and effectively (Al-Daihani and AlAwadhi, 2015). Academic libraries have posted a variety of information for their patrons on Twitter. The trends indicate that the primary groups for disseminating the tweets of academic libraries are within the university community and students (Kim, Abels and Yang 2012). From the users' trend analysis, it is observed that the general "News and announcements" related Tweets receives the maximum attention among the followers. The second most important and popular posting is the "library collections" and "library services". Beside these two categories the following postings are popular; "library marketing and news", "answers and referrals" and "books" and so on. Moreover, there is a global trend that shows that academic libraries have the tendency of posting links more often than other types of contents. Other results show different patterns of communication and interaction between libraries and their Twitter followers (Al-Daihani and AlAwadhi 2015).

Twitter and Indian Libraries

It is now globally recognised that SNSs are very powerful tool today to provide library services. Many libraries are now using online social networking services to make their services popular and user friendly (Vassilakaki and Garoufallou, 2015). Various SNSs for example, Facebook, YouTube, twitter, LinkedIn, Instagram have many applications that could be utilised by the libraries to provide number of services in libraries (Deepthi, Tadasad & Patil 2017). Along with the services provided by the libraries, the SNSs has also changed the nature of library users (Chakravarty and Kiran 2013). Indian libraries have understood the importance of SNS and other Web 2.0 phenomenon of social networking. These kinds of latest and handy tools could enable Indian libraries to engage with their users in the virtual environment for the promotion of the library services. Moreover, SNSs are improving the professional relationships among the LIS profession. More professional contact may result in an increase of information sharing. In this way librarians can meet the demands and needs of their students (Chakravarty and Kiran 2013).

The libraries' use of Twitter and its different pros and cons are quite adequately investigated from developed country's context. A proper investigation of Indian Libraries and their use of Twitter is significantly lacking. This is not only the case of India but valid from the other developed country's context also. The case of developing countries for example in Nigeria's case, it is observed that majority of the library and information professionals have Facebook profiles but the LIS professionals are comparatively less active in Twitter. Findings revealed further that younger librarians showed more positive attitude towards the use of SNSs (Fasola 2015).

As it is mentioned above, Indian libraries are quite interested to adopt ICT tools and techniques in their library services. Contrary to this, they are not that much receptive towards SNSs. It is observed from many empirical evidences that Indian librarian are yet to adopt the popular SNS tools as their daily functioning. For example, based on a study of 54 university websites in Karnataka state showed that 53 of 54 universities (98.14 percent) have their own websites. About 29.62 percent State/Central universities are connected to Facebook, 18.51 percent are connected to YouTube. There are very few universities connected to Twitter and LinkedIn. The study further observed that the university libraries in the study area are lagging behind and trying to catch up with the SNSs. Some of the university libraries are in social network domain. However, their networking services are very limited and used for very basic or elementary purposes. (Deepthi, Tadasad and Patil 2017).

The study on the use of SNS by the students of Tamil Nadu, India shows that university students are quite well versed with the latest SNSs. However, if students require information, they prefer 'Google' search for data (Balamurugan and Thanuskodi 2019). The study observed that Google search engine is the most preferred search engine. Majority of the respondents (about 69 percent) are aware of Google scholar for scholarly literature search. Students have very limited awareness about Research gate, Twitter, SlideShare, Academic.edu. and LinkedIn and so on (Krishnamurthy and Shettappanavar 2019). However, beyond Google, there is a developing pattern of utilizing social media for specific data among students. According to that findings, Social Media is emerging as an alternate source of information from different group. Students find Social Media as a platform for one to one or one-to many ways of communication for subject specific questions or queries. Further the study by Balamurugan and Thanuskodi (2019) found that students are the primary user of social media (Balamurugan and Thanuskodi 2019). So, there are enormous opportunity if the student's community is targeted using these social media platforms. Students can be more attracted towards the respective university of college libraries if they are tapped through the social medias.

Although Twitter is being used by people in various spheres of life. These empirical evidences observed that the use of Twitter by Indian libraries is very limited. Scholarly research in this domain is also very limited (Patra 2019). In this context, this study is an attempt to investigate the Indian libraries' use of Twitter for their various services. This study selects Indian academic libraries as case study to find the following research question:

Research Questions

- How Indian academic libraries Tweets?
- How Indian libraries differs in Tweets in comparison of academic libraries of other developed countries?
- What are the keyword trends in their Tweets?
- What kind of sentiments (positive, negative or neutral and so on) the Tweets carry?

Methodology

For this study, tweets from 10 Indian academic libraries are collected through R interface. These libraries are, Learning Resource Centre, *Silvassa College*, Silvassa, Union Territory of Dadra and Nagar Haveli, *Institute of Hotel Management Catering Technology and Applied Nutrition*, Bhubaneswar, Odisa, Department of Library and Information Science, *Gauhati University*, Guwahati, Library Learning Center, *Indian Institute of Management Raipur*, Vikram Sarabhai Library, *Indian Institute of Management, Ahmedabad*; Central Library of *Indian Institute of Technology Bombay*; MACFAST Library and Information Centre (MLIC) of *Mar Athanasios College for Advanced Studies* Tiruvalla; College library of *Maharshi Dayanand*

College of Arts, Science and Commerce; The Central Library of *Amrita Vishwa Vidyapeetham*; Central Library of *Kalinga Institute of Industrial Technology* (Deemed to be University).

These sample libraries are selected because they have minimum 100 Tweets. The sample is a fair representation of academic libraries from different states in India. Also, in the sample, there are public and private educational institutions including college, universities and technical institutes.

This study further makes a comparison of the Indian academic libraries' Tweets with that of other library Tweets of top ranked global institutes' libraries around the world. For the comparison purpose, the Tweets from the following libraries are downloaded. These libraries are *Trinity College Library*, UK; *National University of Singapore*, *Cornell Library*, USA, *University of Adelaide*, Australia, *York University*, Canada and *Nanyang Technological University Library* Singapore. The Tweets from these different libraries around the globe will act as a comparator to map the position of Indian libraries' activity in Twitter.

Figure 1. Methodology flow chart

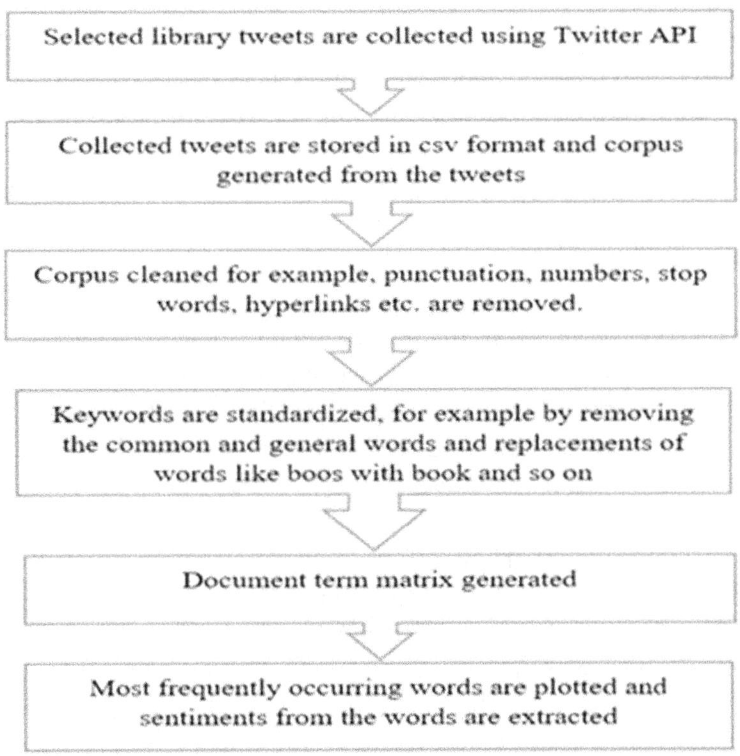

The Tweets are collected form Twitter using the R programming languages. The further analysis is done based on the strong statistical and text mining capabilities of the software R. The figure 1 below shows the step by step methodology for generating word cloud and sentiments

Limitations: this study has the following limitations. *Firstly*, it is based on only one social media, i.e. Twitter. *Secondly*, the study is limited to academic libraries only. Inclusion of other libraries for example; public libraries, school libraries, research libraries, special libraries and other social media like Facebook, LinkedIn will perhaps give a better and holistic picture of Indian libraries' activities on social media. *Thirdly*, the research scope is narrow and only studied the selected libraries activities in microblog Twitter. *Finally*, the Tweets are collected from the library Twitter handle in the particular time of a year. As the field is very dynamic the number of tweets may vary. Future research should focus on the data collection and sorting, make comparative studies from the data of different times including different social network platforms in libraries.

Results

There are altogether about 8,512 Tweets of the 10 different libraries from different parts of India are harvested for this analysis to answer the research questions raised above. It is mentioned in the literature review section that Indian libraries are the early adopter of ICT tools and techniques but their presence in SNSs are not prominent. With the extensive search on the Internet while collecting the Tweets from different library Twitter handles, it is observed that Indian Libraries are generally not that active in Twitter. Many of the famous Indian academic libraries do not even have Twitter account. Many of the library's Twitter handles are inactive and many of them have very limited activities.

The libraries with more than 100 Tweets are selected for this study. The study has taken into account the following 10 libraries. Table 1 shows the profile of different library Tweets harvested from different Indian libraries in the month of August 2019. The table describes different library Tweets and their Twitter handles, their number of Tweets, whom they are following, their followers, the year the Twitter account has been created and from the Indian state or provinces the library or institute is belong to. From the table 1 it is observed that Central Library of Kalinga Institute of Industrial Technology (KIIT) has the maximum number of Tweets followed by Department of Library and Information Science, Guwahati University, Guwahati. Tweets of the rest other libraries are shown in the Table 1 as decreasing order.

For a comparative purpose the following (Table 2) library Tweets from different global academic libraries are chosen. Because of certain limitations, the Twitter API allows to download only 3,500 Tweets at a time. So, the Twitter handles of the

Table 1. Indian Libraries and their Tweets

Sl. No	Name of the Library	Twitter Handle	Number of Tweets	Following	Followers	Year of join in Twitter	State
1.	Central Library of Kalinga Institute of Industrial Technology (Deemed to be University)	@Library_KIIT	3384	79	781	Apr- 2016	Orissa
2.	Department of Library and Information Science, Guwahati University, Guwahati	@DLISGU	2876	29	66	Oct- 2012	Assam
3.	The official Twitter account of Vikram Sarabhai Library, Indian Institute of Management, Ahmedabad	@VSLIIMA	594	648	1225	Dec- 2016	Gujarat
4.	Central Library of Indian Institute of Technology Bombay	@centrallibraryb	520	104	148	Mar-2010	Maharashtra
5.	Institute of Hotel Management Catering Technology and Applied Nutrition, Bhubaneswar	@dash1983	312	52	72	Sep-2013	Orissa
6.	Library Learning Center, Indian Institute of Management Raipur	@IimLibrary	230	19	39	Jul-2018	Chhattisgarh
7.	Learning Resource Centre, Silvassa College, Silvassa, UT of DNH	@SIHL_Library	166	63	52	Mar-2012	Dadra and Nagar Haveli (Indian union territory)
8.	College library of Maharshi Dayanand College is Arts, Science & Commerce	@MDCLibrary	165	70	86	Sep-2011	Mumbai
9.	The Central Library of Amrita Vishwa Vidyapeetham	@ASASLibrary	158	21	51	Jun-2009	Karnataka
10.	MACFAST Library and Information Centre (MLIC) of Mar Athanasios College for Advanced Studies Tiruvalla	@Macfast_Library	107	86	55	Mar-2011	Kerala

following libraries are chosen. In the month of August / September 2019 there were altogether 15,724 Tweets collected form these selected foreign academic libraries. These Tweets are stored in Microsoft Excel comma delimited format for further analysis.

It is evident from the Table 2 that all these libraries have quite significant number of followers. The number of followers shows that these libraries are quite popular among its user. The number of Tweets shows the activity of these libraries and apparently it shows that these libraries are quite active than the Indian academic libraries.

Table 2. Select foreign libraries and their Tweets

Sl. No.	Name of the Library	Twitter Handle	Number of Tweets	Following	Followers	Joined	Country
1.	The Trinity College Library in Cambridge.	@TrinCollLibCam	1423	217	1958	Oct-2014	UK
2.	Cornell University Library	@Cornell_Library	1723	903	2790	Jul- 2017	USA
3.	The University of Adelaide Library	@uofalib	1860	96	1004	Mar-2011	Australia
4.	York University Libraries	@yorkulibraries	3295	825	2569	Dec-2008	Canada
5.	Princeton University Library	@PULibrary	1642	166	1505	Dec-2012	USA
6.	Nanyang Technological University Library	@NTUsgLibrary	2724	140	6013	Aug-2011	Singapore

This study has further observed that there are very few Indian libraries that have separate Twitter accounts (different from their parent institute). It is also not clear who handles these accounts. Moreover, Libraries with Twitter account are very less active. Contrary to this, the libraries from the other developed countries are comparatively more active in Twitter. Those libraries Tweet various information, including new material arrival in the library, seminar announcements and so on.

Topic Modelling

Word frequency analysis or Topic modelling is the concept to extract themes from the textual data. Documents naturally contain words which can represent topics. Hence, Topic modelling can be described as a distribution of concepts over the terms in a corpus of documents. Topic models are applicable in a variety of scientific fields to identify hidden structures in otherwise unstructured text collections (Buckley 2016).

The collected Tweets are further processed by removing the punctuation marks, stop words, space and hyperlinks for word cloud formation and sentiment analysis. From the selected 8,512 Tweets the word corpus is generated. The word cloud shows that 'need' is the most frequently occurring keyword in these words cluster followed by 'delhi.' These words are the most frequently occurred because of the job vacancy announcements. For example, library Tweets, library needs library professionals, librarian and so on. Figure 2 shows the word cloud form the library Tweets.

Figure 3 shows the top 20 most frequently occurring keyword form the Indian academic library's Tweets. The word like assam, kissfoundation kitt, kiss are the prominent keywords. These institutes are the most active in Tweet their contents in Twitter. Hence, it is obvious that these institutes' name will appear and come in priority. Hence it is evident from the Tweet's trends of Indian academic libraries that libraries are more concern about the job-related advertisements and also more towards the contents of their parent institutes in their Tweets rather than their own contents.

Moreover, the word frequency analysis shows that, Indian academic libraries mainly 'Retweet' their parent institute's Tweets with very little contents or value edition of their own. So, it can be concluded that, Indian academic libraries are quite poor in generating content on the Twitter.

Similar to the Tweets collected for the Indian academic libraries, the Tweets from foreign academic libraries are also collected and processed. There are altogether 12,667 Tweets collected form those selected libraries. These tweets are collected as comma delimited format and word corpus created. The figure 4 shows the word cloud generated from the different library Tweets of selected foreign academic libraries. In this case, library is the most prominent keyword, followed by new, book, today and so on. The trends in keywords shows that these libraries are giving more emphasis on library's activities in that day and so on. The words like books and new etc shows the new arrival in the library.

The figure 5 shows the most frequently occurring keywords from the foreign library Tweets. Library is the most frequently occurred keyword with 2,317 occurrences, followed by new, book, today and so on. The word youku is in the fifth position with 741 occurrence represents. The word 'youku' represents York University Libraries is the library system. The topic also shows more towards libraries or library related activities among these libraries. It includes the words like research, students, university and so on.

Figure 2. Word cloud from Indian academic library tweets

Figure 3. The top 20 Tweets collected from the Indian Library Tweets

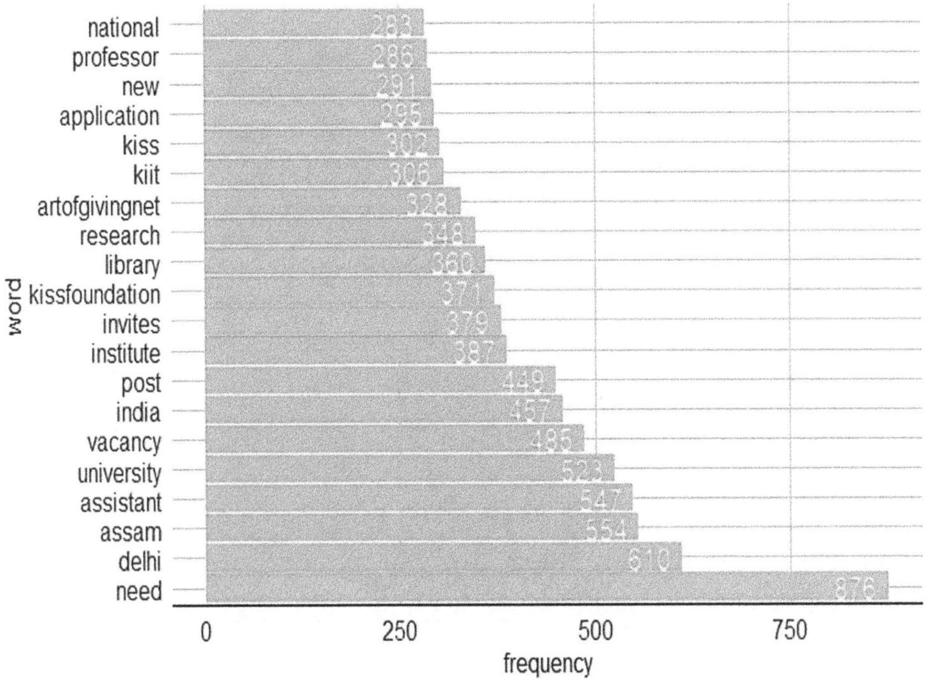

Sentiment Analysis

This section deals with the sentiment analysis of Tweets collected form the selected library's Twitter handles. The objective of this section is to analyse the trends among the library Tweets. By analysing the words in the Twitter, it is trying to identity the sentiments associate with the words.

Sentiment analysis (SA) is about the extraction of sentiment, opinion from the text through the computational treatment of structured or unstructured text (Pang and Lee 2008). With the social media boom in recent years, a vast amount of unstructured data with opinions from various topics are available. With proper treatment of these text many valuable and meaningful information can be extracted (Thelwall, Buckley, and Paltoglou 2011). With the increasing computational power these types of analysis are inexpensive source for opinion analysis of organizations and individuals. Sentiment can be of various categories. For example, a sentiment extracted from the word can be positive, negative, or neutral. Sentiment analysis has widespread applications in various institutes or organization for example in sales prediction, stock management, ad placements, products and so on (Oliveira, Cortez and Areal 2016).

Figure 4. Word cloud of different foreign academic library Tweets

Figure 5. Top 20 most frequently occurring words from selected foreign library Tweets

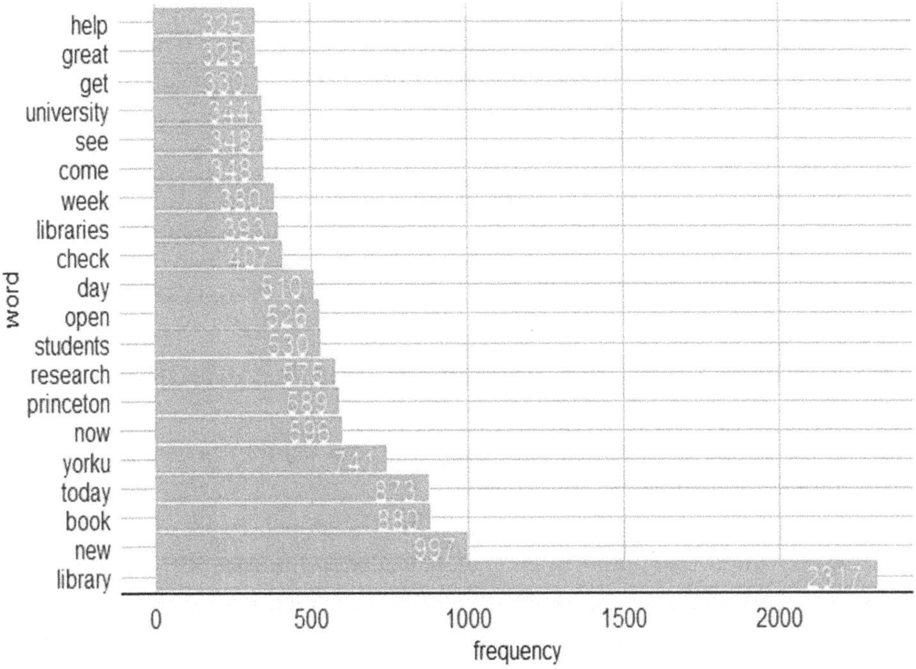

For this study the sentiments extracted from the Tweets are of 10 types. The different types of Tweets are; Positive, Trust, Anticipation, Joy, Negative, Surprise, Fear, Sadness, Anger and Disgust. Figure 6 shows the different types of sentiments extracted from two different type of libraries.

Figure 6. Comparison of sentiments from the words of Indian and Foreign Library Tweets

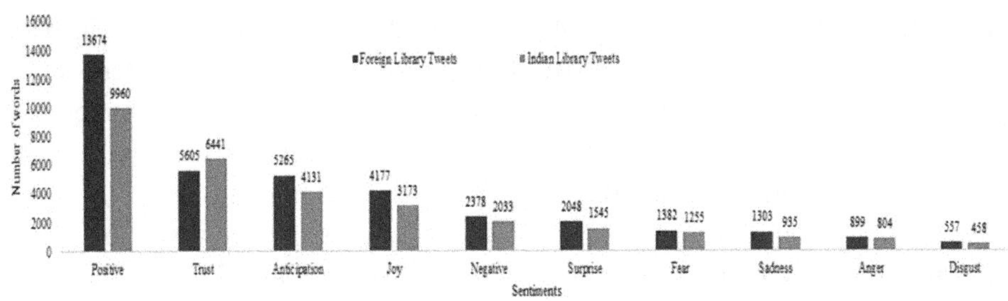

Although the number of Tweets form two different types of libraries varies, the tweets of both types of libraries have similar trends (figure 6). These two different types of Tweets have similar types of sentiment. From the foreign libraries among the 20,808 words 13,674 are positives words (65.72 percent). Similarly, in Indian libraries among 15,401 words 9,960 are positive (64.67 percent) sentiments. However, in case of India libraries 42 percent are trust and in case of foreign libraries are 27 percent trust. Rest other sentiments follow the similar trends. Hence, it is quite optimistic scenario that Indian academic libraries Tweets carry more optimistic and positive sentiment.

CONCLUDING REMARKS AND POLICY IMPLICATIONS

With the increasing availability, popularity and accessibility of SNSs many new opportunities and challenged are opened for the academic libraries. The SNSs are quite popular among the university and college students. In this context, SNSs could be very important platform for Indian academic libraries for self-promotion and marketing of their systemS and services (Liu, Zhang and Ye 2018). Students (both university and college) are the main user of the academic libraries. Students of these age group are quite well versed of using different ICT tools and techniques in their daily routine. With the recent mobile and smartphone penetration among the general population, most of the young people are tech savvy and have Facebook and Twitter accounts. So, Twitter is very helpful to reach these young users. If libraries can be active in social media like Twitter, they can reach these users quite easily and efficiently. The more active twitter handle will certainly be useful to reach the more users.

In comparison to many academic libraries of developed world, Indian academic libraries are not that active in Twitter. Also, it is not evident from the present Twitter handle, who maintains the Twitter account of academic libraries. In this context, it is advisable that, Indian academic libraries should assign an expert LIS professional to maintain their library's Twitter account. A separate division of work with defined job responsibility must be there to look after and coordinate the library Twitter activity regularly. In this way libraries can Tweet their activities to the user or interested patrons. This will in the long run attract more users, particularly the youths in the college and universities who are the primary users of the library.

Indian libraries are early adapter of ICT Tools and services. However, in the case of social media uses, Indian academic libraries are lagging behind in comparison to academic libraries of developed countries. Although, there are difference in social and economic conditions, for example, the financial resources in the libraries, however, Twitter and library Tweeting activity is not an expensive affair. So, Indian libraries could maintain regular Twitter handle to promote their activities. Academic library professional in India must be active in social media include Twitter. More activities on the social media will give a positive picture to the libraries and the librarians as a whole. This will also help to reach their library patrons and other target audience.

The study presented above have used quite simple tools. LIS professionals should use or apply these types of exercises in their libraries regularly. Librarians can adopt this technique to get immediate feedback about their library services and opinions about other things in the library.

REFERENCES

Aharony, N. (2010). Twitter Use in Libraries: An Exploratory Analysis. *Journal of Web Librarianship*, *4*(4), 333–350. doi:10.1080/19322909.2010.487766

Al-Daihani, S. M., & AlAwadhi, S. A. (2015). Exploring academic libraries' use of Twitter: A content analysis. *The Electronic Library*, *33*(6), 1002–1015. doi:10.1108/EL-05-2014-0084

Balamurugan, T., & Thanuskodi, S. (2019). Use of social networking sites among the college students in Tamil Nadu, India. *Library Philosophy and Practice*, *2301*, 1–12.

Buckley, P. (2016). Topic Modelling. In M. Hofmann & A. Chisholm (Eds.), *Text Mining and Visualization Case Studies Using Open-Source Tools*. CRC Press, Taylor and Francis Group.

Carscaddon, L., & Chapman, K. (2013). Twitter as a marketing tool for libraries. *Marketing with social media: A LITA guide*, 147-163.

Chakravarty, R., & Kiran, A. (2013). Social Networking in Libraries: A Case Study of Post Graduate Students and Research Scholars of Panjab University Library, India. In S. Thanuskodi (Ed.), *Challenges of Academic Library Management in Developing Countries*. IGI Global. doi:10.4018/978-1-4666-4070-2.ch009

Deepthi, T. (2017). Use of online social networking services in university libraries: A Study of university libraries of Karnataka, India. *DESIDOC Journal of Library and Information Technology*, *37*(4), 249–258. doi:10.14429/djlit.37.4.10498

Del Bosque, D., Leif, S. A., & Skarl, S. (2012). Libraries atwitter: Trends in academic library tweeting. *RSR. Reference Services Review*, *40*(2), 199–213. doi:10.1108/00907321211228246

Fasola, O. S. (2015). Perceptions and acceptance of librarians towards using Facebook and Twitter to promote library services in Oyo State, Nigeria. *The Electronic Library*, *33*(5), 870–882. doi:10.1108/EL-04-2014-0066

Fields, E. (2010). A unique Twitter use for reference services. *Library Hi Tech News*, *27*(6/7), 14–15. doi:10.1108/07419051011095863

Kim, H. M., Abels, E. G., & Yang, C. C. (2012). Who disseminates academic library information on Twitter? *Proceedings of the ASIST Annual Meeting*, *49*(1), 1-4. 10.1002/meet.14504901317

Krishnamurthy, C., & Shettappanavar, L. (2019). Digital literacy among female postgraduate students of Karnatak University, Dharwad, Karnataka, India: A study. *Library Philosophy and Practice*, *2934*, 1–16.

Liu, L., Zhang, L., & Ye, P. (2018). Research on the application of SNS in university libraries. *The Electronic Library*, *36*(2), 369–386. doi:10.1108/EL-05-2016-0120

Munigal, A. (2014). Use of Microblogs in India: A Study of Twitter Usage by Librarians and in Libraries. *Journal of Library Administration*, *54*(7), 590–608. doi:10.1080/01930826.2014.964021

Oliveira, N., Cortez, P., & Areal, N. (2016). Sentiment Analysis of Stock Market Behavior from Twitter Using the R Tool. In M. Hofmann & A. Chisholm (Eds.), *Text Mining and Visualization Case Studies Using Open-Source Tools*. CRC Press, Taylor and Francis Group.

Palmer, S. (2014). Characterizing university library use of social media: A case study of Twitter and Facebook from Australia. *Journal of Academic Librarianship*, *40*(6), 611–619. doi:10.1016/j.acalib.2014.08.007

Pang, B., & Lee, L. (2008). Opinion mining and sentiment analysis. *Foundations and Trends® in Information Retrieval,* 2(1–2), 1-135.

Patra, S. K. (2019). How Indian libraries tweet? Word frequency and sentiment analysis of library tweets. *Annals of Library and Information Studies*, *66*, 131–139.

Sakas, D. P., & Sarlis, A. S. (2016). Library promotion methods and tools modeling and simulation on Twitter. *Library Review*, *65*(6-7), 479–499. doi:10.1108/LR-06-2015-0068

Shulman, J., Yep, J., & Tomé, D. (2015). Leveraging the power of a Twitter network for library promotion. *Journal of Academic Librarianship*, *41*(2), 178–185. doi:10.1016/j.acalib.2014.12.004

Stuart, D. (2010). What are libraries doing on twitter? *Online (Wilton, Connecticut)*, *34*(1), 45–47.

Thelwall, M., Buckley, K., & Paltoglou, G. (2011). Sentiment in Twitter Events. *Journal of the American Society for Information Science and Technology*, *62*(2), 406–418. doi:10.1002/asi.21462

Vassilakaki, E., & Garoufallou, E. (2015). The impact of Twitter on libraries: A critical review of the literature. *The Electronic Library*, *33*(4), 795–809. doi:10.1108/EL-03-2014-0051

Verishagen, N., & Hank, C. (2014). Are there birds in the library? The extent of Twitter adoption and use by Canadian academic libraries. *First Monday*, *19*(11). Advance online publication. doi:10.5210/fm.v19i11.4945

Chapter 10
Data Visualization and Data Granularity in Delivering Research Data in African Libraries

Oluwaseun David Adepoju
African Leadership University, Kigali, Rwanda

Ruti Dauphin
African Leadership University, Kigali, Rwanda

ABSTRACT

Data has been named the new oil that drives development both in academia and in the business world. It has been used to develop new products across all sectors of the global economy and recently in agriculture through precision agriculture and robotic farming. It should, however, be noted that no matter the potential for change and development a data set contains, it is very important to deploy the right interpretation techniques to make the data useful and meaningful. This chapter explores themes such as data visualization tools, data granularity, and data visualization tools. It also explained the advantages of data visualization and the types of data African libraries should be collecting.

DOI: 10.4018/978-1-7998-3049-8.ch010

INTRODUCTION

The global per-capita capacity to generate data has increased in leaps and bounds in the last two decades. More technological platforms have emerged more than ever before, and the oil they run with is simply data. A cross knowledge from information science noted that data is at the bottom of all experience. As a matter of fact, the lower rung of the knowledge ladder is the Raw Data, it then goes through the transformation from being raw to becoming information to knowledge and then to wisdom. Based on this background, we can boldly say that the foundation of any decision that would be made by humans is a result of the Data that was at the beginning of the decision ladder.

Commenting on the right tools to manage data for the purpose of easy access and use, Panoho (2019) stated that data is one of the most valuable assets a business can have and potentially has a tremendous impact on its long-term success. That's why it's vital to utilize the right tools and technologies to fully leverage all available data and make it as accurate as possible. Data in itself is not meaningful and not useful until the right tools have been used in ensuring its quality, accuracy, arrangement, visualization and accessibility. Data management needs tools such as normalization tools, filing tools, accuracy and cleaning tools, storage tools and visualization tools.

The role of data visualization in the presentation of data is as important as the data content itself. A data user will not benefit from the input if he or she does not understand how to generate insight from the data. According to Marastats (2019), Data visualization is useful for data cleaning, exploring data structure, detecting outliers and unusual groups, identifying trends and clusters, spotting local patterns, evaluating modelling output, and presenting results. It is essential for exploratory data analysis and data mining to check data quality and to help analysts become familiar with the structure and features of the data before them. This is a part of data analysis that is underplayed in textbooks, yet ever-present in actual investigations.

Data is being used for different reasons and purposes across various industries. However, in academia, researchers, students and faculty are always in need of data to generate insights for research outputs and to validate their hypothesis. More often than not, one of the first places they turn to is the academic libraries in their various institutions. They expect to get the Data that will help them in their tasks in a presentable and understandable format, hence, the need for data visualization by academic libraries and academic librarians. The rapid development in technology and the massive growth in the world's capacity to generate data has made it required skill to be able to manage, curate and make sense from raw data. As managers of knowledge, Librarians are at the very center of managing and creating access to useful data for all kinds of organizational and societal decision making. Data is being presented with different innovative visualization tools these days and librarians are well-positioned to master the tools to help the library patrons better.

Given those as mentioned above, this chapter used a qualitative expository methodology in exploring the various skills and tools needed by African Librarians in delivering granular and visualized data to library patrons. Besides, this chapter emphasized the types of African data libraries are meant to be collecting. This will help the librarianship profession to begin to appreciate the concepts of open data, naked statistics, data granularity and data visualization.

Data: The New Oil (Clive Humby, 2006)

In 2006, the renowned British Mathematician and architect by the name of Clive Humby first used the phrase "Data is the new oil'. Bhageshpur (2019) also stated that data is the new oil and that the main impact on humanity isn't how tech giants are monetizing our attention units, but about how data can improve our lives. Since Humby's use of this phrase, the phrase has possibly been used more a million times in different academic and opinion articles globally. Digerati's, technocrats, policymakers, technology enthusiasts and academics working in the data field have confirmed over and over again the phrase "data is the new oil" through various research outputs and intellectual discourse.

Possibly, the earliest articles that made the "data is the new oil" parlance mainstream are Michael Palmer, "Data Is the New Oil," ANA Marketing Maestros published in 2007 and "The World's Most Valuable Resource Is No Longer Oil, but Data," The Economist, May 6, 2017. This article and many more pointed the world to the vast opportunities that abound in the use of data for decision making and innovation disruption. The data is the new oil parlance has generated various schools of thought in validating or maintaining an iconoclastic position on the language.

One of the most exciting research that called the world to caution on reimagining the "data is the new oil" narrative is Loi and Dehaye (2017). They took an approach of institutionalization and policies in approaching data. They also explored how data can lead to a new form of dominance that will not be political but whole technological. Regulations and control were also vital parts of the concerns they raised.

It is, however interesting to note that despite the many concerns on the destructive abilities of data, data has proven to be the force that drives the 21stc century digital economy and all the new technological products. While we cannot deny that data could be the new oil and at the same time the new nuclear bomb, data is proving to be the actual new oil from all the disruptive impacts recorded from the moment Clive Humby (2006) declared data to be the new oil. It will not be a grammatical anomaly to posit that data is not only the new oil but also the currency of the digital age. The comparison of data to crude oil did not only come from the premise of its ability to create wealth but also in its ability to be the foundation of a creative economy for countries and organizations. We are frequently under the definitional pressure of data. There is always this struggle to give a finite definition of data. Still, it has proven over time to carry so much potential that a single description will not suffice to convey its multifarious nature.

As a postgraduate student some years ago, I was in an Electronic Government Class in South Korea, where the Professor was introducing the class to the idea of data and big data. As he proceeded in his explanations of the concept, a student interrupted him with a question. The student asked, and I quote, "What exactly is data"? The Professor smiled, and he answered, "rather than tell you what data is, I would rather tell you what data can do. We are not some students of subject matter but students of problems". The response from the Professor got us all thinking about the pressure to sometimes focus on definitions rather than the use of a thing.

As noted earlier in this chapter, data carries a lot of potentials to change the society positively and also vice versa. Data is what we make out of it. It takes equally the potential to make and to a mare. Data can be a blessing, and it can also be a bane. As technology entrepreneurs explore the use of data in building products and solutions to societal problems, data can also be used to act against the sanity of humanity. These two sides of the coin speak to the deliberate effort that must be put in the gathering, curating, analyzing and the use of data. However, we cannot because of the negative potentials of a thing not explored in full, the positive potential of it. This chapter will explore the positive potential of data through data visualization and data granularity.

Data Visualization and Data Visualization Tools: Speaking Visually

Several academic and business research has established that visual communication is more effective than text communication. Data visualizations combine numeric data with visual representation, and these modes allow them to express certain kinds of knowledge more quickly than others (Rettberg, 2020). Rettberg's explanation of data visualization confirms again that data in its presentation must be easy to comprehend for the users. The same way communication has not taken place until understanding has taken place. Data visualization can also be seen as a graphical representation of information and data. By using visual elements like charts, graphs, and maps, data visualization tools provide an accessible way to see and understand trends, outliers, and patterns in data.

Rettberg (2020) further stated that Data visualizations combine at least two modes of representation: numerical data and visual diagrams. For a computer program to be able to process data, it has to be converted to numbers, to the zeros and ones of machine code. Also, the data need to be visually organized, which often requires dividing them into discrete quantities were lines, size, spatial placement, and other visual elements show specific patterns in the data. Each of these two modes of expression, the numeric and the visible, carries its affordances and constraints for what they can express. Writing on the multimodality of Data visualization, Hippala (2020) took the ideas of Rettberg (2020) further by shedding light on the multimodality of data visualization. He explained multimodality to be how we combine multiple modes of expression, such as written language, photographs, diagrammatic elements, and illustrations, in various printed and digital media.

Inferences from these pieces of the literature show that data visualization is not limited to the use of one mode or tool but a combination of several tools to communicate data effectively. Moreover, presenting data in visuals requires a lot of creativity and ability from the side of the data handler. Data could be clumsy and tiresome in viewing to many. African Libraries should begin to embrace data visualization tools in such a way that they begin to render seemingly boring cumbersome data in an exciting and attractive way to patrons. African Libraries should not only speak in texts, but they should also start to talk visually through infographics, videos, graphics and innovative charts.

Excellent visualization of data highly depends on the type of data being represented; mainly, Qualitative data, Quantitative data and other forms of data. Qualitative Data is the type of data that approximates and characterizes, this type of data is also non-numerical. Generally, it provides insights in determining particular frequency in trends and characteristics. Quantitative Data is the type of data that has value in forms of counts or numbers and hence quantifiable to be used for mathematical calculations and statistical analysis, it usually answers questions such as how many, how often, and how much. Types of data that don't belong to either qualitative or quantitative data such as journey maps, workflows and more, also require tools to best visualize the message to be conveyed.

List of Tools for Data Visualization for African Librarians

Figure 1.

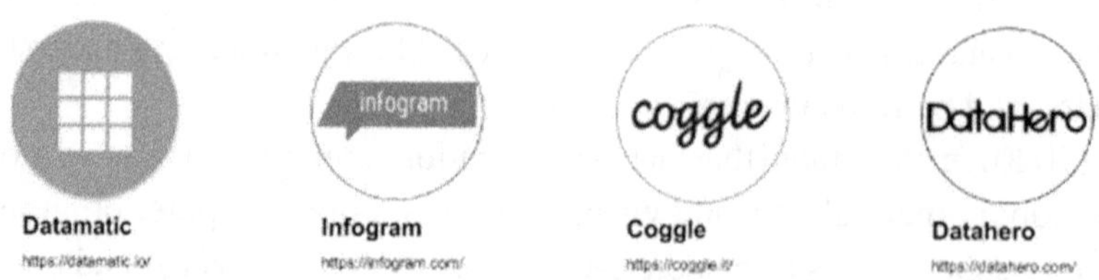

Datamatics (https://www.datamatics.com/)

Datamatic is like Wordpress for interactive data visualizations. It allows you to pick a data visualization template, edit it in a simple online editor and publish on any website. All the models are handcrafted and optimized to be styled and customized.

Infogram (https://infogram.com/)

Infogram is an easy to use infographic and chart maker. Create and share beautiful infographics, online reports and interactive maps.

Coggle (https://coggle.it/)

Coggle is a freeware mind-mapping web application. Coggle produces hierarchically structured documents like a branching tree. This contrasts with other collaborative editors, like Google Docs, which provide either linear or tabular document formats. Its authors promise that it will be free forever.

DataHero (https://datahero.com/)

DataHero is a data visualization solution that enables users to immediately link to cloud-hosted services and import data and drive data to generate insights that help users understand issues.

Figure 2.

amCharts (https://www.amcharts.com/)

amCharts is a set of JavaScript-based data visualization libraries that includes regular chart types like Serial, Pie, etc. as well as advanced ones like Stock Charts and

Maps. Before you can use amCharts, you will need to include required JavaScript Libraries. There is one main library that is necessary for all amCharts operations - amcharts.js. It needs to be added first and is mandatory. Each chart type requires chart-type specific inclusion. For example, Serial chart will also require serial.js; a Pie chart will need pie.js, etc. If on the same web page you will be displaying several different chart types, you will need to include all chart-type-specific includes that are being displayed on that page.

Google Sheets (https://www.google.com/sheets/about/)

Google Sheets is a spreadsheet program included as part of a free, web-based software office suite offered by Google within its Google Drive service. The service also includes Google Docs and Google Slides, a word processor and presentation program, respectively.

LucidChart (https://www.lucidchart.com/pages/)

Lucidchart is a web-based proprietary platform that is used to allow users to collaborate on drawing, revising and sharing charts and diagrams. Lucidchart runs on browsers that support HTML5. This means it does not require updates of third party software like Adobe Flash.

Canva (https://www.canva.com/)

Canva is a graphic design platform that allows users to create social media graphics, presentations, posters and other visual content. It is available on web and mobile and integrates millions of images, fonts, templates and illustrations.

Figure 3.

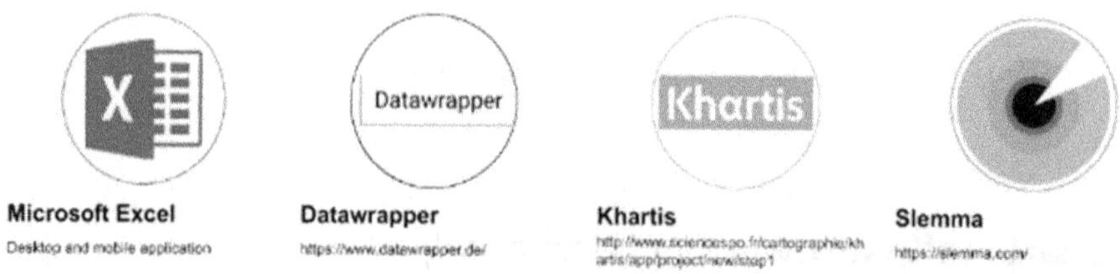

Microsoft Excel (https://www.microsoft.com/en-us/microsoft-365/excel)

Microsoft Excel is a spreadsheet developed by Microsoft for Windows, macOS, Android and iOS. It features calculation, graphing tools, pivot tables, and a macro programming language called Visual Basic for Applications. Excel learns your patterns, organizing your data to save you time. Easily create spreadsheets from templates or on your own and use modern formulas to perform calculations. New charts and graphs help you present your data in compelling ways, with formatting, sparklines, and tables to understand your data better. Easily create forecasts to predict trends with just a click.

Datawrapper (https://www.datawrapper.de/)

Wrapper in data mining is a program that extracts the content of a particular information source and translates it into a relational form. Many web pages present structured data - telephone directories, product catalogues, etc. formatted for human browsing using HTML language. Datawrapper empowers everyone to create digitally optimized charts, maps, or tables. It's as easy as following four steps.

Khartis (https://www.sciencespo.fr/cartographie/khartis/en/)

Khartis helps you to create your thematic maps thanks to a pedagogical accompaniment, accessible to all.

Figure 4.

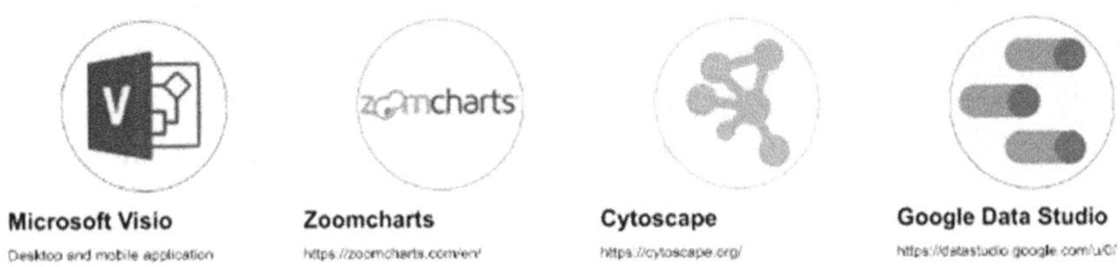

Microsoft Visio (https://www.microsoft.com/en/microsoft-365/visio/flowchart-software)

Microsoft Visio can be used to create simple or complicated diagrams. It offers a wide variety of built-in shapes, objects, and stencils to work with. You can also make your shapes and import them if you're willing to do all that extra work. The driving idea behind Visio is to make diagramming as easy as possible for the user. Visio can be used to create 3D map diagrams, though the built-in tools for this are limited. It works well for simple maps that you might print on a brochure or campus directory.

Zoom Charts (https://zoomcharts.com/en/)

It lets your data tell an engaging story while significantly improving the data exploration process. It also helps to overcome the challenges presented by Big Data and the Internet of Things. The technology lets you explore your data in a fast and straightforward manner. With custom-built multi-touch engine ZoomCharts technology allows you to enjoy dashboards and reports on any device.

Cytoscape (https://cytoscape.org/)

Cytoscape is an open-source bioinformatics software platform for visualizing molecular interaction networks and integrating with gene expression profiles and other state data. Additional features are available as plugins.

Google Data Studio (https://datastudio.google.com/u/0/navigation/reporting)

Easily connect your data from spreadsheets, Analytics, Google Ads, Google BigQuery and more. Transform your raw data into the metrics and dimensions needed to create easy-to-understand reports and dashboards — no code or queries required. Arm people with the knowledge of your critical parameters by sharing automated data dashboards that regularly update, so they can focus more on what matters.

Visualization Diagrams

Figure 5. Venn Diagram

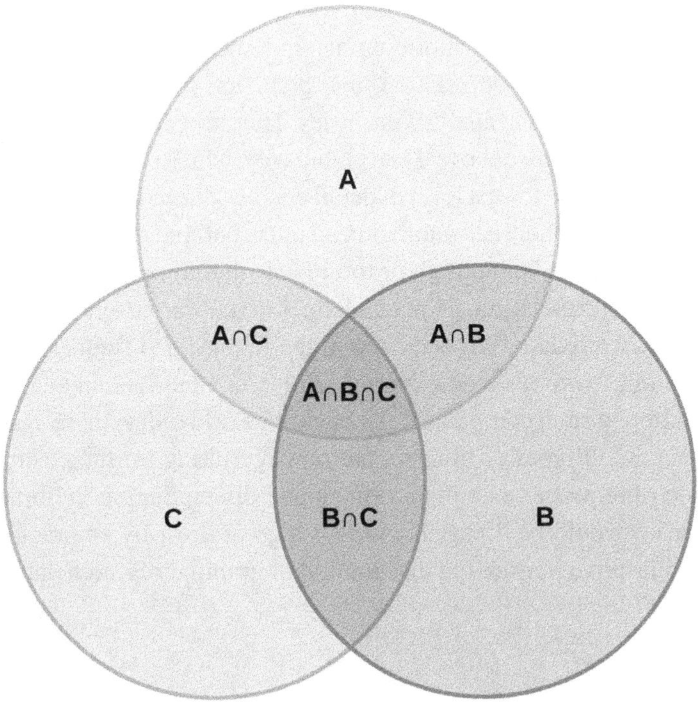

Data Granularity: Breaking the Rock to Chaffs

According to Technopedia, Granular Data is Data that is in pieces, as small as possible, to be more defined and detailed. The advantage of granular data is that it can be molded in any way that the data scientist or analyst requires, just like granules of sand that conform to their container. Granular data can be aggregated and disaggregated to meet the needs of different situations. If data is not granulated, such as a name or address field being saved as a whole, then it is challenging for analysts to mine and analyze data because they are in large chunks. Granular data can be easily merged with data from external sources and can be effectively integrated and managed.

More often than not, it has been observed that data collection and data analysis is not the only issue in Africa. There is yet a more significant challenge of know-how on breaking complex data down to granular states which enables a layperson to understand and probably use for decision making. Data is just like a rock; it needs granular interpretation and meaning addition from the most complex field to the simplest area. Data is not useful, either structured or unstructured if the user cannot understand it. When the level of granularity in building a data warehouse in African libraries are appropriately set, the remaining aspects of implementation will run smoothly and vice versa.

Proper data granularity allows for more robust analysis and reduction of decision errors to the barest minimum. Shortcomings in a measurement system's accuracy (bias, linearity, stability or correlation) and precision (resolution, repeatability or reproducibility) can obstruct analysis purposes. Therefore, data granularity will help immensely in avoiding those above. Data granularity, which is the process of breaking a data model down to the lowest level of detail enables data administrators to transfer data from one data warehouse to another in an interoperable manner. Granularity for data, however, must not be too high or too low. It should instead meet the users at the right level of interpretation. Most academics and library users have complained of complex data from data files accessed in the library, and frequently, librarians, especially the ones who have no experience in data analysis and analytics do not have any solution to such complaints. All over the world today, more specifically in the United States, all types of libraries are now recruiting for the position of Data Librarian to ensure proper data management and dissemination to library patrons. African libraries would be doing themselves a great favor by embracing this new field of librarianship to ensure the distribution of granular research data to patrons.

Figure 6. Pie Chart

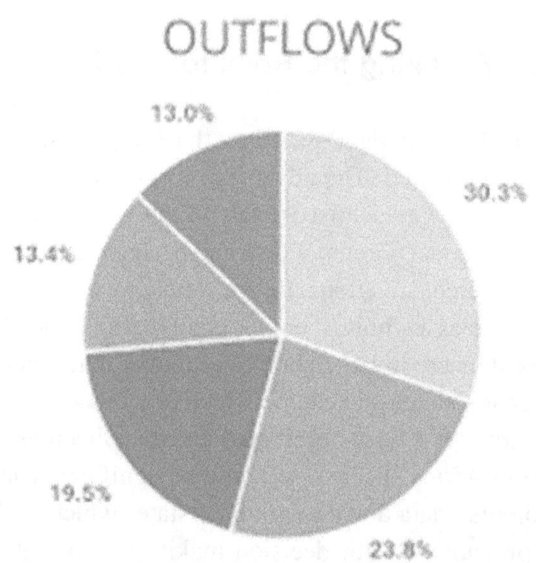

Figure 7. Maps

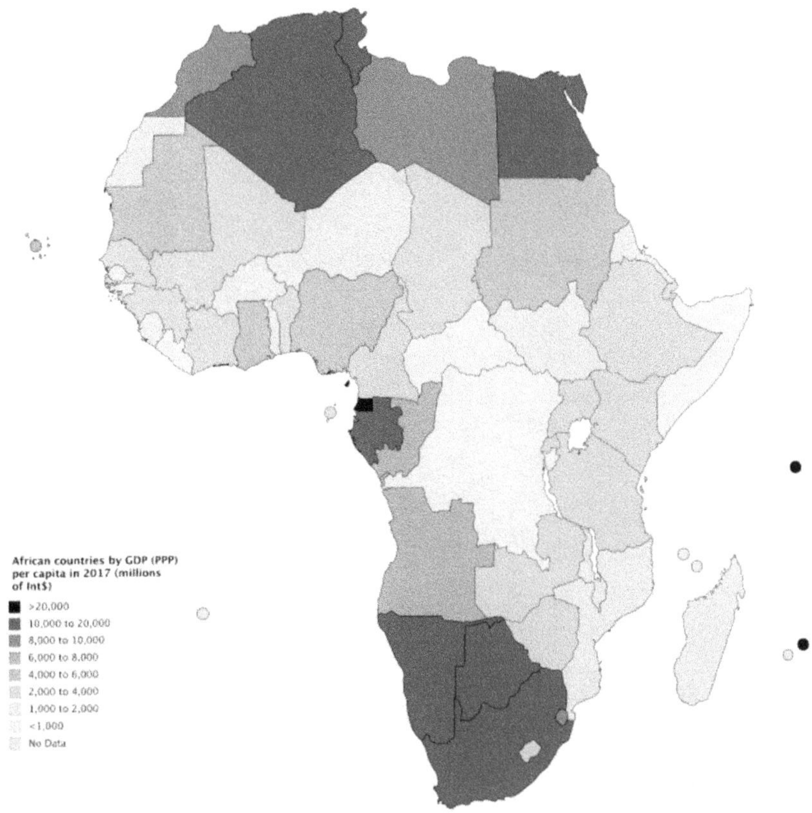

Figure 8. Bar Chart

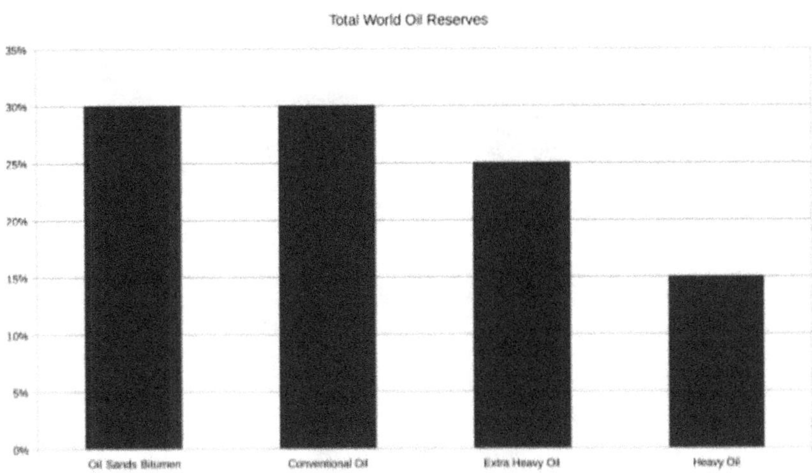

Figure 9. Line Chart

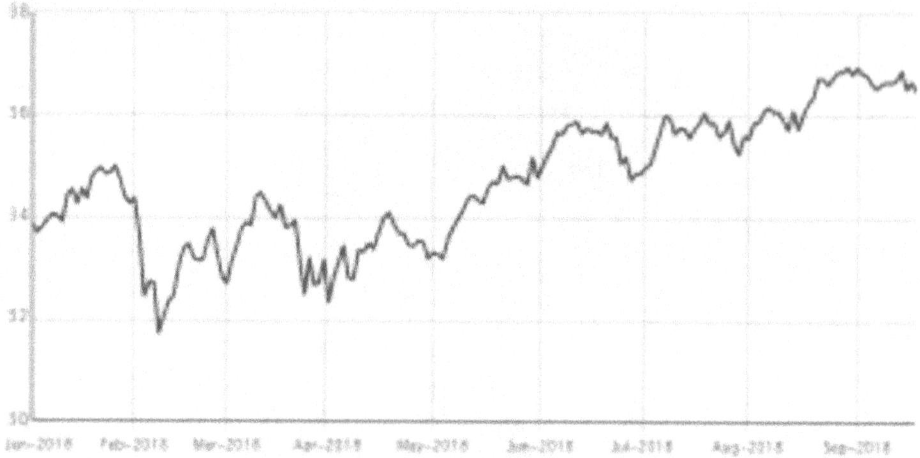

Figure 10. Rose Chart

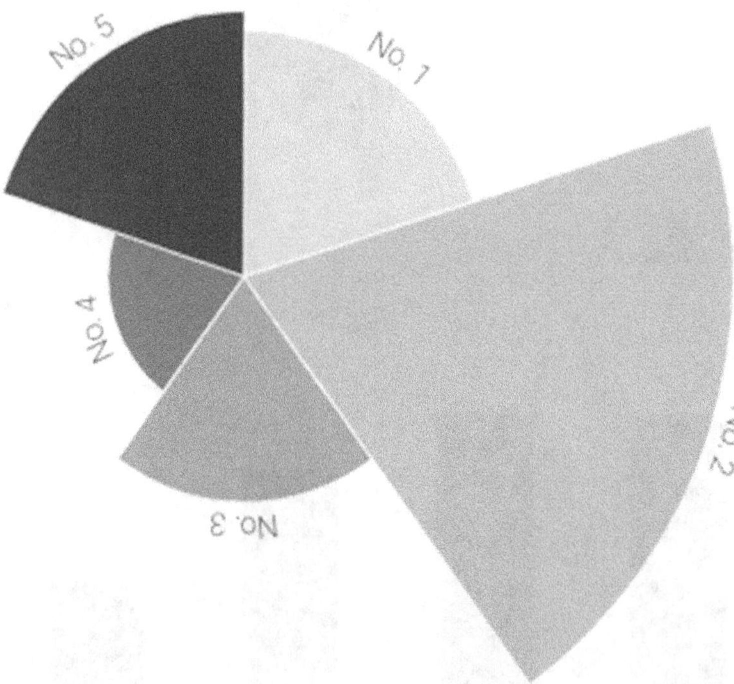

Figure 11. Scatter Chart

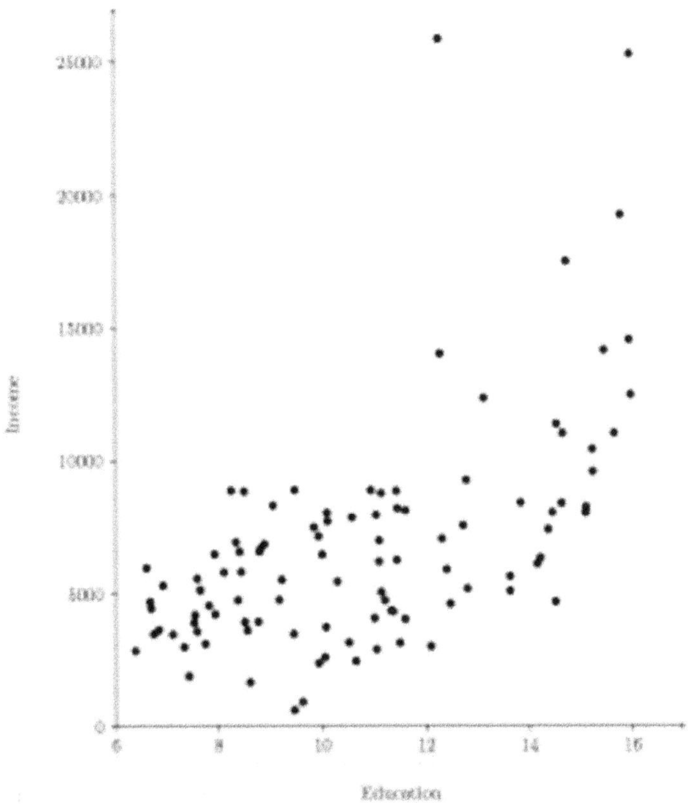

Figure 12. Timeline

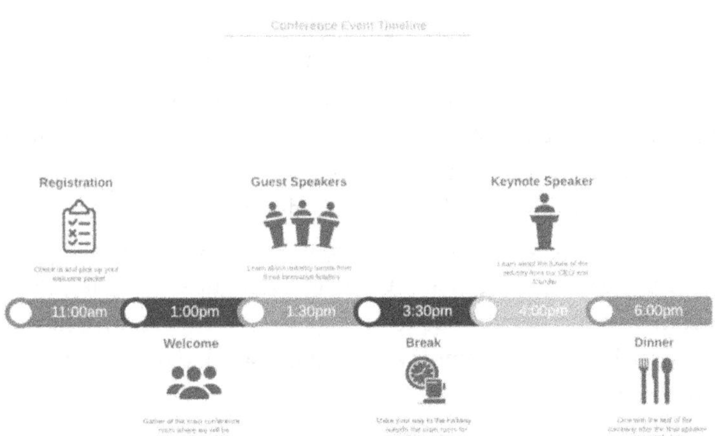

Figure 13. Mindmap

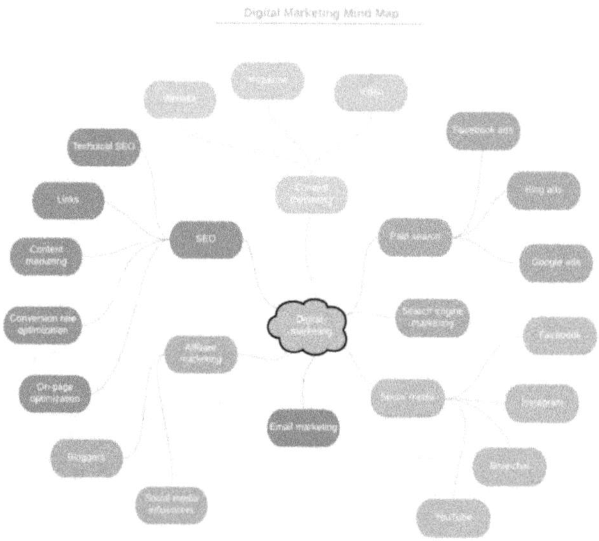

Data librarians will be responsible for the further breaking down of multiple data files to meet the specific needs of users. Users, academics are most likely to come back to the library when they get granular, usable, easily understandable, and decision focused data from the library. Data Librarians will be instrumental to the 21st-century African libraries in ways unimaginable in the coming days and this by implication requires deploying all our intellectual and financial arsenals in making it a reality in Africa. It is very imperative to address the issues of skills development for African librarians in the continually changing world. Change is inevitable in all human endeavors, and it is essential for African libraries to begin to invest more in capacity building, train-retrain and upskilling for its workforce. I have also observed in my years of practice that the biggest sabotage to investment on capacity building in most African libraries is what I would best describe as "Getting new skills and doing old job's syndrome". The lack of data management skills sometimes might not be because the library institutions are not investing in upskilling for the workforce. Still, the inability of the institutions to engage the workforce with new challenges that push them to deploy the unique skills and knowledge they have acquired from the upskilling process.

Figure 14. Flow Chart

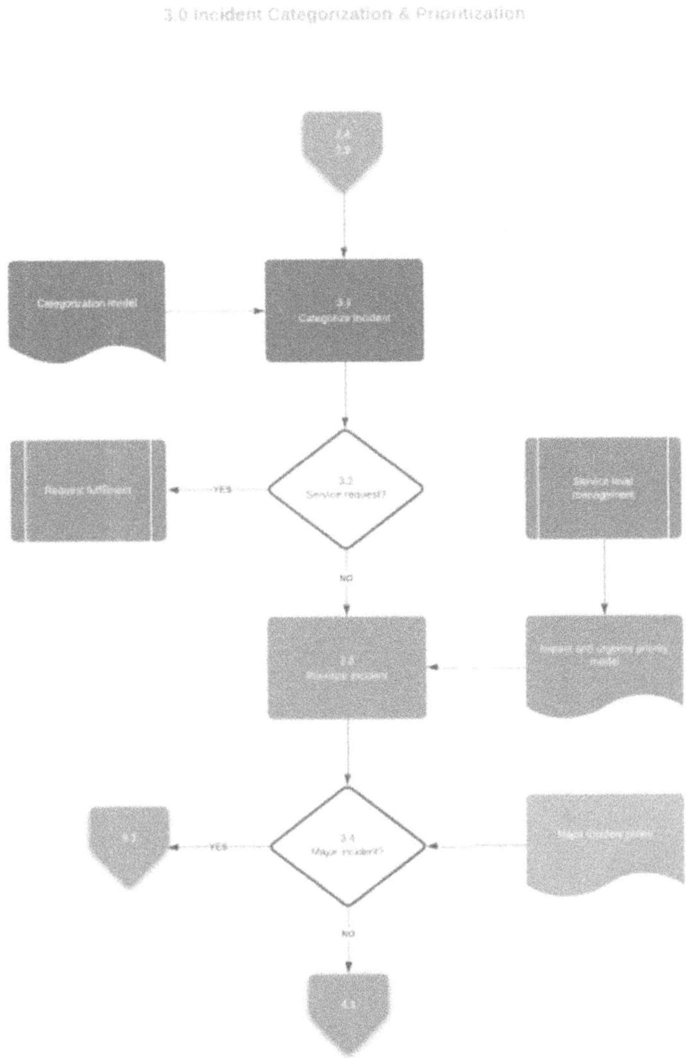

Figure 15. Workflow

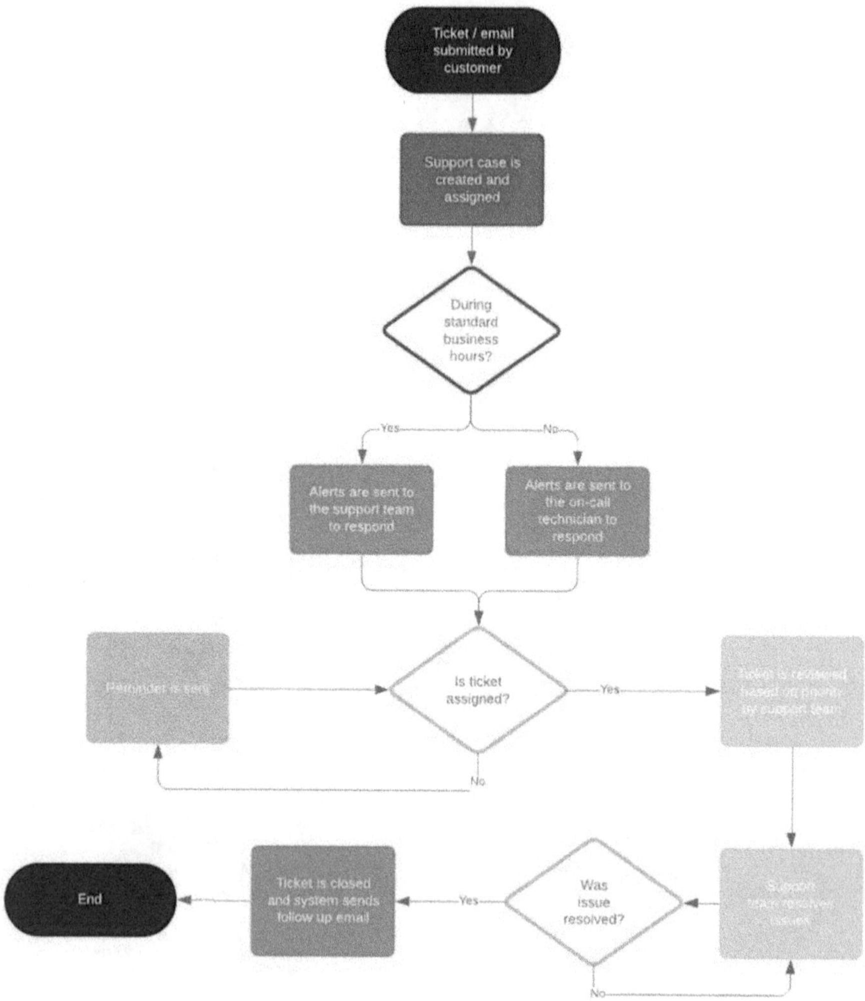

What Data Should African Libraries be Collecting?

Librarianship, as a profession has experienced a paradigm shift both in its service delivery and societal roles. The evolution of information provision as a profession has not been without its attendant challenges, especially in the rapidly changing techno-deterministic era. Librarianship has a long-standing history as one of the most critical professions that are central to achieving learning and teaching goals. Before the advent of information technologies, librarians were known to be people who did due diligence to know something about everything through the study of information sources. In the 21st century where disruptive technologies have affected the way things are done in all spheres of life, librarians' role and relevance as information providers were threatened with the arrival of search engines and information metadata. Many library users began to abandon the library desks because they feel Search engines would meet all their information needs.

Figure 16. Radial Bar Chart

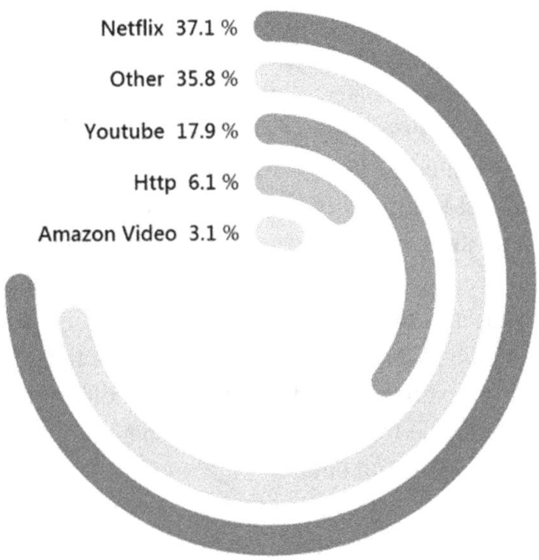

This relevance threat by technology has unanimously changed the roles of librarians from people who are seen as those who sit by some old books, arranged on some wooden shelves to the 21st-century tech-savvy cyborg librarians. A cyborg librarian is one who is part machine and part human. The machine part describes the skill sets of such a librarian in navigating the vast information terrain that has been introduced by technology and the human section describes how such a librarian can still use his or her human intuitions and psychology in discovering the information needs of patrons.

It is very pertinent to note that as the information architecture space is changing, the needs of library patrons are also evolving concurrently. It has been observed that as data becomes central to decision making globally, the demand for different types of data is also on the rise by students, researchers, startups and policymakers. Instead of those mentioned above, one of the places people in need of data would decide to check for their needed data will be the library. However, most African libraries are falling short in curating both structured and unstructured data to satisfy the data needs of patrons by organizing a significant data infrastructure that accommodates all kinds of data.

If African libraries maintain their level of relevance in the rapidly changing data-driven era, they must begin to collect valuable and re-usable data for their users. The following are the types of Data African Libraries should begin to curate;

Internal Patron Data

Most African libraries are guilty of not collecting and generating insights from patron data. This is the beginning of a data collection journey for most African Libraries. Libraries should be able to give without any equivocation, the data insights of the number of patrons that visited the library over a while, the number of books borrowed and returned, the subject field mostly used by patrons and so on. African libraries should also be able to show which gender uses which collection most and which group is least used by patrons. All these forms of data would enable the library the questions of why what and where in their decision making. It will also help the library to track progress and the areas of shortcomings of the library. In a nutshell, generating insights from patrons' data is the best form of feedback for any library. Numerous ideas can be made from library patrons' data for libraries that are ready to explore the potentials of patron data.

There are possibilities for African Academic Libraries to generate data insights that identify the best patron of the library every month and invariably develop a celebratory structure for such a patron. This can also be done to determine the highest users of subject collections in the library. This will not only reposition the academic to be innovative but will also automatically increase the use of the library collection by patrons.

Indigenous Knowledge Data

One of the most significant challenges of Africa as a continent is that it does not tell its own stories unapologetically. Other people who know little or nothing about the continent say to her stories for her with all sorts of wrong data and information. If Africa can get her data and information, she can counter all forms of misinformation that have been evangelized globally about her. African culture and history were also mostly oral, and this has led to a considerable loss of vital data for her as a continent.

African libraries are pivotal to changing the narratives of misinformation about Africa on a global scale. Africa, as a continent, has not been able to counter a lot of stereotypical perspectives because there is a lack of data. Even though Africa has lost a lot of her history because of the foundational purely oral tradition, however, it should not wait till the remaining historical custodians fade off before it begins to collect these data.

It should be noted that there is data unique to Africa in terms of culture, arts, religion, food, governance and language, and Africa is gradually losing a lot of these data. Some words are slowly fading away in some parts of Africa while some unique traditions have also been thrown in the trash of forgettable history. To discourage the culture of selective memory that is taking over the historical data about Africa, African libraries must begin to rise to the occasion by collecting detailed indigenous data that posterity can appreciate.

The most disadvantaged people are the people who lack knowledge of their history. In place of this, the most significant gift African libraries can give to African society is the data (Structured and unstructured) about Africa across all spheres of life. The campaign against stereotypical perspectives about Africa is not the role of a few individuals but a joint responsibility of all the types of Libraries in Africa, but more importantly Public Libraries through a steady and deliberate Indigenous Data collection system. A considerable investment in information repackaging will be needed in achieving indigenous Data collection, but it is achievable with commitments from African Libraries. Information Repackaging will enable the raw data to be transformed, interpreted and presented in various formats to serve the needs of different patrons.

Government Data

It is essential to consider what the government means to an ordinary citizen in any country, especially in the African context. In Nigeria, for example, the system of government being run is a democracy which means "the government of the people, by the people, for the people". If this is true in the real sense of it, it then means that the people must be aware of every single thing going on in government. Transparency, which is the most significant hallmark of democracy, should be evident in the way the democratic government provides information and data to its citizens directly without any blockage. However, the ideal has not been the case in most African countries, where citizens feel too far from the government by default.

In this situation where the people are from the government in terms of information and data access, there is a need for a corporate curator or a government information aggregator that will facilitate the data access to the citizens. This is the role of African libraries, most notably, public libraries. African libraries must begin to engage directly with policymakers and government ministries through Open Government

Data Advocacy, especially in countries where there are no OpenGov Portals where citizens can get the government data they want.

The libraries in the people's immediate community are ideally supposed to reflect if not entirely, to a considerable extent, the government of the country through reliable data and information provision. African libraries will begin to gain even more relevance and people's trust when they can provide the type of data or information the citizens are interested in. In the highly techno-deterministic era, African libraries who have significant traffic on their online channels can also begin to aggregate OpenGov data of the country they serve. This will not only increase the accessibility of government data, but it will also increase the involvement of Libraries in National Governance through Government Data Provision.

Benefits of Data Visualization for African Libraries

1. Easy Information Comprehension

Libraries in Africa can begin to present data and information using graphical representations. This will, by implication, enable library patrons and researchers to see a large amount of data in a clear, cohesive way and draw all kinds of conclusions from that information. Academics especially do not need to do a lot of desktop analysis before they can drive insights from research data they get from the library. It is not impossible to have a whole document full of data, but tedious to understand. However, I can have a page of the paper on Data visualization with an entire book of interpretation in text because of the direct insights we are getting from the visualized data.

2. Pattern Relationship

There is always a relationship pattern when a dataset is adequately visualized. We can generate patterns of relationships between or among two or more variables, factors or subjects in sophisticated data curation. This patterned relationship helps patrons, especially researchers, to make quick inferences and generalization from academic resources. The best way to understand patterned relationships among many variables is to use visualization tools such as Scatter Plots of Venn Diagram. These tools will not only show the patterned links but will also show the degree or level of relationship between or among variables.

3. Trends Identification

It has often been said that before we can fully understand the future, we must have a good grip of the past. The best way to have a good grasp of the past is to use historical data to understand trends. Data visualization will help African libraries to see the history and to predict the future both in their institutional operations and information provision to patrons. There can be no predictive without a retrospective. Any prediction made without a proper understanding of the past in retrospect might be a dangerous prediction. African Libraries, as custodians of knowledge, are well-positioned to become innovative in their data presentation to patrons using data visualization tools that show trends.

CONCLUSION

Data will remain the currency of the information age for a long time to come. African libraries must begin to appreciate this precious resource and also to find innovative ways to collect, curate and present it to library patrons. African Libraries will be more positioned to create a more significant impact with the full embrace of data visualization and data granularity tools in presenting research data to their patrons yet.

AREAS OF FURTHER RESEARCH

Even though this chapter has explored the types of data visualization tools and the kinds of African data Librarians should be collecting, there remains a knowledge gap on the process of breaking data down to the most granular and straightforward forms by libraries. Further research can be done in this area to expose African librarians to the various techniques of breaking data down granular and understandable bits for research and decision making.

REFERENCES

Bhageshpur, K. (2019). Data is the new oil -- And that's a good thing. *Forbes*. https://www.forbes.com/sites/forbestechcouncil/2019/11/15/data-is-the-new-oil-and-thats-a-good-thing/#916053d73045

Data is the new oil. (2006, November 3). *ANA Marketing Maestros*. https://ana.blogs.com/maestros/2006/11/data_is_the_new.html

Hiippala, T. (2020). A multimodal perspective on data visualization. *Data Visualization in Society*, 277–294. doi:10.2307/j.ctvzgb8c7.23

Loi and Dehaye. (2017). *If data is the new oil, when is the extraction of value from data unjust? (2017, January 1)*. ResearchGate. https://www.researchgate.net/publication/326200389_If_Data_Is_The_New_Oil_When_Is_The_Extraction_of_Value_From_Data_Unjust/citations

Marastats. (n.d.). *Marathon and Half Marathon Statistics*. https://marastats.com/

Panoho, K. (2019). Council post: The age of analytics and the importance of data quality. *Forbes*. https://www.forbes.com/sites/forbesagencycouncil/2019/10/01/the-age-of-analytics-and-the-importance-of-data-quality/#1d759a435c3c

Rettberg, J. W. (2020). Ways of knowing with data visualizations. *Data Visualization in Society*, 35–48. doi:10.2307/j.ctvzgb8c7.8

The world's most valuable resource is no longer oil, but data. (2017, May 6). *The Economist*. https://www.economist.com/leaders/2017/05/06/the-worlds-most-valuable-resource-is-no-longer-oil-but-data

What is granular data? - Definition from Techopedia. (n.d.). *Techopedia.com*. https://www.techopedia.com/definition/31722/granular-data

KEY TERMS AND DEFINITIONS

Data Granularity: Data granularity is the level of detail considered in a model or decision-making process or represented in an analysis report. The higher the granularity, the deeper the level of detail.

Data Visualization: Data visualization is the graphic representation of data. It involves producing images that communicate relationships among the represented data to viewers of the pictures. This communication is achieved through the use of a systematic mapping between graphic marks and data values in the creation of the visualization.

Data Visualization Skills: The ability to present data in a graphical or pictorial format in an attempt to help people understand its significance is known as data visualization skills. Data visualization skills simply refer to the ability to identify or uncover patterns, correlations, and trends.

Data Visualization Tools: Data visualization tools provide an accessible way to see and understand trends, outliers, and patterns in data.

Chapter 11
Real-Time Recommendation Engine for Readers

Sangeeta Namdev Dhamdhere
https://orcid.org/0000-0002-0037-5617
Modern College of Arts, Science, and Commerce, Pune, India

Deepak Mane
Tata Consultancy Services, India

ABSTRACT

In today's world, every reader or social media user has different choices/hobbies in terms of reading. For example, if any social media user is searching for a book to read without any specific idea of what s/he wants, s/he wastes a lot of time browsing around on the internet and crawling/trawling through various sites hoping that s/he might get good book. To avoid confusion, the authors are building a recommendation system for every reader/user that helps to recommend a book based on his choices, hobbies, or what s/he had read previously that will be massive help for users instead wasting time on various sites. Data from social media is the powerful fuel that can be used to helps in decision making and building a recommendation engine. Social media data in the different format is biggest challenge for the business to ingest data at the reasonable speed and further process. In social media data, it is difficult to detect and capture data. Real-time recommendation engine for users, which includes data ingestion methods, challenges, metadata problem, analysis, and consumption, is discussed here.

DOI: 10.4018/978-1-7998-3049-8.ch011

BACKGROUND

In today's world, every reader or social media user has different choices/hobbies in terms of reading. For example, if any social media user is searching for a book to read without any specific idea of what s/he want, s/he waste a lot of time browsing around on the internet and crawling/trawling through various sites hoping that s/he might get good book. To avoid confusion, we are building a recommendation system for every reader user that helps to recommends book based on his choices, hobbies or what s/he had read previously that will be massive help for users instead wasting time on various sites. Data from social media is the powerful fuel that can be used to helps in decision making and building a Recommendation engine, Data of social media in the different format, it's the biggest challenge for the business to ingest data at the reasonable speed and further process, in social media data it is difficult to Detection and capture of changed data. Once data is available, it is difficult to prepare data for analysis, transform (cleansing and normalizing the data) and convert data into structured format. In this Chapter, we are describing a case study about Real Time Recommendation Engine for users which includes data ingestion methods, challenges, metadata problem, analysis and consumption.

What is Recommendation Engine

Recommendation Engine is a black box which analysis some set of users and recommends the items which a user may like. The analysis uses the user details like Gender, Age, Geographical Location, Online searches, book information, previous hobbies/books readers are interested (Techtarget, n.d.)

Before we learn deeper aspects of recommendation engines. Let's first understand about the real life and online recommendation engines.

Recommendation engine is a field that involves the, collection, analysis, and presentation of social media data and efficient decision making and recommendation of books of readers The goals of a recommendation engine include:

- Properly recommendation of books to readers based on their interest and offers
- Collecting the data from social media in a sound manner for analytics
- Producing analysis that accurately describe user requirements, interest

Benefits of Recommendation Engine

Following benefits are provided by implementing Recommendation Engine

Figure 1. Benefits of a Recommendation Engine

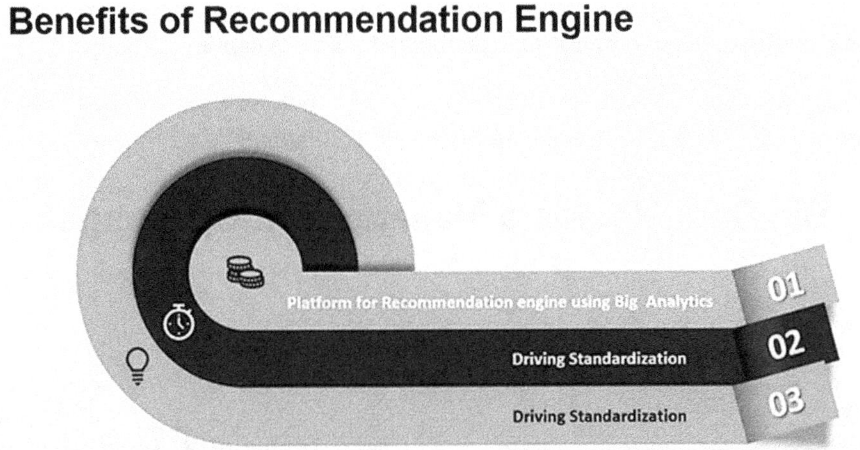

1. **Platform for Recommendation engine using Big Analytics: Once** Data (Volatile and static) has been captured, stored and properly preserved in a secure manner, analysis of it can begin. Domain expert/Data Scientist/Business analyst use data mining and analytics tools to extract information from a large set of Library unstructured data from social media, which is then transformed into an understandable structured data for further use Recommendation Engine is providing capability to provide quick recommendation based on search and analyse a mountain of data quickly and efficiently. They can search keywords related to library science such as book name, journals, interest etc. in a big data clusters in different languages which is beneficial
2. **Driving Standardization: In** one sense, creating recommendation engine standards in big data is merely a temporary first step on a much longer journey then Analytics for building recommendation engine will give a huge impetus for the standardization of recommendation process in big data domain and library data management. infrastructure. That key shift will inevitably catalyse IT modernization and improve internal IT services maturity, quick way of resolution recommendation issues, effective decision making etc. Also helps in Application security portfolio rationalization
3. **Geographic Transparency and Traceability:**Big Data (Library's Data such as book name) and reader's data (such as name, location, is frequently sensitive and its location is therefore important, since data entering or exiting national borders can contravene national and international regulations, such as the EU Data Protection Directive .To address this, big data defines process which is transparent about the geographic location where data and services are stored, and allows clients to keep data on their own servers, using a VPN connection

Big Data Governance Management Challenges

Some of Big data governance management challenges capture as below

Figure 2. Big Data Governance Management Challenges

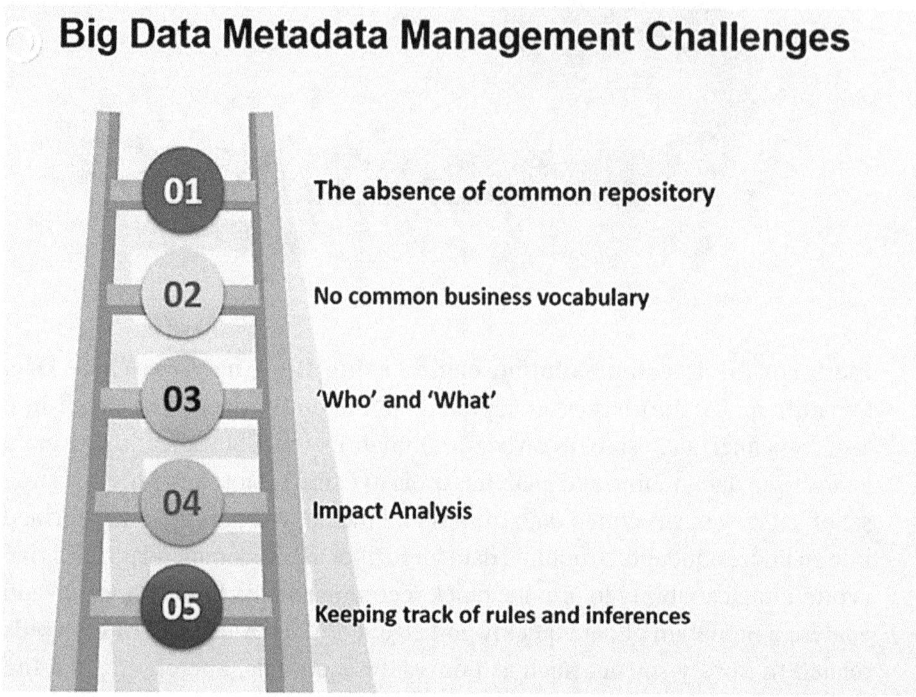

1. **Need for Synchronization Between Disparate Data Sources (Data Integration, n.d.):** As data about books, journals, comments from social media are becoming diverse and bigger, there is a big challenge to incorporate them into a single analytical platform for building a unique data model for analysis. If this data mode is overlooked, it will create gaps and lead to wrong analytics and insights, non-effective decision making and building recommendation engine
2. **Shortage of Library Professionals Who Understand domain and Library data analysis (Data Integration, n.d.):** The analysis of data is important to make this voluminous amount of data being produced in every minute, useful. With the exponential rise of data, a huge demand for library domain analytics, big data scientists and Big Data analysts has been created in the market. It is important for business organizations/universities to hire a data scientist,

domain experts having skills that are varied as the job of a data scientist is multidisciplinary. Another major challenge faced by universities is the shortage of professionals who understand domain of library science, big data. There is a sharp shortage of data scientists, domain experts in comparison to the massive amount of data being produced.

3. **Getting Meaningful Insights about library data Through the Use of Big Data Analytics:** It is imperative for universities to gain important insights from Big Data analytics, and also it is important that only the relevant department/ users has access to this information. A big challenge faced by the universities/ libraries in the Big Data analytics is mending this wide gap in an effective manner.
4. **Getting Voluminous Data into The Big Data Platform (New Gen Apps, n.d.):** It is hardly surprising that data is growing with every passing day. This simply indicates that business organizations need to handle a large amount of data on daily basis. The amount and variety of data available these days can overwhelm any data engineer and that is why it is considered vital to make data accessibility easy and convenient for brand owners and managers.
5. **Uncertainty of Data Management Landscape:** With the rise of Big Data, new technologies and companies are being developed every day. However, a big challenge faced by the universities in the Big Data analytics is to find out which technology will be best suited to them without the introduction of new problems and potential risks.
6. **Data Storage and Quality:** data about libraries, books and journals are growing at a rapid pace. With the tremendous growth of the companies and large book publications, journals publications increase the amount of data produced. The storage of this massive amount of data is becoming a real challenge for everyone. Popular data storage options like data lakes/ warehouses are commonly used to gather and store large quantities of unstructured and structured data in its native format. The real problem arises when a data lakes/ warehouse try to combine unstructured and inconsistent data from diverse sources, it encounters errors. Missing data, inconsistent data, logic conflicts, and duplicates data all result in data quality challenges.
7. **Security and Privacy of Data (Dataconomy, n.d.):** Once library discover how to use Big Data, it brings them a wide range of possibilities and opportunities. However, it also involves the potential risks associated with big data when it comes to the privacy and the security of the data (Dataconomy, n.d.) The Big Data tools used for analysis and storage utilizes the data disparate sources. This eventually leads to a high risk of exposure of the data, making it vulnerable. Thus, the rise of voluminous amount of data increases privacy and security concerns.

Big Data Metadata Management Challenges

Here some challenges about metadata management captured as below

Figure 3. Big Data Metadata Management Challenges

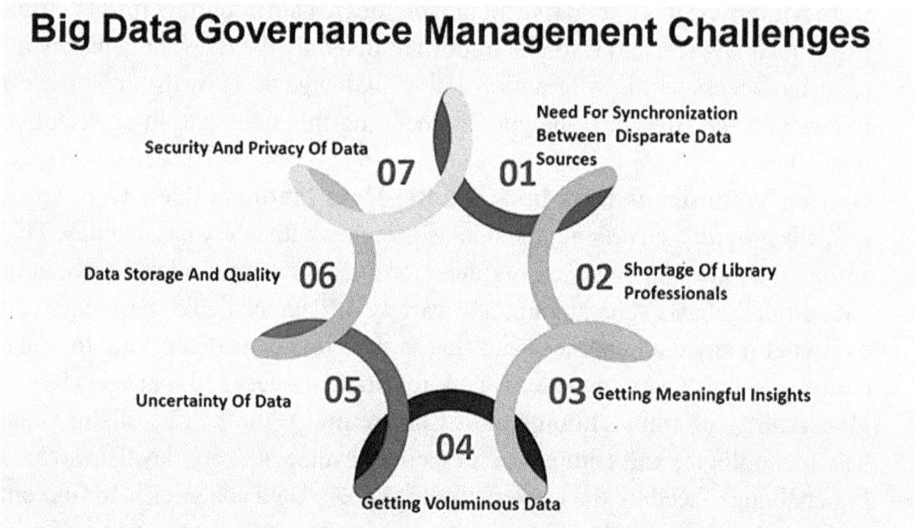

1 **The absence of common repository for library terms** – There is a dearth of single repository which captures the entire metadata of the library data includes books names, topics, classification, publication dates, author etc.
2 **No common business vocabulary** – It becomes difficult for common users, Domain analyst and IT to maintain consistency of information about user's information, books information across different channels.
3 **'Who' and 'What'** – Answering who is doing what on the environment, and keeping a track from accountability perspective is the need of library management activities.
4 **Impact Analysis** – It requires a lot of effort for the IT team to see the impact of a proposed change and understand cross-table dependencies.
5 **Keeping track of rules and inferences** – It becomes difficult for businesses to keep a track of the rules and the inferences drawn by analysts.

Big Data Mashup/ Collection/Ingestion Challenges

Gathering data from multiple sources and in different forms for business use cases presents a variety of challenges in data ingestion. These challenges can include: multiple source ingestion, managing streaming/real-time data, speed of ingestion, and change detection.

Figure 4. Big Data Collection/Ingestion Challenges

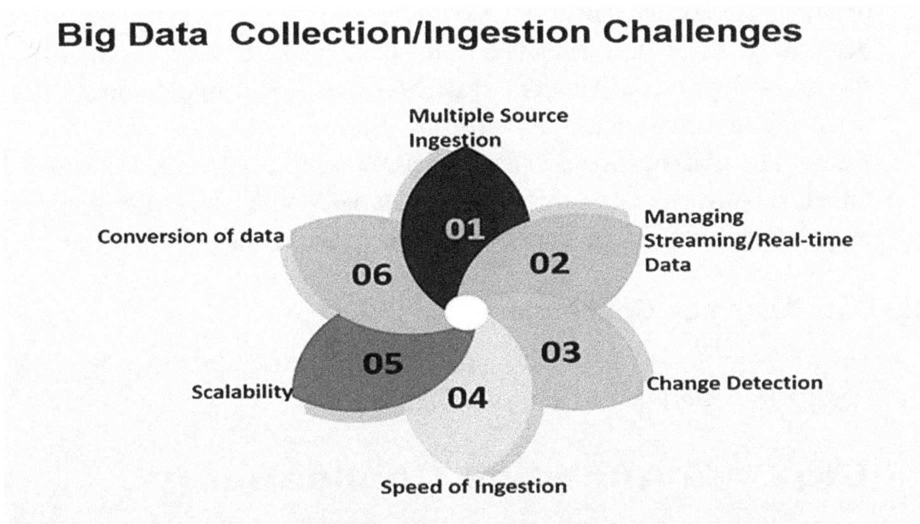

1 **Multiple Source Ingestion** (Intersys Consulting, n.d.) — This is a challenge when you have to manage and decide which data to include from social media because it can generate an enormous amount of data These datasets can include reader's data, books information, hobbies, interest, journal information etc. from various social media website such as Facebook, twitter, google plus etc.

2 **Managing Streaming/Real-time Data** – This type of ingestion challenging occurs when managing data coming from sources like different social media like (Facebook, Twitter). We need to develop Real Time Steam management (RTSM) which help to manage continuous data streams. Since most RTSM are data-driven, a continuous query produces new results as long as new data arrive at the system.

3 **Change Detection** – The detection and capture of change data is a big problem in data ingestion (Xenon Stack, n.d.). This problem has been extensively studied

for scalar or multivariate data streams and has been largely left unattended in the Big Data scenario.

4 **Speed of Ingestion** – Since data from different social media deliver at varying frequencies. For example, information about very popular books, Journals information's which occur at a low frequency. However, information, comments such as tweets of can be seen as small volumes of data that occur at a high frequency (Mariadb, n.d.) and require more rapid ingestion. We need build an ingestion platform to ingest, process big data, including advanced SQL (sometimes called NoSQL) databases that adapt SQL to handle larger volumes of structured data with greater speed

5 **Scalability**- Since data generated from social media is large, it pays off to choose a storage that will built for scale, horizontally including automatic data balancing across clusters/nodes

6 **Conversion of data** - Since all data generated from social media is instructed format, it is difficult task convert into structured format(tables) after applying proper data cleaning, data quality, metadata management

Big Data Analytics Challenges

Figure 5. Big Data Governance Analytics Challenges

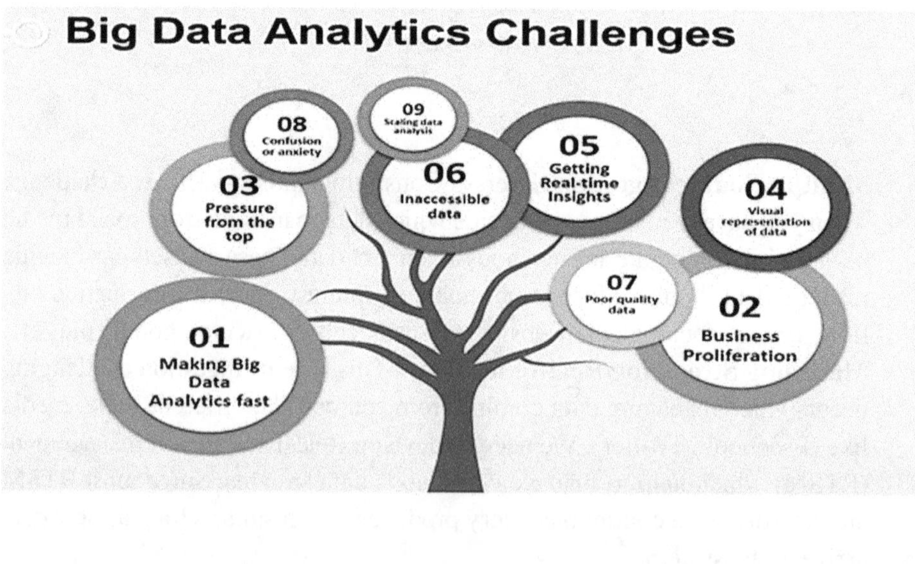

1 **Making Big Data Analytics fast (Knowledge Hut, n.d.):** Relevant data needs to be identified quickly to be of value. This requires high processing speeds

that can be achieved by installing hardware that can process large amounts of data extremely quickly.

2 **Business Proliferation:** Big Data is currently used by universities for research, students project all of which lead to university proliferation and give universities a competitive advantage. By analysing social media platforms, they can gauge reader response and roll out in-demand books

3 **Getting Real-time Insights:** A great deal of complexity is added when we move from analysing stagnant data from different social media to handling real-time inputs. This requires a new range of data analysis tools that can handle data of high veracity and velocity. These tools include ETL engines, visualization, computation, frameworks, and libraries. Universities/library often loses on important relevant information because of failure to keep pace with the rapidly originating data

4 **Visual representation of data** (Mariadb, n.d.): To be understood and impactful, library data often needs to be visually presented in graphs or charts. While these tools are incredibly useful, it's difficult to build them manually. Taking the time to pull information from multiple areas and put it into a reporting tool is frustrating and time-consuming. Strong data systems enable report building at the click of a button. Employees and decision-makers will have access to the real-time information they need in an appealing and educational format.

5 **Inaccessible data:** Moving data into one centralized system has little impact if it is not easily accessible to the people that need it. Decision-makers and risk managers need access to all of an organization's data for insights on what is happening at any given moment, even if they are working off-site. Accessing information should be the easiest part of data analytics.

6 **Poor quality data:** Nothing is more harmful to data analytics than inaccurate data. Without good input, output will be unreliable. A key cause of inaccurate data is manual errors made during data entry. This can lead to significant negative consequences (Xenon Stack, n.d.) if the analysis is used to influence decisions. Another issue is asymmetrical data: when information in one system does not reflect the changes made in another system, leaving it outdated

7 **Pressure from the top:** As risk management becomes more popular in universities, Directors and program sponsors demand more results from risk managers. They expect higher returns and a large number of reports on all kinds of data. With a comprehensive analysis system, risk managers can go above and beyond expectations and easily deliver any desired analysis. They'll also have more time to act on insights and further the value of the department to the organization.

8 **Confusion or anxiety:** Library Users/analytics/data scientists may feel confused or anxious about switching from traditional data analysis methods, even if they

understand the benefits of automation. Nobody likes change, especially when they are comfortable and familiar with the way things are done

9 **Budget:** Another challenge risk manager regularly face is budget. Risk is often a small department, so it can be difficult to get approval for significant purchases such as an analytics system. Risk managers can secure budget for data analytics by measuring the return on investment of a system

10 **Scaling data analysis:** Finally, analytics can be hard to scale as a universities and the amount of data it collects grows. Collecting information and creating reports becomes increasingly complex. A system that can grow with the university is crucial to manage this issue (Xenon Stack, n.d.). While overcoming these challenges may take some time, the benefits of data analysis are well worth the effort. Improve your organization today and consider investing in a data analytics system.

Key Consideration for Building Recommendation Engine

1 Data Quality and Integrity across multiple data sources impacting the richness of reader's view

2 Scalable and efficient data aggregation ecosystem essential to correct value out of readers' data

3 Data governance and Monitoring as a key to compliance

4 Tight Coupling between reader's interest/hobbies and Recommendation engine essential to unlock actionable real-time reader's insights

5 Evolve Recommendation Engine model based on aggregated reader's date and machine-learning driven decision support system to deliver the right reader's customer recommendation

Data Characteristics

Since we are collecting all data from social media, all data are unstructured format containing more than 250+ fields, using big data technology stack, we need to convert unstructured data into structured format

Technology Stack Used to Build Recommendation Engine

Identified technologies gaps in existing DWH, based on gaps, TCS recommended technology stack classified into 4 categories

- Common in bundle across all vendors
- Open Source

- License individual products
- Available with selective vendor only

Figure 6. Big Data Recommended Technology Stack

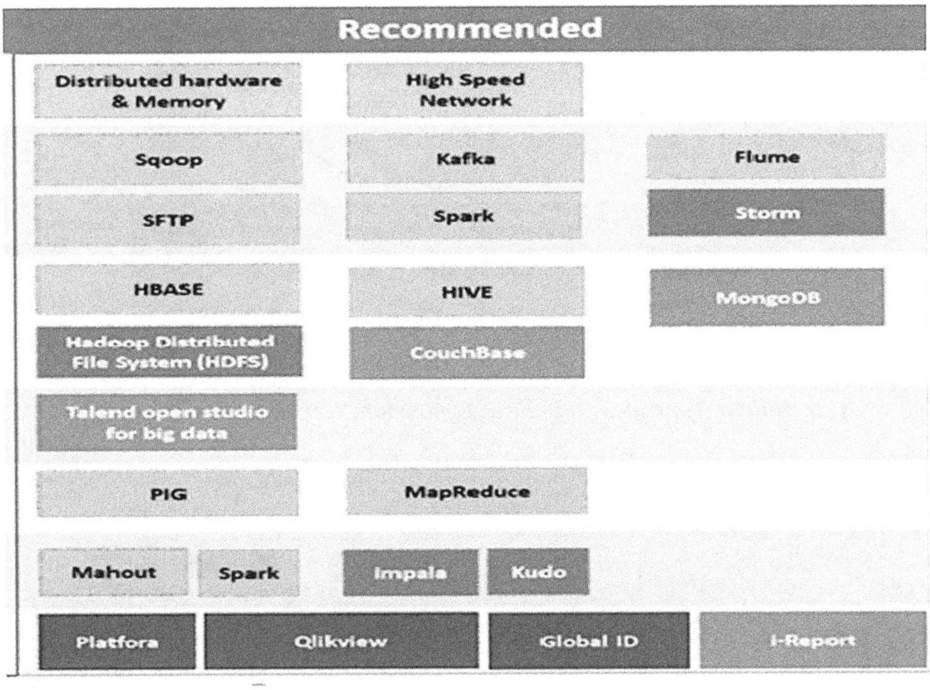

Logical Solution Approach for Build Recommendation Engine

provides an end to end view of integrating the data sources, storing and transforming the data in the Enterprise Data Lake which will be consumed by downstream systems

Technology Solution Approach for Build Recommendation Engine

provides a mapping of tools, technologies and framework towards to data ingestion, transformation, store and presentation of components of logical architecture

Figure 7. Logical Solution Approach to build recommendation engine

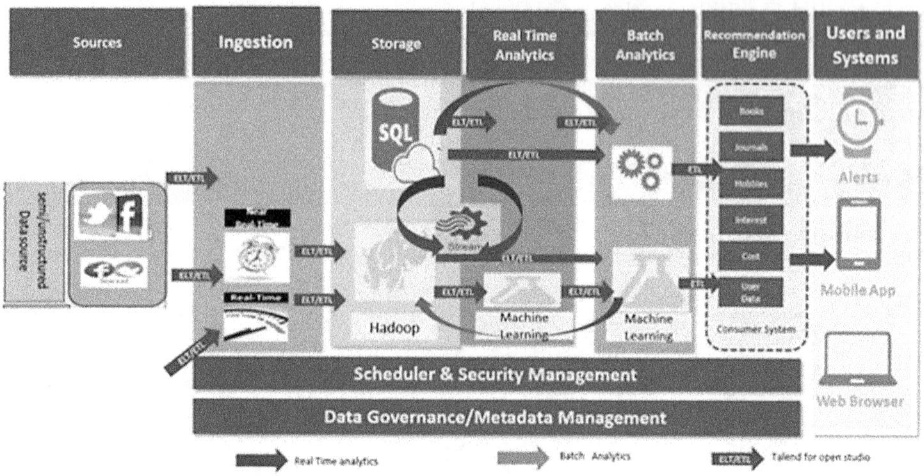

Figure 8. Technical Approach to build recommendation engine

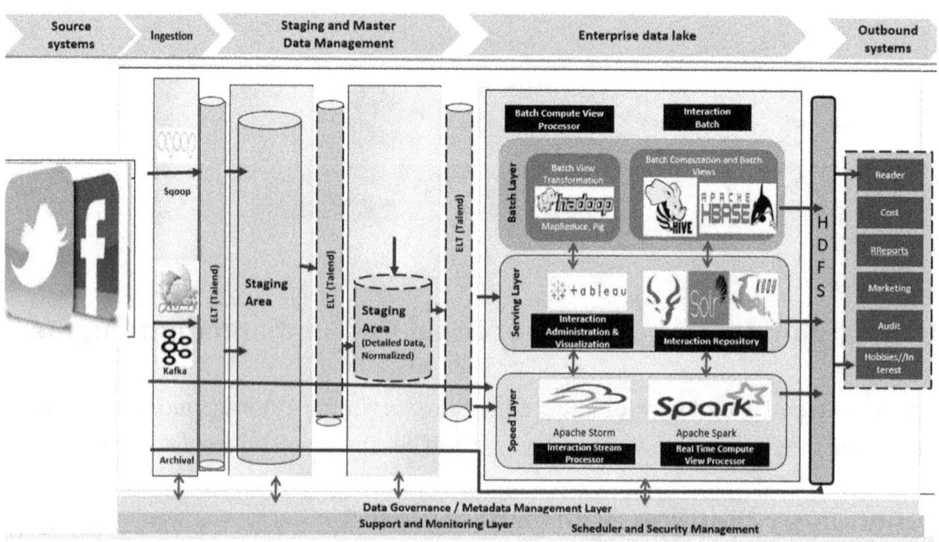

CONCLUSION

In this chapter authors have discussed a case study of real time recommendation engine used for offering new library services. All basic to technical details have given with the help of properly explained figures like what recommendation engine is? What are big data governance management, big data collection, ingestion and analytics challenges along with all possible key considerations for building recommendation engine with the technological, legal solutions. This chapter will help all Library professionals, software professions and application developers to develop real time recommendation platform for effective services to the library patrons in future in low price.

REFERENCES

Big Data Analytics. (n.d.). http://big-data-analytics-challenges-faced-business-enterprises-7-top

Data Integration. (n.d.). https://www.dataintegration.info/data-synchronization

Dataconomy. (n.d.). https://dataconomy.com/2017/07/10-challenges-big-data-security-privacy

Intersys Consulting. (n.d.). https://www.intersysconsulting.com/services/data/data-ingestion

Knowledge Hut. (n.d.). https://www.knowledgehut.com/blog/big-data/big-data-analytics-challenges-and-opportunities

Mane, D., & Shibe, K. (2018). Big Data Forensic analytics. *ICDMAI 2018*. https://www.springer.com/gp/book/9789811312731

Mariadb. (n.d.). https://mariadb.com/kb/en/library/data-warehousing-high-speed-ingestion

New Gen Apps. (n.d.). https://www.newgenapps.com/blog/top-big-data-challenges-solutions-problems

Oxfrod Royale. (n.d.). https://www.oxford-royale.co.uk/articles/business-english-vocabulary.html

Techtarget. (n.d.). https://whatis.techtarget.com/definition/recommendation-engine

Xenon Stack. (n.d.). https://www.xenonstack.com/blog/ingestion-processing-big-data-iot-stream

Chapter 12
Landscape of Big Data Research in India:
A Scientometric View

Ravindra Sopan Bankar
https://orcid.org/0000-0002-3488-3695
Department of Library and Information Science, Shivaji University, Kolhapur, India

Shalini Ramdas Lihitkar
Department of Library and Information Science, Rashtrasant Tukadoji Maharaj Nagpur University, India

ABSTRACT

We all know that data has become a new fuel to the fast paced technology-driven world. And the academicians and researchers are doing their best for getting better into moulding the data-driven society to keeping it updated every day. Indian academicians and researchers are also doing their best in field of big data research studies. This chapter will focus the research landscape of big data research in India. This scientometric evaluation will let us know how India is going forward in this research area with some specific statistics in scientific community.

INTRODUCTION

The term has been in use since the 1990s, with some giving credit to John Mashey for popularizing the term. Big data usually includes data sets with sizes beyond the ability of commonly used software tools to capture, curate, manage, and process data

DOI: 10.4018/978-1-7998-3049-8.ch012

within a tolerable elapsed time (Mashey, 1997)8. Big data philosophy encompasses unstructured, semi-structured and structured data, however the main focus is on unstructured data.(Lohr, 2013)6. Big data is a field that treats ways to analyse, systematically extract information from, or otherwise deal with data sets that are too large or complex to be dealt with by traditional data-processing application software. Particularly Big Data techniques used in libraries and repositories are to handle and maintain the databases of members, collections and various services provided by them. The chapter will conclude the research trends in the field in Indian context.

DATA AND MATERIAL

In this chapter, researcher have selected most comprehensive and well known literature database, the WoSCC (Web of Science core collection) as the source of data. As researchers aims to find various bibliographical data for systematic analysis of "Big Data" research- Researchers set the conditions by restricting the search conditions as " TS=Big Data AND CU=India" (Here TS= Topic and CU= Country/Region) confining the timespan between 1989 to 2019. All the data taken was updated till date May 16, 2020. Indexes accessed was: SCI-EXPANDED, SSCI, A & HCI. Using mentioned search conditions, total 1231 records were obtained.

METHODOLOGY AND SOFTWARE USED

Researchers aim is to analyse Big Data research in terms of basic bibliometrics, most relevant research communities, key research topics, and discipline-level interactions. To complete these tasks, the following methods and Software were used: The downloaded data from WoSCC was in plain text format and in bunches of 500, 500 and 231 in each plain text file. These files were concatenated with the help of Bibexcel software (Olle Persson, n.d.). Then data was processed and the analysis of basic metrics was conducted with Histcite(Eugene Garfield, n.d.), a bibliometric analysis software The basic metrics include yearly publication output, Document Types, Most Prolific Authors, core journals, and countries. Researchers used R-Bibliometrix package (Aria & Cuccurullo, 2017) for some Metrix processes such as Most Globally Cited Documents, Most Locally Cited Documents and Lotka's Law for Author Productivity. For Visualizations and graphs researchers used VOSviewer (Van Eck & Waltman, 2013) and Microsoft Excel (Microsoft, 2018) software.

BACKGROUND

We are known about the fact that scientometric or bibliometric studies are applied for analysing the usability and impact of particular scientific communications/ publications. Researchers have been gone through various similar studies to know about different aspects that can be explored.

(Ruiz-Rosero et al., 2017) in their work Internet of Things: A Scientometric Review -done scientometric review of Internet of things. These review covers surveys was focussed to IoT vision, enabling technologies, applications, key features, co-word and cluster analysis, and future directions. Also, they used scientific databases to perform a quantitative analysis. This work develops a scientometric analysis of IoT research of bunched data set of 19,035 records published in timespan of (2002–2016) about 15 years in two renowned science databases (WoS and Scopus). The researchers developed a Python script called ScientoPy to perform this analysis. This research throws light into research trends by exploring a top author's, country collaborations, affiliations, most productive authors, top research applications, communication protocols, software processing, hardware, operating systems, and various hot topics in research.

(Bright Winsley & Muthukannan M., 2020) studies scientometric analyses in their work-Information Security: A Scientometric Study. Researchers collected data related to information security research from the Web of Science core collection and applied through Scientometrics for finding literature growth in years, high productive country, collaborating institutions, and authors, their funding agencies, top contributing journals, and the area of research (Keywords). This study reveals USA is the top contributing country while China is parallel stakeholder in this field. Chinese funding agencies fund most of the research. And English is the preferred language of communication.

(Sab, Parashappa & Biradar 2019) have published their work in scientometric studies-Marketing Research in India: A Scientometrics Study. Their work contributes towards trends and growth in marketing field. They have analysed several parameters like output, impact, collaborative patterns, research trend, affiliation, and collaborating countries. They claims study will be helpful in benchmarking of the field in the research field.

(Özen Çınar, 2020) does scientometric study in his work-Bibliometric analysis of breast cancer research in the period 2009–2018. They explored the various metrics in field such as research growth, top ranking authors in the field, various co-authorship patterns, and keywords analyses. The research shows how cancer research is growing up steadily and helping in the public health as a good cause.

BIBLIOMETRIC ANALYSIS, RESULTS AND DISCUSSION:

Yearly Publication Output

When we see the research in quantitative terms one can find the growth of the research field. The following Table No.1 shows the statistics of yearly output of big data

Table 1. Yearly Publication Output

Sr.No.	Publication Year	Records	Percentage	TGCS
1	1991	1	0.08	13
2	1993	1	0.08	3
3	1994	2	0.16	54
4	1995	5	0.41	47
5	1996	5	0.41	102
6	1997	7	0.57	237
7	1998	2	0.16	9
8	1999	4	0.32	82
9	2000	4	0.32	96
10	2001	7	0.57	143
11	2002	4	0.32	3208
12	2003	6	0.49	127
13	2004	8	0.65	4347
14	2005	10	0.81	892
15	2006	10	0.81	8000
16	2007	14	1.14	331
17	2008	12	0.97	5108
18	2009	19	1.54	735
19	2010	23	1.87	4855
20	2011	23	1.87	530
21	2012	26	2.11	523
22	2013	33	2.68	385
23	2014	31	2.52	12714
24	2015	80	6.50	1175
25	2016	99	8.04	6681
26	2017	148	12.02	2100
27	2018	265	21.53	2817
28	2019	382	31.03	1062
	Total	**1231**	**100**	

research in India during the time span of 29 years. The research shows continuous and steady growth in the field (in terms of research productivity). From the year 2017 it has increased more in output. The highest yield is in year 2019.

Figure 1. Yearly growth trend

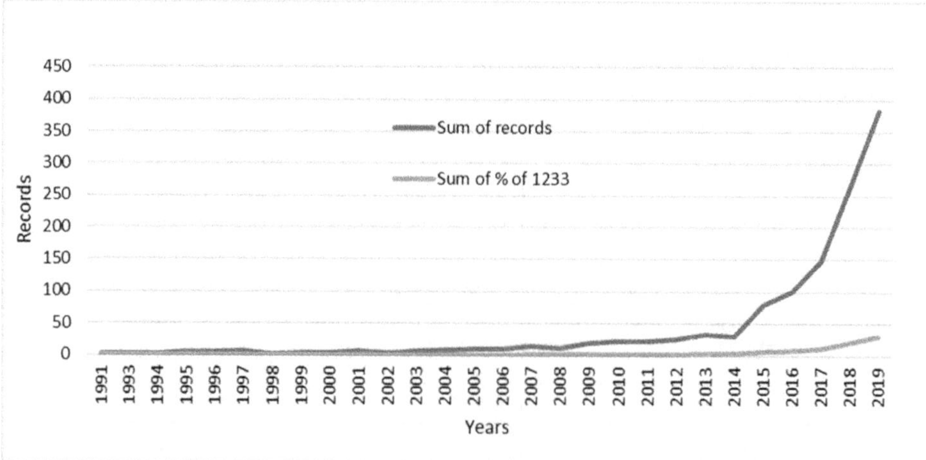

Table 2. Documents Types of Publications

Sr. No.	Document Type	TNP	Percent	TLC	TGC
1	Article	1041	82.6	281	28937
2	Review	104	8.1	63	27029
3	Editorial Material	37	3	7	119
4	Proceedings Paper	15	1.2	0	245
5	Meeting Abstract	20	1.6	11	32
6	Book Chapter	6	0.4	0	1
7	Book Review	4	0.3	0	1
8	Letter	4	0.3	0	7
	Total	**1231**			

TNP: Total number of Publications, TLC: Total Local Citations, TGC: Total Global Citations.

The graph illustrates the yearly increasing growth in research output. We can see higher and steadily increasing trend line after year 2017.

Document Types of Publications

The following Table No. 2 reveals various document types published in the research field of big data in India. It's seen that Article is highest published type (1017 nos.), then review (100 nos.) comes after articles and 3rd type is Editorial material type (37 nos.).

Figure 2. Graph of Types of Documents

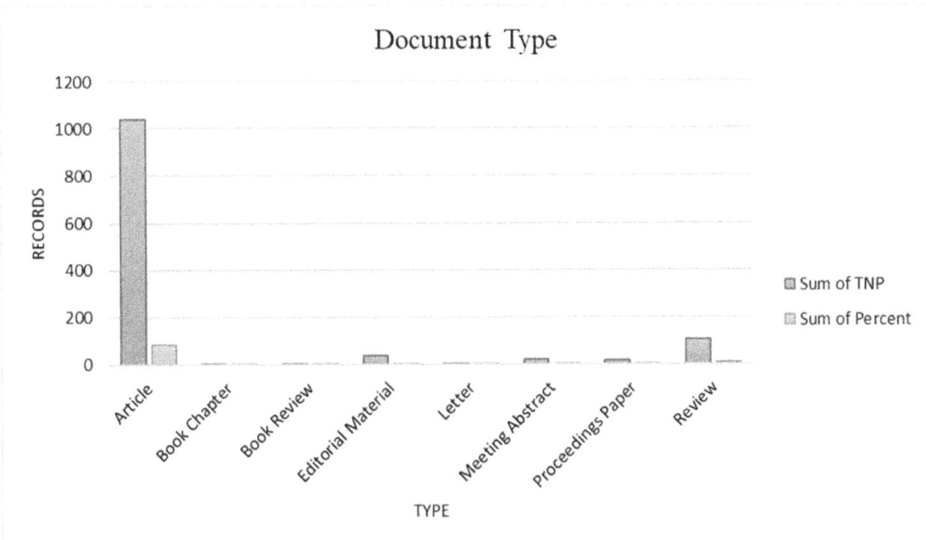

The graph illustrates the various types and their percentage in publications of big data research.

Author Productivity

In this section, Researcher collected data of top productive authors in the research field. The following table shows authors with high productivity. Kumar N is highest productive author with 29 records, Kumar S is at 2nd with 21 records Gupta S and Sanghaiah AK are at 3rd in list with 16 record in their account. Various indexes are also shown in the table accordingly from analyses (please refer appendix). Authors CPP (Citation Per Paper) and RCI(Relative Citation Impact) also counted for measuring the prolific authors impact. Kumar N was topped at the list with 14.17 CPP and 1.95 RCI. And Gupta is at 2nd place with 9.25 CPP and 1.27 RCI.

Table 3. Most Productive Authors

Sr. No.	Author	TNP	Percent(Records)	TNC	CPP	RCI
1	Kumar N	29	2.4	411	14.17	1.95
2	Kumar S	21	1.7	120	5.71	0.78
3	Gupta S	16	1.3	148	9.25	1.27
4	Sangaiah AK	16	1.3	132	8.25	1.13
5	Kumar A	15	1.2	120	8.00	1.10
6	Baldini C	14	1.1	57	4.07	0.56
7	Brito-Zeron P	14	1.1	57	4.07	0.56
8	Hernandez-Molina G	14	1.1	57	4.07	0.56
9	Mariette X	14	1.1	57	4.07	0.56
10	Praprotnik S	14	1.1	57	4.07	0.56

TNP: Total number of Publications, TNC: Total number of Citations, CPP: Citations Per Paper, RCI: Relative Citation Impact.

CPP is average number of citations per paper, CPP= Total Number of Citations (TNC)/Total number of Papers (TNP). It has been widely used in Bibliometric assessments as it normalizes large disparities in volumes of productivity among various prolific authors, organizations/Institutions and countries. And RCI (Relative Citation Impact) RCI measures both the influence and visibility of an author's research in the global context. It was developed by the Institute of Scientific Information (now Thomson Reuters, USA) and has been used by Dwivedi et al.[4] to examine the impact of the research output from India in organic chemistry.

$$RCI = \frac{Authors'\,share\,of\,citations\,(C\%)}{Authors'\,share\,of\,publications\,(P\%)}$$

(RCI = 1 indicates that a Authors 'citation rate is equal to the world's citation rate; RCI > 1 indicates that a Authors' citation rate is higher than the world's citation rate and RCI < 1 indicates that a Authors' citation rate is less than the world's citation rate.)

Authors Impact

The following Table No. 4. Shows the authors impact in the field of Big Data in India. The top authors' are- Kumar N with total count of 411 citations, author started publications in year 2012. Kumar S at 2nd in list with total count of 114 citations and started their publications in year 2008 and Baldini comes next with 57 numbers of citation and started their publication during 2016.

Table 4. Authors with high impact

Sr. No.	Author	h_index	g_index	m_index	Citation Count	PY start
1	Kumar N	12	19	1.333	411	2012
2	Kumar S	6	9	0.462	114	2008
3	Baldini C	2	7	0.4	57	2016
4	Gupta S	7	12	0.7	148	2011
5	Praprotnik S	2	7	0.4	57	2016
6	Retamozo S	2	7	0.4	57	2016
7	Sangaiah AK	6	11	2	132	2018
8	Gottenberg JE	2	7	0.4	57	2016
9	Kumar A	6	10	0.667	120	2012
10	Mariette X	2	7	0.4	57	2016

PY: Publication Year

Highly Cited Indian Publications

The following Table No. 5 reveals the statistics of the top-cited documents. Analyses shows the research documents have minimal citation count as compared to global citation count. In this rankings top local cited document is-The impact of big data on world-class sustainable manufacturing and it is authored by Dubey R with total count of 17 local & 108 global citations. The 2nd ranked document is <i>Planck</i> 2013 results. XVI. Cosmological parameters and its authored by Ade Par with 15 local and 6326 global citations. Subsequently, 3rd publication is - Dynamics of Dark Energy and its authored by Copeland EJ with total count of 14 local and 3478 global citations.

Table 5. Highly Cited Publications

Sr. No.	Record	DOI	Year	Total Local Citations	Total Global Citations
1	Dubey R, 2016, The impact of big data on world-class sustainable manufacturing	10.1007/s00170-015-7674-1	2016	17	108
2	Ade Par, 2014, <i>Planck</i> 2013 results. XVI. Cosmological parameters	10.1051/0004-6361/201321591	2014	15	6326
3	Copeland EJ, 2006, Dynamics of Dark Energy	10.1142/S021827180600942X	2006	14	3478
4	Gunasekaran A, 2017, Big data and predictive analytics for supply chain and organizational performance	10.1016/j.jbusres.2016.08.004	2017	12	149
5	Lopez D, 2016, Climate change and disease dynamics - A big data perspective	10.1016/j.ijid.2016.02.084	2016	11	30
6	Wamba SF, 2017, Big data analytics and firm performance: Effects of dynamic capabilities	10.1016/j.jbusres.2016.08.009	2017	11	212
7	Akter S, 2016, How to improve firm performance using big data analytics capability and business strategy alignment?	10.1016/j.ijpe.2016.08.018	2016	9	133
8	Gupta S, 2018, Big data with cognitive computing: A review for the future	10.1016/j.ijinfomgt.2018.06.005	2018	9	33
9	Manogaran G, 2018, A Gaussian process based big data processing framework in cluster computing environment	10.1007/s10586-017-0982-5	2018	9	34
10	Ade Par, 2016, <i>Planck</i> 2015 results: XIII. Cosmological parameters	10.1051/0004-6361/201525830	2016	8	4702

DOI: Digital Object Identifier, TLC: Total Local Citations, TGC: Total Global Citations

High Impact Journals

The following Table No. 6 shows the metrics of high impact journals in the big data research field. The top journal in the list is Cluster Computing-The Journal of Networks Software Tools and Applications with 36 Net Points according to various index metrics, 2nd in top list is Future Generation Computer Systems-The International Journal of E-science with 27 points, and IEEE Access holds 3rd rank in the list with 21 Net Points. Netherlands based Journal- Future Generation Computer Systems-The International Journal of E-science have highest impact factor (5.768) and England's- Journal of Network and Computer Applications (5.273) is at 2nd Position. USA and Netherlands have most high-impact journals in field of Big Data.

Table 6. High Impact Journal

Sr.No.	Source/Journal Name	Publishing Country	h_index	g_index	m_index	TNC	JIF
1	Cluster Computing- The Journal Of Networks Software Tools And Applications	USA	6	12	1	158	1.851
2	Future Generation Computer Systems- The International Journal Of E-science	Netherlands	13	23	2.6	533	5.768
3	IEEE Access	USA	7	21	1.4	477	4.098
4	Multimedia Tools And Applications	Netherlands	6	11		125	2.101
5	Wireless Personal Communications	Netherlands	4	8	0.8	77	0.929
6	Computers & Electrical Engineering	England	6	9	1.2	98	2.189
7	Physical Review D	USA	9	15	0.38	3457	4.368
8	Journal Of Medical Systems	USA	5	9	1.25	88	2.415
9	Journal Of Supercomputing	USA	3	6	-	42	2.157
10	Journal Of Network And Computer Applications	England	5	11	1	131	5.273

TNC: Total number of Citations, JIF: Journal Impact Factor.

Top Productive Institutions

The following Table No. 7 depicts us about the Top productive institutes in big data research field in India. Indian Institute of Technology, Bombay is top in research of big data field 72 records shares 5.8% productivity of all the records. Subsequent is VIT University with 47 record and shares 3.8% productivity of all record. And 3rd is Thapar University with 31 records and 2.5% share of all the records.

Table 7. Top Productive Institutions

Sr. No.	Institution	TNP	Percent	TLC	TGC
1	Indian Institute Technology, Bombay	72	5.8	22	1933
2	VIT University	47	3.8	45	636
3	Thapar University	31	2.5	26	431
4	Anna University	28	2.3	1	78
5	Indian Institute Technology, Delhi	26	2.1	39	444
6	Indian Statistical Institute	25	2	0	240
7	Natl Institute Technology	25	2	4	153
8	University of Melbourne	22	1.8	20	17988
9	Indian Institute Science	21	1.7	1	246
10	Tata Institute Fundamental Research	20	1.6	10	20783

TNC: Total number of Publications, TLC: Total Local Citations, TGC: Total Global Citations

Table 8. Highly Cited Countries

Sr.No.	Country	TNC	CPP
1	United Kingdom	15560	486.25
2	USA	11796	153.19
3	India	9036	10.01
4	Japan	7832	979
5	Italy	4724	1181
6	Russia	4021	4021
7	France	1108	69.25
8	China	326	11.24
9	Canada	222	20.18
10	Egypt	186	37.2

TNC: Total number of Citations, CPP: Citations per Paper

Table 9. Language of Published records

Sr. No.	Language	TNP	Percent	TLC	TGC
1	English	1230	99.9	362	56376
2	French	1	0.1	0	0

TLC: Total Local Citations, TGC: Total Global Citations

Table 10. Author Productivity through Lotka's Law

Sr. No	Documents written	Number of Authors	Proportion of Authors
1	One	4704	0.742
2	Two	850	0.134
3	Three	306	0.048
4	Four	247	0.039
5	Five	49	0.008
6	six	80	0.013
7	Seven	29	0.005
8	Eight	8	0.001
9	Nine	15	0.002
10	Ten	5	0.001
11	More than 10	55	0.008

Highly Cited Countries

Researchers explored the highly cited countries of documents published under big data research. The following Table No.8 reveals that United Kingdom is top cited country with total 15560 citations. Subsequently, USA and India are with 11796 and 9036 total citations respectively.

Language of Published Records

Language plays vital role in the scientific communication. Researchers explored the languages that all the big data researches have been published in India. Total 1230 records are in English and only one research is in French language.

Author Productivity through Lotka's Law

The Lotka's law is considered here in analyses to prove the author productivity. The Law is, - As the number of articles published increases, authors producing that many publications become less frequent.(Lotka, 1926)[6]

The general formula says:

$X^nY=C$ *or* $Y=C/X^n$

{Where X is the number of publications, Y the relative frequency of authors with X publications, and n and C are constants depending on the specific field.}

Researchers tested Lotka's Law for the dataset and found proven, that table shows the mentions of the authors has been decreased as if the number of published records are increased.

Keywords Occurrences: The following VOSviewer visualization shows us about the trending keywords used in research. The most used keywords are: Big data, Cloud Computing, Model, Classification, Management, Big data analytics, Predictive Analytics, etc.

Figure 3. Keywords Occurrences

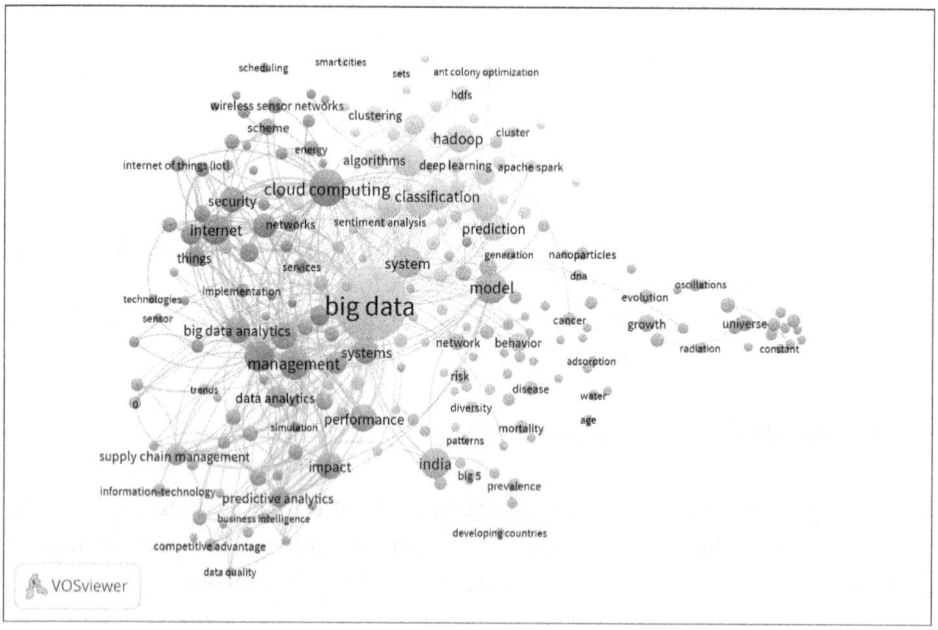

CONCLUSION

Based on above scientometric analysis of Big Data Research field we can conclude the following:

1. The annual growth rate is seen fluctuating still year slots of 2003-04, though the output seen grow steadily afterwards.

2. Indian authors shown good impact in research output most of the authors have RCI index more than 1 or near to 1. h-index and m-index were significant to authors performance.
3. Identification of highely cited indian publications show quality and usability of research in the field.
4. Most prolific publishing journals are from USA and Netherlands, all these journals have high impact factor. Netherlands based Journal- Future Generation Computer Systems-The International Journal of E-science topped in the list with highest impact factor (5.768).
5. Top Productive Institutions such as IITB, VIT University, Thapar University and Anna University have leading researches in the field of Big Data.
6. In the list of Highly Cited countries United Kingdom was top, USA was 2nd and India ranked 3rd in the list.
7. Mostly used language for research is English and only one research was published in French Language.
8. Testing of Lotka's Law shows that authors has been decreased as number of publication increases in the field. 4704 authors have only one output in their account.
9. Most used keywords in the Big Data Research field are: Big data, Cloud Computing, Model, Classification, Management, Big data analytics, Predictive Analytics, etc.

REFERENCES

Aria, M., & Cuccurullo, C. (2017). Bibliometrix: An R-tool for comprehensive science mapping analysis. *Journal of Informetrics*, *11*(4), 959–975. doi:10.1016/j.joi.2017.08.007

Garfield. (n.d.). *HistCite*. Clarivate Analytics. http://www.garfield.library.upenn.edu/

Garg, K. C., Kumar, S., & Lal, K. (2006). Scientometric profile of Indian agricultural research as seen through Science Citation Index Expanded. *Scientometrics*, *68*(1), 151–166. doi:10.100711192-006-0088-y

Gorjiara, T., & Baldock, C. (2014). Nanoscience and nanotechnology research publications: A comparison between Australia and the rest of the world. *Scientometrics*, *100*(1), 121–148. doi:10.100711192-014-1287-6

Lotka, A. J. (1926). The frequency distribution of scientific productivity. *Journal of the Washington Academy of Sciences*, *16*(12), 317–323.

Microsoft. (2018). *Microsoft Excel*. Microsoft Corporation. https://office.microsoft.com/excel

Olawumi, T. O., & Chan, D. W. (2018). A scientometric review of global research on sustainability and sustainable development. *Journal of Cleaner Production, 183*, 231–250. doi:10.1016/j.jclepro.2018.02.162

Özen Çınar, İ. (2020). Bibliometric analysis of breast cancer research in the period 2009–2018. *International Journal of Nursing Practice*. Advance online publication. doi:10.1111/ijn.12845

PerssonO. (2007). *Bibexcel*. https://homepage.univie.ac.at/juan.gorraiz/bibexcel/

R Core Team. (2018). *R: A Language and Environment for Statistical Computing*. R Foundation for Statistical Computing. https://www.R-project.org

Ruiz-Rosero, J., Ramirez-Gonzalez, G., Williams, J., Liu, H., Khanna, R., & Pisharody, G. (2017). Internet of Things: A Scientometric Review. *Symmetry, 9*(12), 301. doi:10.3390ym9120301

Sab, C. (2019). Marketing Research in India: A Scientometrics Study. *Webology, 16*(1), 172–186. doi:10.14704/WEB/V16I2/a197

Van Eck, N. J., & Waltman, L. (2013). *VOSviewer*. https://www.vosviewer.com/

Winsley & Muthukannan. (2020). *Information Security: A Scientometric Study*. IGI Global Publishers. https://www.igi-global.com/gateway/chapter/238176

Compilation of References

10Acker, F., & Saunders, S. (2017). Approaching big data: harnessing app information in social marketing. In *Formative Research in Social Marketing* (pp. 33–52). Springer. doi:10.1007/978-981-10-1829-9_3

Affelt, A. (2015). *The Accidental Data Scientist: Big Data Applications and Opportunities for librarians and information professionals*. Information Today.

Aharony, N. (2010). Twitter Use in Libraries: An Exploratory Analysis. *Journal of Web Librarianship*, *4*(4), 333–350. doi:10.1080/19322909.2010.487766

Al-Barashdi, H., & Al-Karousi, R. (2018). Big Data in academic libraries: Literature review and future research directions. *Journal of Information Studies and Technology*, *2*(13), 2–16.

Al-Daihani, S. M., & AlAwadhi, S. A. (2015). Exploring academic libraries' use of Twitter: A content analysis. *The Electronic Library*, *33*(6), 1002–1015. doi:10.1108/EL-05-2014-0084

Alotaibi, N. M., & Abdullah, M. A. (2016). Big data mining: a classification perspective. *Communication, Management and Information Technology, Proceedings of the International Conference on Communication, Management and Information Technology*, 687-696.

American Library Association (ALA). (1989). *ALA Presidential Committee on Information Literacy Final Report*. American Library Association ALA.

Aria, M., & Cuccurullo, C. (2017). Bibliometrix: An R-tool for comprehensive science mapping analysis. *Journal of Informetrics*, *11*(4), 959–975. doi:10.1016/j.joi.2017.08.007

Armstrong, J. S., & Overton, T. S. (1977). Estimating nonresponse bias in mail surveys. *JMR, Journal of Marketing Research*, *14*(3), 396–402. doi:10.1177/002224377701400320

Association of College and Research Libraries (ACRL). (2005). *Information Literacy Competency Standards for Higher Education*. Chicago: ACRL. Retrieved from http://www.ala.org/acrl/ilcomstan.html

Bakti, I. G. M. Y., & Sumaedi, S. (2013). An analysis of library customer loyalty: The role of service quality and customer satisfaction, a case study in Indonesia. *Library Management*, *34*(6/7), 397–414. doi:10.1108/LM-05-2012-0025

Balamurugan, T., & Thanuskodi, S. (2019). Use of social networking sites among the college students in Tamil Nadu, India. *Library Philosophy and Practice*, *2301*, 1–12.

Ball, F. (2019). Big data and their impact on libraries. *American Journal of Information Science and Technology*, *3*(1), 1–9. doi:10.11648/j.ajist.20190301.11

Bello-Orgaz, G., Jung, J.J., & Camacho, D. (2016). Social big data: recent achievements and new challenges. *Information fusion, 28*(March), 45-59.

Bello-Orgaz, G., Jung, J. J., & Camacho, D. (2016). Social big data: Recent achievements and new challenges. *Information Fusion*, *28*, 45–59. doi:10.1016/j.inffus.2015.08.005

Bhageshpur, K. (2019). Data is the new oil -- And that's a good thing. *Forbes*. https://www.forbes.com/sites/forbestechcouncil/2019/11/15/data-is-the-new-oil-and-thats-a-good-thing/#916053d73045

Big Data Commission. (2012). Demystifying Big Data: A practical guide to transforming the business of government, *Transportation Science*, *6*(1), 61–79. Available at: http://www.techamerica.org/Docs/techAmerica-BigDataReport-FINAL.pdf

Boland, M. V. (2016). Big Data, Big Challenges. *Ophthalmology*, *7–8*. doi:10.1016/j.ophtha.2015.08.041

Boyd, D., & Crawford, K. (2012). Critical questions for big data. *Information Communication and Society*, *15*(5), 662–679. doi:10.1080/1369118X.2012.678878

Broome, M. E. (2016). Big data, data science, and big contributions. *Nursing Outlook*, *113–114*. doi:10.1016/j.outlook.2016.02.001

Buckley, P. (2016). Topic Modelling. In M. Hofmann & A. Chisholm (Eds.), *Text Mining and Visualization Case Studies Using Open-Source Tools*. CRC Press, Taylor and Francis Group.

Carlson, J., Fosmire, M., Miller, C. C., & Nelson, M. S. (2011). Determining Data Information Literacy Needs: A Study of Students and Research Faculty. *Portal (Baltimore, Md.)*, *11*(2), 629–657. doi:10.1353/pla.2011.0022

Carlson, J., Nelson, M. S., Johnston, L. R., & Koshoffer, A. (2015). Developing Data Literacy Programs: Working with Faculty, Graduate Students and Undergraduates. *Bulletin of the Association for Information Science and Technology*, *41*(6), 14–17. doi:10.1002/bult.2015.1720410608

Carscaddon, L., & Chapman, K. (2013). Twitter as a marketing tool for libraries. *Marketing with social media: A LITA guide*, 147-163.

Chakravarty, R., & Kiran, A. (2013). Social Networking in Libraries: A Case Study of Post Graduate Students and Research Scholars of Panjab University Library, India. In S. Thanuskodi (Ed.), *Challenges of Academic Library Management in Developing Countries*. IGI Global. doi:10.4018/978-1-4666-4070-2.ch009

Chen, C. P., & Zhang, C. Y. (2014). Data-intensive applications, challenges, techniques and technologies: A survey on Big Data. *Information Sciences*, *275*(10), 314–347. doi:10.1016/j.ins.2014.01.015

Chen, M., Mao, S., & Liu, Y. (2014). Big data: A survey. *Mobile Networks and Applications*, *19*(2), 171–209. doi:10.100711036-013-0489-0

Chigwada, J. P. (2020). The Role of the Librarian in the Research Life Cycle: Research Collaboration Among the Library and Faculty. In C. Chisita (Ed.), *Cooperation and Collaboration Initiatives for Libraries and Related Institutions* (pp. 335–346). IGI Global. doi:10.4018/978-1-7998-0043-9.ch017

Collegiate Education. (n.d.). Retrieved on March 14, 2020 from http://www.dce.karnataka.nic.in

Cowan, S. R., & Campbell, D. G. (2016). The paradox of privacy: Revisiting a core library value in an age of big data and linked data. *Library Trends*, *64*(3), 492–511. doi:10.1353/lib.2016.0006

Daniel, B. (2014). Big data analytics in higher education: Opportunities and challenges. *British Journal of Educational Technology*, *46*(5), 1–10.

Daniel, K. B. (Ed.). (2017). *Big Data and Learning Analytics in Higher Education*. doi:10.1007/978-3-319-06520-5

Data is the new oil. (2006, November 3). *ANA Marketing Maestros*. https://ana.blogs.com/maestros/2006/11/data_is_the_new.html

Data, B. I. G., & Big, M. A. (2011). *Big data makes a big impact*. NewBay Media.

Data, L. B. (2017). *Leveraging Big Data : Exploring the New Frontier in Construction*. Initiafy.

De Mauro, A., Greco, M., & Grimaldi, M. (2015). Article. *AIP Conference Proceedings*, *1644*, 97–104. doi:10.1063/1.4907823

De Mauro, A., Greco, M., & Grimaldi, M. (2016). A formal definition of Big Data based on its essential features. *Library Review*, *65*(3), 122–135. doi:10.1108/LR-06-2015-0061

Deepthi, T. (2017). Use of online social networking services in university libraries: A Study of university libraries of Karnataka, India. *DESIDOC Journal of Library and Information Technology*, *37*(4), 249–258. doi:10.14429/djlit.37.4.10498

Del Bosque, D., Leif, S. A., & Skarl, S. (2012). Libraries atwitter: Trends in academic library tweeting. *RSR. Reference Services Review*, *40*(2), 199–213. doi:10.1108/00907321211228246

E-granthalaya. (n.d.). Retrieved on April 5, 2020 from http://egranthalaya.nic.in

Emani, C. K., Cullot, N., & Nicolle, C. (2015). Understandable big data: A survey. *Computer Science Review*, *17*(August), 70–81. doi:10.1016/j.cosrev.2015.05.002

Eynon, R. (2013). The rise of Big Data: What does it mean for education, technology, and media research? *Learning, Media and Technology*, *38*(3), 237–240. doi:10.1080/17439884.2013.771783

Fagan, J. C. (2014). The dimensions of library service quality: A confirmatory factor analysis of the LibQUAL instrument. *Library & Information Science Research*, *36*(1), 36–48. doi:10.1016/j.lisr.2013.10.003

Fasola, O. S. (2015). Perceptions and acceptance of librarians towards using Facebook and Twitter to promote library services in Oyo State, Nigeria. *The Electronic Library*, *33*(5), 870–882. doi:10.1108/EL-04-2014-0066

Federer, L. (2016). Research data management in the age of big data: Roles and opportunities for librarians. *Information Services & Use*, *36*(1/2), 35–43. doi:10.3233/ISU-160797

Feng, J. A. (2014). A scheme to improve the international inter-library loan service in the National Library of China. *Interlending & Document Supply*, *42*(2), 88–91. doi:10.1108/ILDS-01-2014-0005

Ferran, N., Mor, E., & Minguillón, J. (2005). Towards personalization in digital libraries through ontologies. *Library Management*, *26*(4/5), 206–217.

Fields, E. (2010). A unique Twitter use for reference services. *Library Hi Tech News*, *27*(6/7), 14–15. doi:10.1108/07419051011095863

Fosso Wamba, S., Akter, S., Edwards, A., Chopin, G., & Gnanzou, D. (2015). How big data can make big impact: Findings from a systematic review and a longitudinal case study. *International Journal of Production Economics*, *165*(July), 234–246. doi:10.1016/j.ijpe.2014.12.031

Fuller, M. (2015). Big data: New science, new challenges, new dialogical opportunities. *Zygon*, *50*(3), 569–582. doi:10.1111/zygo.12187

Gandomi, A., & Haider, M. (2015). Beyond the hype: Big data concepts, methods, and analytics. *International Journal of Information Management*, *35*(2), 137–144. doi:10.1016/j.ijinfomgt.2014.10.007

Gantz, J., & Reinsel, D. (2011). Extracting value from chaos. *IDC iView*, *1142*, 1-12.

Garfield. (n.d.). *HistCite*. Clarivate Analytics. http://www.garfield.library.upenn.edu/

Garg, K. C., Kumar, S., & Lal, K. (2006). Scientometric profile of Indian agricultural research as seen through Science Citation Index Expanded. *Scientometrics*, *68*(1), 151–166. doi:10.100711192-006-0088-y

Gordon-Murname, L. (2012). Big data: A big opportunity for librarians. *Online (Bergheim)*, *36*(5), 30–34.

Gorjiara, T., & Baldock, C. (2014). Nanoscience and nanotechnology research publications: A comparison between Australia and the rest of the world. *Scientometrics*, *100*(1), 121–148. doi:10.100711192-014-1287-6

Gorman, M. (2015). *Our enduring values revisited: librarianship in an ever-changing world.* Available at: http://books.google.com/books

Gunther, W. A., Mehrizi, M. H. R., Huysman, M., & Feldberg, F. (2017). Debating big data: A literature review on realising value from big data. *The Journal of Strategic Information Systems*, *26*(3), 191–209. doi:10.1016/j.jsis.2017.07.003

Haendel, M. A., Vasilevsky, N. A., & Wirz, J. A. (2012). Dealing with Data: A Case Study on Information and Data Management Literacy. *PLoS Biology*, *10*(5), e1001339. doi:10.1371/journal.pbio.1001339

Han, Y. J. (2016). *China library development report, rural library volume*. Chinese National Library Press.

Hashem, I. A. T., Yaqoob, I., Anuar, N. B., Mokhtar, S., Gani, A., & Khan, S. U. (2015). The rise of 'big data' on cloud computing: Review and open research issues. *Information Systems*, *47*, 98–115. doi:10.1016/j.is.2014.07.006

Head, S. R., Komori, H. K., LaMere, S. A., Whisenant, T., Van Nieuwerburgh, F., Salomon, D. R., & Ordoukhanian, P. (2014). Library construction for next-generation sequencing: Overviews and challenges. *BioTechniques*, *56*(2), 61.

Hiippala, T. (2020). A multimodal perspective on data visualization. *Data Visualization in Society*, 277–294. doi:10.2307/j.ctvzgb8c7.23

Hoy, M. B. (2014). Big data: An introduction for librarians. *Medical Reference Services Quarterly*, *33*(3), 320–326. doi:10.1080/02763869.2014.925709

Hu, C. P., Hu, J. M., Deng, S. L., & Liu, Y. (2013). A co-word analysis of library and information science in China. *Scientometrics*, *97*(2), 369–382.

Hurwitz, J., Nugent, A., Halper, F., & Kaufman, M. (2013). *Big data for dummies*. John Wiley & Sons, Inc.

IFLA. (2018). *IFLA trend report 2018 update*. https://trends.ifla.org/update-2018

Ishwarappa & Anuradha. (2014). A Brief Introduction on Big Data 5Vs Characteristics and Hadoop Technology. *Procedia Computer Science*, *48*, 319–324. doi:10.1016/J.PROCS.2015.04.188

Jaakkola, T., & Analytics, B. D. (2014). *Big Data Analytics Machine Learning Tools*. Tackling The Challenges of Big Data.

James, M., Michael, C., Brad, B., Jacques, B., Richard, D., Charles, R., & Angela, H. (2011). Big Data: The Next Frontier for Innovation, Competition, and Productivity. McKinsey Global Institute.

Jin, X., Wah, B.W., & Cheng, X. (2015). Significance and challenges of big data research. *Big Data Research*, *2*(2), 59-64.

Joshi, P. (2015). Analysing big data tools and development platforms. *International Journal of Multidisciplinary Approach and Studies*, *2*(2), 45–56.

Jules, J. (2013). Simple but powerful big data techniques, principles of big data. In *Principles of big data. Burlinton* (pp. 99–127). Morgan Kaufmann.

Kaisler, S., Armour, F., Espinosa, J. A., & Money, W. (2013, January). Big data: Issues and challenges moving forward. In *2013 46th Hawaii International Conference on System Sciences* (pp. 995-1004). IEEE.

Kalra, S. (2014). *Applications of big Data: Current Status and Future Scope*. Academic Press.

Katal, A., Wazid, M., & Goudar, R. H. (2013). Big data: issues, challenges, tools and good practices. In *Contemporary computing (IC3), 2013 Sixth International Conference*. IEEE. 10.1109/IC3.2013.6612229

Kaul, H. K. (2013). Library Networks: The Futuristic Trends and the Emerging Roles and Responsibilities. In *Knowledge, Library and Information Networking: NACLIN 2013. Papers of sixteenth National Convention on Knowledge, Library and information Networking (NACLIN 2013)*. Delhi: DELNET – Developing Library Network.

Kellam, L. M., & Thompson, K. (2016). *Datalibrarianship: the academic data librarian in theory and in practice*. ALA.

Kellam, L., & Peter, K. (2011). *Numeric data services and sources for the general reference librarian*. Elsevier. doi:10.1533/9781780632599

Khan, H. R., & Du, Y. (2018). What is a data Librarian? A content analysis of job advertisements for data librarians in the United States Academic Libraries. IFLA WLIC 2018.

Khurshid, A. (2019). An analysis of academic librarians competencies and skills for implementation of Big Data analytics in libraries A correlational study. *Data Technologies and Applications*, *53*(2), 201–216. doi:10.1108/DTA-09-2018-0085

Kim, S., & Choi, M. S. (2016). Study on data center and data librarian role for reuse of research data. *Knowledge and Smart Technology (KST), 2016 8th International Conference on IEEE*, 303-308. 10.1109/KST.2016.7440517

Kim, H. M., Abels, E. G., & Yang, C. C. (2012). Who disseminates academic library information on Twitter? *Proceedings of the ASIST Annual Meeting*, *49*(1), 1-4. 10.1002/meet.14504901317

Kitchin, R., & McArdle, G. (2016). What makes Big Data, Big Data? Exploring the ontological characteristics of 26 datasets. *Big Data and Society*, *3*(1), 1–10. doi:10.1177/2053951716631130

Knapp, M. (2013). Big data. *Journal of Electronic Resources in Medical Libraries*, *10*(4), 215–222. doi:10.1080/15424065.2013.847713

Krishnamurthy, C., & Shettappanavar, L. (2019). Digital literacy among female postgraduate students of Karnatak University, Dharwad, Karnataka, India: A study. *Library Philosophy and Practice*, *2934*, 1–16.

Kumar, N., Iqbal, R., Misra, S., & Rodrigues, J. J. (2015). An intelligent approach for building a secure decentralized public key infrastructure in VANET. *Journal of Computer and System Sciences*, *81*(6), 1042–1058. doi:10.1016/j.jcss.2014.12.016

Laney, D. (2001). *3D Data Management: Controlling Data Volume, Velocity and Variety*. META Group Research Note, 6.

Lariviere, V., Sugimoto, C. R., & Cronin, B. (2012). A bibliometric chronicling of Library and Information Science's first hundred years. *Journal of the American Society for Information Science and Technology*, *63*(5), 997–1016. doi:10.1002/asi.22645

Lawton, A., & Burns, J. (2015). A review of competencies needed for health librarians-a comparison of Irish and international practice. *Health Information and Libraries Journal*, *32*(2), 84–94. doi:10.1111/hir.12093

Leyenaar, K., Big, P., & Engineer, D. (2016). Big Data Opportunities. *Express Computer*. Available at:http://search.ebscohost.com/login.aspx?direct=true&db=edsnbk&AN=14138C05E25EA138&site=eds-live

Li, J., Lu, M., Dou, G and Wang, S. (2017). Big data application framework and its feasibility analysis in library. *Information Discovery and Delivery*, *45*(4), 161-168.

Li, J., Lu, M., Dou, G., & Wang, S. (2017). Big data application framework and its feasibility analysis in library. *Information Discovery and Delivery*, *45*(4), 161-168.

Li, S. (2019). Problems and Changes in Digital Libraries in the Age of Big Data from the Perspective of User Services. *The Journal of Academic Librarianship*, *45*(2), 22-30.

Li, B. Y., & Zhang, X. Y. (2013). The problem of large data in the construction of digital library. *Information Sciences*, *11*, 26–29.

Li, C., Zhu, L., & Luo, Z. (2016). Big time-frequency domain data mining for underdetermined BSS using density component analysis, *2016 IEEE International Symposium on Signal Processing and Information Technology (ISSPIT)*, 188-192.

Li, S., Jiao, F., Zhang, Y., & Xu, X. (2019). Problems and changes in digital libraries in the age of big data from the perspectives of user services. *Journal of Academic Librarianship*, *45*(1), 22–30. doi:10.1016/j.acalib.2018.11.012

Liu, L., Zhang, L., & Ye, P. (2018). Research on the application of SNS in university libraries. *The Electronic Library*, *36*(2), 369–386. doi:10.1108/EL-05-2016-0120

Loi and Dehaye. (2017). *If data is the new oil, when is the extraction of value from data unjust? (2017, January 1)*. ResearchGate. https://www.researchgate.net/publication/326200389_If_Data_Is_The_New_Oil_When_Is_The_Extraction_of_Value_From_Data_Unjust/citations

Long, R., & Harvey, P. (2014). Technologies for Libraries. *The ANZTLA EJournal*, *10*(10), 2–9. doi:10.31046/anztla.vi10.242

Lotka, A. J. (1926). The frequency distribution of scientific productivity. *Journal of the Washington Academy of Sciences*, *16*(12), 317–323.

Lu, J. (2014). The evaluation and prospects of big data research in library in China. *Library Journal, 33*(1), 20–25.

Luna, D. R. (2014). Challenges and potential solutions for big data implementations in developing countries. Yearbook of Medical Informatics, 9(1), 36–41.

MacMillan, D. (2015). Developing data literacy competencies to enhance faculty collaborations. *LIBER Quarterly, 24*(3), 140. doi:10.18352/lq.9868

Making, D. D. (2012). *Big data. Data Revolut. Big Data, Open Data, Data Infrastructures Their Consequences*. doi:10.1089/big.2013.0037.Published

Manovich, L. (2011). Debates Digit. *Humanit,*. 1.

Manyika, J., Chui, M., Brown, B., Bughin, J., Dobbs, R., & Roxburgh, C. (2011). *Big data: The next frontier for innovation, competition, and productivity*. McKinsey Global Institute.

Marastats. (n.d.). *Marathon and Half Marathon Statistics*. https://marastats.com/

Marvin, H. (2014). Big data in Libraries: Content and policies for librarians. *Government Information Quarterly, 31*(4), 681.

McAfee, A., Brynjolfsson, E., Davenport, T. H., Patil, D., & Barton, D. (2012).. . *Harvard Business Review, 90*, 61.

Microsoft. (2018). *Microsoft Excel*. Microsoft Corporation. https://office.microsoft.com/excel

Munigal, A. (2014). Use of Microblogs in India: A Study of Twitter Usage by Librarians and in Libraries. *Journal of Library Administration, 54*(7), 590–608. doi:10.1080/01930826.2014.964021

Narayanan, A., & Shmatikov, V. (2008). Article. *Proceedings of IEEE Symposium on Security and Privacy*, 111–125.

Narendra, A. P. (2016). Big Data, data analyst, and improving the competence of librarian. *Record and Library Journal, 1*(2), 83–93. doi:10.20473/rlj.v1i2.1162

Noh, Y. (2015). Imagining library 4.0: Creating a model for future libraries. *Journal of Academic Librarianship, 41*(6), 786–797. doi:10.1016/j.acalib.2015.08.020

Noor, A. (2013). Putting big data to work. *Mechanical Engineering (New York, N.Y.), 135*(10), 32–37. doi:10.1115/1.2013-OCT-1

Normandeau, K. (2013). *Variety and Velocity is the Issue of Big Data Veracity*. Available at https://insidebigdata.com/author/kevin/

Oladokun, O. (2014). Library cooperation and resource sharing: Some lessons from the University of Botswana. *African Journal of Library Archives and Information Science, 24*(2), 187–193.

Olawumi, T. O., & Chan, D. W. (2018). A scientometric review of global research on sustainability and sustainable development. *Journal of Cleaner Production, 183*, 231–250. doi:10.1016/j.jclepro.2018.02.162

Oliveira, N., Cortez, P., & Areal, N. (2016). Sentiment Analysis of Stock Market Behavior from Twitter Using the R Tool. In M. Hofmann & A. Chisholm (Eds.), *Text Mining and Visualization Case Studies Using Open-Source Tools*. CRC Press, Taylor and Francis Group.

Özen Çınar, İ. (2020). Bibliometric analysis of breast cancer research in the period 2009–2018. *International Journal of Nursing Practice*. Advance online publication. doi:10.1111/ijn.12845

Palmer, S. (2014). Characterizing university library use of social media: A case study of Twitter and Facebook from Australia. *Journal of Academic Librarianship*, *40*(6), 611–619. doi:10.1016/j.acalib.2014.08.007

Pang, B., & Lee, L. (2008). Opinion mining and sentiment analysis. *Foundations and Trends® in Information Retrieval, 2*(1–2), 1-135.

Panoho, K. (2019). Council post: The age of analytics and the importance of data quality. *Forbes*. https://www.forbes.com/sites/forbesagencycouncil/2019/10/01/the-age-of-analytics-and-the-importance-of-data-quality/#1d759a435c3c

Patra, S. K. (2019). How Indian libraries tweet? Word frequency and sentiment analysis of library tweets. *Annals of Library and Information Studies*, *66*, 131–139.

Pawar, A. M. (2016). Big Data mining: Challenges, technologies, tools and applications. *Database Systems Journal*, *7*(2), 28–33.

Pearson, T and Wegener, R. (2013). *Big Data: The Organizational Challenge.* Bain & Company report.

PerssonO. (2007). *Bibexcel*. https://homepage.univie.ac.at/juan.gorraiz/bibexcel/

Pokorny, J. (2013). NoSQL databases: A step to database scalability in web environment. *International Journal of Web Information Systems*, *9*(1), 69–82. doi:10.1108/17440081311316398

Provost, F., & Fawcett, T. (2013). Data science and its relationship to big data and data-driven decision making. *Big Data*, *1*(1), 51–59. doi:10.1089/big.2013.1508

R Core Team. (2018). *R: A Language and Environment for Statistical Computing*. R Foundation for Statistical Computing. https://www.R-project.org

Reinhalter, L., & Wittmann, R. J. (2014). The library: Big data's boomtown. *The Serials Librarian*, *67*(4), 363–372. doi:10.1080/0361526X.2014.915605

Rettberg, J. W. (2020). Ways of knowing with data visualizations. *Data Visualization in Society*, 35–48. doi:10.2307/j.ctvzgb8c7.8

Ruiz-Rosero, J., Ramirez-Gonzalez, G., Williams, J., Liu, H., Khanna, R., & Pisharody, G. (2017). Internet of Things: A Scientometric Review. *Symmetry*, *9*(12), 301. doi:10.3390ym9120301

Sab, C. (2019). Marketing Research in India: A Scientometrics Study. *Webology*, *16*(1), 172–186. doi:10.14704/WEB/V16I2/a197

Sakas, D. P., & Sarlis, A. S. (2016). Library promotion methods and tools modeling and simulation on Twitter. *Library Review*, *65*(6-7), 479–499. doi:10.1108/LR-06-2015-0068

Salo, D. (2010). *Retooling libraries for the data challenge*. Academic Press.

Semeler, A. R., Pinto, A. L., & Rozados, H. B. F. (2017). Data science in data librarianship: Core competencies of a data Librarian. *Journal of Librarianship and Information Science*, *51*(3), 771–780. doi:10.1177/0961000617742465

Shulman, J., Yep, J., & Tomé, D. (2015). Leveraging the power of a Twitter network for library promotion. *Journal of Academic Librarianship*, *41*(2), 178–185. doi:10.1016/j.acalib.2014.12.004

Simovic, A. (2018). A big data smart library recommender system for an educational institution. *Library Hi Tech*, *36*(3), 498–523. doi:10.1108/LHT-06-2017-0131

Sin, K., & Muthu, L. (2015). Application Of Big Data In Education Data Mining And Learning Analytics – A Literature Review. *ICTACT Journal on Soft Computing*, *5*(4), 1035–1049. doi:10.21917/ijsc.2015.0145

Singh, P. (2019). *Recommender Systems: With Natural Language Processing and Recommender Systems*. . doi:10.1007/978-1-4842-4131-8_7

Smith, K., Hallam, G., & Ghosh, S. B. (2012). *Guidelines for professional library / Information Educational Programs-2012*. http://www.ifla.org/publications

Stuart, D. (2010). What are libraries doing on twitter? *Online (Wilton, Connecticut)*, *34*(1), 45–47.

Teets, M., & Goldner, M. (2013). Libraries' role in curating and exposing big data. *Future Internet*, *5*(3), 429–438. doi:10.3390/fi5030429

The world's most valuable resource is no longer oil, but data. (2017, May 6). *The Economist*. https://www.economist.com/leaders/2017/05/06/the-worlds-most-valuable-resource-is-no-longer-oil-but-data

Thelwall, M., Buckley, K., & Paltoglou, G. (2011). Sentiment in Twitter Events. *Journal of the American Society for Information Science and Technology*, *62*(2), 406–418. doi:10.1002/asi.21462

Thomas, C., & Urban, R. (2018). What do data librarians think of the MLIS? Professionals perceptions of knowledge transfer, trends, and challenges. *College & Research Libraries*, *79*(3), 401–423. doi:10.5860/crl.79.3.401

Van Eck, N. J., & Waltman, L. (2013). *VOSviewer*. https://www.vosviewer.com/

Vassilakaki, E., & Garoufallou, E. (2015). The impact of Twitter on libraries: A critical review of the literature. *The Electronic Library*, *33*(4), 795–809. doi:10.1108/EL-03-2014-0051

Verishagen, N., & Hank, C. (2014). Are there birds in the library? The extent of Twitter adoption and use by Canadian academic libraries. *First Monday*, *19*(11). Advance online publication. doi:10.5210/fm.v19i11.4945

Viceconti, M., Hunter, P., & Hose, R. (2015). Big Data, Big Knowledge: Big Data for Personalized Healthcare. *IEEE Journal of Biomedical and Health Informatics*, *19*(4), 1209–1215. doi:10.1109/JBHI.2015.2406883

Wang, C., Xu, S., Chen, L., & Chen, X. (2016). Exposing library data with big data technology: A review. In *2016 IEEE/ACIS 15th International Conference on Computer and Information Science (ICIS),* 1-6). IEEE. 10.1109/ICIS.2016.7550937

Wani, M. A., & Jabin, S. (2018). Big Data: Issues, Challenges, and Techniques in Business Intelligence. In *Big Data Analytics* (pp. 613–628). Springer. doi:10.1007/978-981-10-6620-7_59

What is granular data? - Definition from Techopedia. (n.d.). *Techopedia.com.* https://www.techopedia.com/definition/31722/granular-data

Winsley & Muthukannan. (2020). *Information Security: A Scientometric Study.* IGI Global Publishers. https://www.igi-global.com/gateway/chapter/238176

Wu, J. Z. (2009). On information need and service for digital library client. *Hebei Sci-Tech Library Journal*, *22*(5), 59–61.

Wu, J., Zhang, Y., & Mu, Z. (2014). Predicting nucleosome positioning based on geometrically transformed Tsallis entopy. *PLoS One*, *9*(11), e109395. doi:10.1371/journal.pone.0109395

Xu, R., & Yang, Y. (2019). Study of user behaviour data, mining and applications in university libraries: taking the Central China Normal University Library as an example. *Advances in Computer Science Research* Volume 87. *3rd International Conference on Mechatronics Engineering and Information Technology (ICMEIT 2019).* 10.2991/icmeit-19.2019.44

Xu, Z., Liu, Y., Mei, L., Hu, C., & Chen, L. (2015). Semantic based representing and organising surveillance big data using video structural description technology. *Journal of Systems and Software*, *102*(April), 217–225. doi:10.1016/j.jss.2014.07.024

Yuehua, F. (2014). Library personalized information push service based on Smartphone APP. *Journal of Library Science*, *3*, 116–118.

Zaharia, M., Xin, R. S., Wendell, P., Das, T., Armbrust, M., Dave, A., & Ghodsi, A. (2016). Apache spark: A unified engine for big data processing. *Communications of the ACM*, *59*(11), 56–65. doi:10.1145/2934664

Zhang, X. L. (2001). Mechanisms of digital library: Evolution of paradigms and its challenges. *Journal of the Library Science in China*, *27*(6), 3–8.

Zhang, X. L. (2005). From digital library to e-knowledge mechanism. *Journal of Library Science in China*, *31*(4), 5–10.

Zhan, M., & Widen, G. (2017). Understanding big data in librarianship. *Journal of Librarianship and Information Science*, *51*(2), 561–576. doi:10.1177/0961000617742451

Zhou, Q. (2016). eBook Service in Shanghai Library. *International Journal of Librarianship*, *1*(1), 66–73. doi:10.23974/ijol.2016.vol1.1.16

About the Contributors

Sangeeta Dhamdhere is a Library professional from India having a more than 19 years of experience in Library and Information Science. She has been instrumental in installing top-class Library and Information management practices in a number of places and in her current role as the Chief Librarian of Modern College in Pune (India), she constantly strives to find and optimize newer and newer ways of segregating and delivering information to her users. She completed her Masters in Library and Information Science from University of Pune and has cleared both, the National and State level Eligibility Tests for Lecturership in Libraries and Information Science. She has also picked up a couple of computing, etc. diplomas on the way and is adept at using computers to her advantage. She has got Scholarship for International training Programme on "Scientific and Technological Information Management in Universities and Libraries" Sponsored by the Belgium Government and Vrije University, Brussels, Belgium for the Period 1st October 2008 to 19th December, 2008 and again for three weeks workshop on E-Discovery Tools in December 2015 at Antwerp University. She has completed her PhD in Library Science at Nagpur University in July 2018 and recipient of couple of awards in academic field. She has very good experience of library automation and digital library software systems. She has guided many bachelor and masters students for library related projects and is an active member of various library communities and various associations. She has completed two assignments for BIREME, DocBiblios, UNESCO and one research project sponsored by Savitribai Phule Pune University. She is recipient of three national and three International Awards. She has travelled many countries for her academic assignments and study like USA, Europe, Japan, UAE, China. She has published and presented more than 55 research publications at national and International level in conferences, seminars and reputed peer reviewed journals and edited two book and one National Seminar proceedings namely "Cloud Computing and Visualization Technologies in Libraries" and "E-Discovery tools and applications in modern libraries" published by IGI Global, USA and National seminar proceedings on Intellectual Property Rights (IPRs) and Research Ethics-2020, sponsored by ICSSR, New Delhi.. She is also author of two books namely " Knowledge Management in Indian Higher Education System: Strategies, Processes and Planning, published by Lap Lambert Publishing, Germany and "Web-based services: a transforming revolution in modern libraries" by ESS ESS Publications, New Delhi. She is Chief editor of "Granthavedh" Library E_Newsletter and "Aakanksha" Annual magazine of her college and editorial board member and reveiwer of about 14 reputed peer reviewed International Journals in Library Science and Computer Science. Sangeeta is wholly committed to this uplifting task which she calls 'maintaining humanity of humans'. Her mission statement is also "To give maximum information for maximum number of time by maximum number of ways in minimum time".

* * *

Oluwaseun David Adepoju bagged a first-class degree in Library and Information Studies from the University of Ibadan Nigeria and also a masters in Library and Information Science from the same University. He is a published technology researcher with special interest Open Data and Technology Applications in the society. He is a two time TED speaker and a GIZ recognized Digerati working in Africa. He is currently a Research Methods Faculty and the Institution Librarian at the African Leadership University in Kigali Rwanda.

Nandeesha B., working has Asst. Library & Information Officer at All India Institute of Speech and Hearing, Mysore having 15 years of experience. He is pursuing a Ph.D. from the University of Mysore. He has published 13 research articles in various National and International Journals and also presented and published a number of research papers in various National and International Conferences.

Ravindra Bankar is a Sr. Research Fellow at the Department. of Library and Information Sciences, Rashtrasant Tukadoji Maharaj Nagpur University, Nagpur. Working on ICMR funded Extramural Research Project. He graduated from the Department of Library & Information Sciences at Shivaji University with a Masters in Information Science in April 2018. and currently doing PhD in the same department.

Josiline Chigwada is the Sub Librarian responsible for the Reader and Information services at Bindura University of Science Education Library. She has worked in university libraries since September 2006. She holds a Doctor of Literature and Philosophy in Information Science from the University of South Africa, Master and Bachelor of Science Honours Degree in Library and Information Science from the National University of Science and Technology – Bulawayo, Zimbabwe. Her research interests are big data, open science, research data management, indigenous knowledge systems, Information Literacy, Generation X, Y and Z, open access, reference services, marketing library products and services, digital libraries, and the changing role of librarians. She has vast experience in academic librarianship and her career is centred on academic and special libraries. She has presented in various national, regional and international conferences.

Ruti Dauphin is a Computer Science Faculty at the African Leadership University, Kigali Rwanda. He is a certified Cyber-security expert with more than 5 years of experience.

Pravin Dusane is Assistant Professor in Physics serving Abasaheb Garware College for 15 years his area of Interest are nanotecnology,2D materials, magnetic materials, etc.

Mahesh G T working as Selection Grade Librarian at Government First Grade College, Saligrama having 18 years of Professional experience.He had the opportunity to work in IISC, Bangalore and IIMB Library Bangalore. Has published more than 15 research articles in various National and International Journals, presented and published more than 10 research papers in various National conferences and seminars. Has edited one National Conference Proceedings on the theme "Exploring the Gateways in Higher Education: Culture, Transition and Transformations". His areas of interests include User Behavior, Application of Cloud Computing in Libraries, Networking of Libraries and Knowledge Management.

Swapnaja Hiray is professor at Sinhgad College of Engineering, Computer Engineering Department. Pursuing Ph.D in Big data Analytics. Has 20 years of Teaching Experience.

Justice Kasiroori is a Technology Librarian at Bindura University of Science Education. His areas of responsibility include overseeing the adoption and management of library related technology. His current research interests include Big Data, Research Data Management, Data Analytics and open source technologies.

Shweta Kaushik received her BE degree in Computer Science and Engineering from Uttar Pradesh Technical University, Lucknow, India in 2010 and MTech degree in Computer Science and Engineering from Jaypee Institute of Information Technology (JIIT) Noida, India in 2012. She is pursuing her PhD degree in Cloud Computing from Jaypee Institute of Information Technology (JIIT), Noida, India. In 2012, she joined the Department of Computer Science and Information Technology, UPTU as an Assistant Professor. Since August 2015, she has been with the

Department of Master of Computer Application, Indraprastha University (IP) Delhi, where she was an Assistant Professor. Her current research interests include cloud computing, network security, distributed system, algorithms and big data. She is a member of ACM.

Shalini Lihitkar is Associate Professor at Department of LISc, Rashtrasant Tukdoji Maharaj Nagpur University, Nagpur. She has been previously worked as Professor and Head at Department of LISc, Shivaji University, Kolhapur from August 2017.She has been in LIS Profession Since 2002, she is a Gold Medalist from Nagpur University. She worked as Head of the Department of LISc, Rashtrasant Tukadoji Maharaj Nagpur University, Nagpur. She has experience of teaching and guiding for UGC-NET/SET, P.O. and other competitive examinations. She has 15 years teaching experience in LIS field. She has published several papers in seminars, conferences and Journals at National and International level and has more than 180 papers to her credit. She has edited 16 conferences and workshops proceedings.

Deepak Mane is an IT Evangelist, Project Manager in TCS. Published many research papers in an international journals. Managed many projects related to big data.

Soochitra Paatil, M. Lib.II. Sc., PGDLIM, working in Dr. D. Y. Patil Institute of Management Studies, Akurdi, Pune 411044, Maharashtra, India.

Sukhada Dinesh Pandkar, M.Lib. I. Sc. SET/NET, PGDLIM, working in P. E. Society's Modern College of Arts, Science and Commerce, Shivajinagar, Pune 411005, Maharashtra, India.

Swapan Kumar Patra is a Career Advancement Research Fellow at Industrial Engineering Department, Faculty of Engineering and the Built Environment, Tshwane University of Technology, Pretoria, South Africa. Dr. Patra is a PhD in Science Policy from Centre for Studies in Science Policy, School of Social Sciences, Jawaharlal Nehru University, New Delhi, India. His research interests are in the areas of big data, Innovation and Development, Globalization, Multinational Enterprises, Innovation System, Science Technology Indicators, Social Network Analysis, Big Data, Data Mining. He is Associate Editors of African Journal of Science Technology, Innovation and Development (AJSTID); Journal of Scientometric Research (JSCIRES); Tshwane University of Technology - Journal of Creativity, Innovation and Social Entrepreneurship (TUT-JCISE). Dr. Patra has received the "Academic Excellence Award 2018" from Tshwane University of Technology, Pretoria, South Africa.

Amita Pradhan completed Ph.D in 2012. Topic- "Developing a Model for Information Audit for Engineering college Libraries". 12 conference and Journal papers on credit. 20 years of Administrative Experience. Passion to adopt new technologies in Libraries.

Index

A

B

C

D

T

V

Ensure Quality Research is Introduced to the Academic Community

Become an IGI Global Reviewer for Authored Book Projects

The overall success of an authored book project is dependent on quality and timely reviews.

In this competitive age of scholarly publishing, constructive and timely feedback significantly expedites the turnaround time of manuscripts from submission to acceptance, allowing the publication and discovery of forward-thinking research at a much more expeditious rate. Several IGI Global authored book projects are currently seeking highly-qualified experts in the field to fill vacancies on their respective editorial review boards:

Applications and Inquiries may be sent to:
development@igi-global.com

Applicants must have a doctorate (or an equivalent degree) as well as publishing and reviewing experience. Reviewers are asked to complete the open-ended evaluation questions with as much detail as possible in a timely, collegial, and constructive manner. All reviewers' tenures run for one-year terms on the editorial review boards and are expected to complete at least three reviews per term. Upon successful completion of this term, reviewers can be considered for an additional term.

If you have a colleague that may be interested in this opportunity, we encourage you to share this information with them.

www.ingramcontent.com/pod-product-compliance
Lightning Source LLC
LaVergne TN
LVHW081322300926
849161LV00008B/1850

* 9 7 8 1 7 9 9 8 3 0 4 9 8 *